D1035234

Arthur O. Lovejoy
AND THE QUEST FOR INTELLIGIBILITY

Arthur O. Lovejoy

AND THE QUEST FOR INTELLIGIBILITY

BY DANIEL J. WILSON

THE UNIVERSITY OF NORTH CAROLINA PRESS

CHAPEL HILL

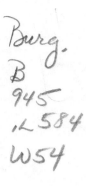

Manufactured in the United States of America

Library of Congress Catalog Card Number 79-25902

ISBN 0-8078-1431-8

Library of Congress Cataloging in Publication Data
Wilson, Daniel J   1949–
Arthur O. Lovejoy and the quest for intelligibility.
Bibliography: p.
Includes index.
1. Lovejoy, Arthur Oncken, 1873-1962.
2. Philosophers—United States—Biography.
3. Rationalism—History. I. Title.
B945.L584W54   191 [B]   79-25902
ISBN 0-8078-1431-8

For my mother,

MARY P. WILSON,

and for the memory of my father,

RUSSELL S. WILSON

CONTENTS

Contents

ILLUSTRATIONS

PREFACE

Arthur O. Lovejoy was a very private man. During his lifetime he did not want a biography written and, I suspect, he would not welcome the appearance of this volume. Like his contemporary, philosophical adversary, and friend John Dewey, Lovejoy seldom reminisced. There are a few hints in his published writings, a few details conveyed to friends and students, and perhaps a dozen references in his manuscripts. His reluctance to reveal his past and to speculate on its influence was in part shyness and a way of keeping unpleasant memories at bay; it was also, and to his mind most importantly, the result of his conviction that what mattered about an individual were not the biographical details, but what a man thought.

If Lovejoy did not encourage biographical inquiry, neither did he systematically destroy the evidence a biographer requires. His parents preserved his letters and family documents and he, in turn, preserved their letters. After his father and stepmother died in 1921, Lovejoy kept the papers his parents had preserved. He also kept much of what a scholar accumulates in some sixty years of correspondence, research, writing, and teaching. At Lovejoy's death in 1962, George Boas turned this material over to The Johns Hopkins University, where it fills nearly two hundred manuscript boxes. When this is combined with his published work and the reminiscences of those who knew him, a reasonably complete portrait of Lovejoy begins to emerge.

But why undertake the biography of a man who maintained that his past was a very private matter? If Lovejoy had played only a minor role in the intellectual and academic life of the early twentieth century, then a biography would hardly be justified. He was, however, a major figure in the development of American philosophy, the chief exponent of the history of ideas, and a leader in the effort to mold college teaching into an effective profession that would serve the nation within the university and without. It is not self-evident why one man, especially one celebrated as "reason-in-action," should have such diverse interests, or should mix the life of the mind with social and political activism. Previous studies of Lovejoy have taken up various facets of his writing or of his professional life, but none have attempted to examine in detail Lovejoy's intellectual and personal development or to uncover the relationships among the various elements of his career. This study is an attempt to trace the personal and intellectual roots of Lovejoy's devotion to rational scholarship and to outline the development of his religious beliefs, his philosophical positions, his historical studies, and his social and political activism.

The questions a biographer needs to ask about a soldier, or politician, or even a novelist are quite different from those that must be asked about a philosopher. Although he is perhaps best known today as a historian of ideas, Lovejoy was first and foremost a philosopher. Two related considerations underlie this study, and the reader's task may be eased if they are made explicit. In a short study of William James, Lovejoy wrote that "all philosophies . . . are the result of the interaction of a temperament (itself partly molded by a historical situation) with impersonal logical considerations arising out of the problems with which man's reason is confronted." Some sixty years later Allan Janik and Stephen Toulmin, in their study of Ludwig Wittgenstein, argued that a fruitful way of approaching a philosopher is to ask what were the most basic problems he confronted and thus tried to resolve in his philosophizing.[1] When one examines the life of Lovejoy with these considerations in mind, the seemingly disparate elements of his life and work begin to reveal their interrelations. Possessed of a rational temperament, he faced the problem of making the diverse, evolving modern universe intelligible. The quest for intelligibility and the answer he suggested —reason as the sole guiding principle in a pluralistic universe— shaped his entire career. This quest and its ramifications are the focus of this biography.

To understand why Lovejoy needed to establish a rational basis for choice in a pluralistic universe requires peeling away some of the layers of privacy within which he enveloped himself. Reason-in-action was a part of Lovejoy's persona that fulfilled a deeply felt temperamental need and preserved the privacy he valued. But Lovejoy's desire for an intelligible, rational account of the world cannot be fully understood without understanding its roots in the emotional turmoil of his youth and the protracted religious dispute with his father. His mother's death when he was eighteen months old, his father's subsequent mental and physical breakdown, and his separation from his father for three years took an emotional toll that is impossible to calculate. Only with his father's remarriage in the early 1880s did Lovejoy experience a normal family life. Lovejoy's father found the solution to his problems in evangelical religion and tried to pass that belief to his son. Lovejoy resisted vigorously in a struggle that lasted more than ten years. But that struggle, too, shaped his search for a rational theology and his participation in social service and political affairs. Reason became a sound alternative to the uncertainty of emotion and faith.

Because reason and thought lay at the center of Lovejoy's life, this biography is very much a life of the mind. I have tried to suggest the roots of that life, but I have not probed deeply into possible psychological explanations. The evidence simply does not exist for what has come to be known as a psychobiography. Nor am I convinced that it would do more than trace the development of Lovejoy's thought and career. My approach does, however, tend to slight the personal side of Lovejoy, but with justification. Lovejoy never married and his personal life was largely uneventful. He took considerable pleasure in his work, both intellectual and service, and his diversions tended to be solitary, from reading detective fiction and Civil War history to listening to baseball on the radio and attending plays. Often formal and demanding in his relations with students and colleagues, he could be warm and open with children. George Boas recounts tales of Lovejoy's taking the part of Owl in reading *The House at Pooh Corner* and, on another occasion, lecturing the dog he had given the Boas children on the evils of killing chickens.[2] He was understanding and sympathetic with colleagues who were having problems as well as with the immigrants he helped in the settlements.

For all this, the real interest and drama in studying Lovejoy is in the life of the mind: in his efforts, ultimately successful, to establish independence from his father, in the rejection of the idealisms of his teachers, in the adoption of pluralism and the realization that intelligibility was still elusive, in the development of a dualistic epistemology that explained how we know anything and pointed toward the intelligibility he sought, in his tracing the historical antecedents of his own thought in the history of ideas, and in his vigorous defense of academic freedom in the university and freedom of thought in the nation and the world. Lovejoy remains, in many ways, a very private man, but the real interest in his life, in any case, was his effort to establish a coherent account of the world in which he lived, and then to act on that conception.

ACKNOWLEDGMENTS

Since much of this book rests on manuscript sources, my first debt is to the archivists who responded to my inquiries and provided access to their holdings. I would like to thank Tom Truss, Jr., of the American Association of University Professors; J.R.K. Kanter, Archivist, University of California, Berkeley; Rodney G. Dennis, Curator of Manuscripts, Houghton Library, Harvard; Bonnie B. Salt, Harvard University Archives; Julia Morgan, of the Ferdinand Hamburger, Jr., Archives, The Johns Hopkins University; Susan Reynolds Rosenberg, Stanford University Archives; and Beryl H. Manne, Washington University Archives. I would particularly like to thank Carolyn Smith and Carol Beechen and the rest of the staff in Special Collections, The Johns Hopkins University, for their always friendly assistance during the many months I spent working with the Lovejoy Papers.

I would like to thank Morton S. Baratz, General Secretary of the American Association of University Professors, for permission to cite material in their files; Professor Stanley Cavell, Chairman Department of Philosophy, Harvard University, for permission to quote from Lovejoy's correspondence in the Department of Philosophy Files, Harvard University Archives; and George Boas for permission to quote from the papers of Lovejoy. The letters of Lovejoy to George Holmes Howison are quoted by permission of the University Archivist, Bancroft Library, University of California, Berkeley; the letters of Lovejoy to William James and George Sarton are quoted by permission of Houghton Library, Harvard University; the letters of Lovejoy to David Starr Jordan are quoted by permission of Stanford University Archives; the letters from Lovejoy to W. S. Chaplin are quoted by permission of Washington University Archives; and Lovejoy's resigna-

Acknowledgments

tion letter from the University of Maryland Board of Regents is quoted by permission of Peter F. O'Malley, Chairman of the Board of Regents.

Chapter Six, "The Moral of *The Great Chain of Being*," originally appeared in the *Journal of the History of Ideas*, and is reprinted here, with minor revisions, by their permission. The final revisions on the manuscript were aided by a Faculty Research Grant from Muhlenberg College.

Colleagues and students of Lovejoy have not only encouraged my work, but have also responded to my inquiries and shared their knowledge of Lovejoy with me; for that I owe them a debt of gratitude. Sidney Hook and Roy Harvey Pearce responded to my inquiries in correspondence. I would like to thank Lewis S. Feuer, Victor Lowe, Frank N. Trager, and Philip P. Wiener for taking time to share their recollections with me. I would especially like to thank George Boas; my visits with him were always interesting, informative, and enjoyable, and I came away from them with renewed enthusiasm.

Although writing is essentially an individual task, I have been fortunate to receive good advice and encouragement from many people over the last five years. Since the inception of this study Kenneth S. Lynn has provided encouragement, searching criticism, and a sense of humor that improved the biography and eased the work. John Higham and Maurice Mandelbaum read an early version of the biography, and the later revision owes much to their counsel. Lewis S. Feuer, David A. Hollinger, Bruce Kuklick, and Ludwig F. Schlecht read all or part of the manuscript and offered helpful criticism, for which I am grateful. I would also like to thank Malcolm Call of The University of North Carolina Press.

One of the joys of working on this biography has been the friendships that developed at Johns Hopkins and have continued since. We all had our own work, but many were willing to help as they could with anything from listening as one talked out a problem to providing a bed on a research trip. For that, I would like to thank Richard Golden, who suggested the subject, Peter B. Hirtle, Thomas M. Jacklin, Kathy Kobayashi, Kathy Ogren, and Linda Burcher Ramsey. My special thanks, for things that cannot be stated in an acknowledgment, to A. Roger Ekirch,

Acknowledgments

André-Philippe Katz, Paul F. Paskoff, Peter A. Poggioli, and Carolyn Date Wagner.

Finally, I owe the greatest thanks to my mother, Mary P. Wilson, my sister Marjorie, and brother Stewart. Without their help and support, this book never would have been written.

Arthur O. Lovejoy
AND THE QUEST FOR INTELLIGIBILITY

CHAPTER I

THE MAKING OF A

PHILOSOPHER, 1873–1899

In late June 1903, on vacation from Washington University, Arthur O. Lovejoy revisited his childhood home of Ironton, Ohio. He had taken the train east from St. Louis and in Cincinnati realized that it stopped at Russell, Kentucky, across the Ohio River from Ironton. He left the train at Russell, arriving in Ironton at one in the morning. The next day he visited old friends and walked the streets. Little had changed, except that everything seemed curiously smaller. As he continued to Washington, Lovejoy recalled with pleasure memories of his years in the sleepy river town.[1] The letters to his father and stepmother in which he recalled his years in Ironton were among the rare occasions when Lovejoy reminisced about his childhood.

The source of Lovejoy's family heritage was not the Midwest, but New England and Germany. His father, Wallace William Lovejoy, the son of a carpet merchant, was born in Boston in 1847. The Lovejoys traced their lineage to John Lovejoy, an indentured servant who landed in Massachusetts in the 1630s. In the following decade, John Lovejoy was among the first settlers of Andover, where the family prospered and, as one historian noted, "epitomized some of the principal characteristics of family life in seventeenth-century Andover." Wallace Lovejoy's memories of his father mixed fondness and guilt. Joseph Lovejoy had been affectionate and a good companion on summer trips. Nonetheless, Wallace, in later years, deeply regretted rejecting his father's advice to enter the Protestant Episcopal ministry. Instead, he had followed his own instincts into medicine.[2] Wallace remembered his mother as conscientious, but unemotional and reserved, even with her nine children. She first converted to Episcopalianism in the 1850s and eventually brought the rest of the family into the church, including her husband, who, after an initial reluctance, became an enthusiastic convert.[3]

In February 1872, having received a medical degree from Harvard, Wallace Lovejoy left New York to continue his studies in Germany. He carried a letter of introduction to the Reverend J. G. Oncken of Hamburg, whom he immediately visited after landing at Bremerhaven. The young American, a stranger in Germany, hoped to board with the Oncken family. On his first visit he met Sara, the youngest daughter of Mr. Oncken. A week later, he took up residence as a boarder. Less than a month after arriving in Hamburg, Wallace announced his love for Sara Oncken and the formal engagement took place on 22 May 1872.[4]

This young woman, who would become Arthur Lovejoy's mother, was the daughter of a prominent Baptist missionary and religious publisher in Germany. The Reverend Mr. Oncken was of Scotch as well as German descent and had been educated in Scotland. While a young man he had been converted to the Baptist faith by an American sea captain. With missionary zeal he preached in Germany and published religious tracts to support himself. His evangelical labors had resulted in imprisonment and heavy fines before religious liberty was established in Germany. Though he respected the achievements of J. G. Oncken, Wallace regarded him as "the most consummate egotist" he had ever met. Wallace never knew Sara's own mother; she died of cancer shortly after Sara's birth on 22 April 1845. Although raised largely by her older sister Margaret, Sara was friendly with her father's second wife.[5]

Sara Oncken received a good education, graduating from a school at Kornthal, in southern Germany, at seventeen. First employed as a governess to the family of the Reverend F. Stanley in Yorkshire, England, she returned to Hamburg after three years to teach the children of several wealthy merchants. Shortly before she met her future husband she had begun teaching English in private schools.[6]

In May, after his engagement to Sara had been formalized, Wallace left Hamburg for Berlin to begin his medical studies. The separation was difficult for the young lovers, but Wallace returned to Hamburg several times during the summer for long

and happy weekends. There were, however, more serious problems than the separation. Wallace's family in Boston, when it
learned of the engagement, was almost uniformly hostile to the
marriage plans. The reasons are not clear, although the family's
hostility may have rested on religious grounds. Wallace's older
brother Arthur came to Germany in July 1872 to investigate the
situation for the family. After meeting Sara, Arthur changed his
mind and gave his approval for an early marriage. Thus, Wallace
Lovejoy and Sara Oncken were married on 24 September 1872 at
a Baptist church in Hamburg.[7]

Following the marriage Wallace resumed his medical studies.
He and his new wife spent the fall in Leipzig but were separated
in December by the illness of Sara's stepmother. Much of the first
half of 1873 they spent apart, Wallace pursuing his studies in
Leipzig and Prague while Sara cared for her stepmother in Hamburg until the latter's death. By fall the Lovejoys were reunited
in Berlin. There, in a boarding house on Louisen Strasse, early in
the morning of 10 October 1873 Sara Lovejoy gave birth to a
son, who was named Arthur Schauffler Lovejoy.[8]

Arthur's arrival complicated matters in the troubled Lovejoy
marriage. Sara was unable to nurse her son and a week of artifi-
cial feeding proved ineffective. Wallace hired a good nurse for
Arthur, but repeated attempts to find a wet-nurse failed. Neither
country nor city girls were satisfactory; all were more interested
in making money than in providing adequate nourishment. Wallace finally found an acceptable woman, but he remained convinced that the irregular nursing was the cause of his son's continued restlessness as a baby.[9]

The winter was difficult for the young family. In addition to
the problems with the nurses, Wallace was often separated from
his wife and child as his medical studies took him to Dublin and
London. While he was in Dublin, Sara wrote her husband urging
him not to forget Arthur during his busy days. She described her
fear "that we may not keep him—there is something so heavenly
in his expression every now & then & he is too intelligent and
bright." In April, Wallace returned to Germany and took his
small family to London preparatory to sailing for America in
May 1874.[10]

Wallace hoped that Boston and the new life in America would
usher in a peaceful, settled life for his family. Instead, the prob-

lems only increased. Although Sara had been separated from her sister Margaret previously, this time the separation disturbed her greatly. The icy reception of the Lovejoys deepened her depression. The family, especially Wallace's mother, had never been completely reconciled to the marriage. Wallace later recalled that only his father had accepted his "German" wife. Sara and her father-in-law enjoyed each other, and his death shortly after her arrival in Boston was an unexpected blow to her. On top of these family difficulties, the restlessness of young Arthur remained a problem. Even though he was well attended by nurses, Sara worried about her son and spent long hours caring for him. Wallace finally prescribed something to quiet Arthur at night, partly so his wife could also rest: three drops of fluid extract of gelsemium.[11]

Unknown to her husband, Sara found the glass-stoppered bottle in Wallace's inner office. Ignorant of its dangers, she began taking the drug herself to help her sleep. Wallace later speculated that the normal side effects would also have relieved some of her depression. On Sunday evening, 25 April 1875, Sara and Wallace went to the Boston Music Hall to hear Henry Varley, an English revivalist. About an hour after they retired, Sara's labored breathing woke her husband. As paralysis began to numb her body, she confessed to Wallace that she had taken the drug several times previously and that night had taken about a teaspoon and a half. Sara Lovejoy died before morning on Monday, 26 April.[12]

Sara's life in America had not been particularly happy. Separated from her sister, surrounded by unfriendly relatives, and troubled by her restless son, she had become despondent. Yet, if her husband's description is accurate, her death was inadvertent. Unaware of the drug's power and buoyed by its euphoric effects, Sara Lovejoy increased her own self-prescription.[13] On that Sunday in April 1875, she took an overdose.

Before his mother's death, the eighteen-month-old Arthur had already experienced a great deal of emotional uncertainty. There were the repeated difficulties with wet-nurses, his father's recurring separation from the family, and his mother's depression after the move to Boston. Although Sara seems to have been a loving and caring mother, her own problems may have affected her son. With her death, even this reassuring presence and familiar source of security disappeared.

It is difficult to reconstruct the events of succeeding years, for the Wallace Lovejoy family all but disintegrated following the death of Sara. Wallace plunged into a depression that left him incapable of overseeing his son's care. Wallace's mother, in cooperation with several of Wallace's sisters, removed Arthur from his father's supervision. During the summer of 1875 they took the young boy to Germany, where they remained for three years, while Wallace paid for their stay. Back in Boston he became totally absorbed in his medical practice.[14]

Father and son were reunited in 1878, but not without difficulty. Wallace's sisters opposed Arthur's return to his father until Wallace threatened to make things "hot as hell." They were finally brought together at the home of Auntie Bates, one of Wallace's sisters, where Arthur was staying. With his father sitting in a large chair, Arthur was called from his play. As the youngster walked slowly across the room, Auntie Bates asked, "Who is it? Arthur." The reply was simply, "Papa," and Arthur climbed into his father's lap.[15] Shortly after this reunion, Wallace moved to Germantown, Pennsylvania, where he was later joined by Arthur, Wallace's mother, and several of his sisters. Suffering from pneumonia and overwork, and with a ready supply of drugs, Wallace soon developed an addiction that crippled his ability to function as a doctor and a father.[16]

Arthur Lovejoy's experiences during these five years shaped how he would respond to the world as a mature adult. The extent of the emotional uncertainty was striking. Separation, from both his father and mother, was a recurring event that may well have made him cautious about personal relationships throughout his life. A current of hostility and emotional turbulence raged about him. Tension had characterized the family's relationship with the Lovejoy clan in Boston, and later, when he was removed from his father's care, his grandmother and aunts were determined to keep Wallace at a distance. Even as he returned to his father there were heated quarrels over the propriety of the reunion. In all of this, the young child learned he could not depend upon ties of emotion and sentiment. When, as an adult, Lovejoy sought some basis for coherence in the world, he knew well where he would not find it.

These traumatic events in Lovejoy's early years cannot be ignored for their effect on his mature life, but neither should they

be overemphasized. The caution inculcated in these years probably inhibited his forming intimate personal relationships as an
adult and may partially explain why he never married. Beyond
this, his early unfortunate experiences with emotion and sentiment influenced his work as a philosopher and historian. He
knew that the nonrational aspects of man's being were capricious
and impermanent. He was incapable of building anything on the
quicksand of the nonrational. The most important effect of these
early experiences on Lovejoy's later career was to close off the
nonrational as the foundation for erecting a philosophy. That
left, however, the rational, and on that firmer ground Lovejoy
built.

The events of Lovejoy's life between the time he was reunited
with his father and 1891, when he entered the University of California at Berkeley, are only partially recorded. These years, however, were less turbulent than those preceding them. Stability returned to the Lovejoy family in the early 1880s. Sometime in the
late seventies or early eighties Wallace gave up the practice of
medicine. Wracked by guilt and convinced that his wife's death
and his other problems flowed from his disobedience of his father's will, Wallace entered the Episcopal ministry. This change
helped him to fight his drug addiction and to turn his attention
to his family and his ministry. In January 1881 Wallace remarried,
his bride this time Emmeline Dunton of Germantown, Pennsylvania. Emmeline, perhaps more than any other factor, brought
father and son back together and provided the solid basis for a
family life. Arthur later alluded to her role when he, in a Christ-
mas note to his stepmother, called her "the dear Lady from Philadelphia who, in spite of tribulations, has fetched us all through
safe and sound, packed us off and welcomed us home again several times and still keeps the heart and centre of the family where
she is."[17]

In the early 1880s Wallace moved his family to Ironton, Ohio,
a small town on the Ohio River east of Cincinnati. Here he
served his first ministry in the Protestant Episcopal church. Arthur, reassured by the presence of his father and new mother,
enjoyed the pleasures the river town offered a growing boy. Jynx,
as his parents often called him, and his friends spent many hours
acting out great adventures. The barn of his friend Walter Davis
became in turn "a warship, a fort, a blockhouse besieged by In-

EMIL LEWETZ   HAMBURG.

Arthur O. Lovejoy at the age of two
(Special Collections: The Johns Hopkins University)

Lovejoy's parents, Sara Oncken Lovejoy and Wallace W. Lovejoy
(Special Collections: The Johns Hopkins University)

Lovejoy's stepmother, Emmeline Dunton Lovejoy
(Special Collections: The Johns Hopkins University)

dians, and a circus tent." Romantic adventuring could not last and in the winters gave way to a "lamentable struggle with the multiplication table." The Lovejoys were not in Ironton long, for Wallace soon decided to return East, probably to continue his ministerial studies.[18]

Arthur and his stepmother returned to the Philadelphia area while Wallace continued his studies, first at the Worcester Academy in Worcester, Massachusetts, and later at a school for Protestant ministers established by William Rainey Harper in Philadelphia. They lived in Germantown and then across the Delaware River in Palmyra and Trenton. Arthur continued his schooling and, in addition, attended some classes with his father at Harper's school. Lovejoy remembered taking, at the age of fourteen, a class in Hebrew. His presence in the class was somewhat incongruous; not only was he the youngest, his were the only feet that could not touch the floor. Although the early training in classical languages would prove invaluable, Lovejoy resented his father's pressure to study them. He did not, however, spend all his time in the classroom; there was plenty of time for rowing on the river and for long walks with his dog Karlie along its banks. His last year in the area Arthur spent at the Germantown Academy, where he graduated in 1891.[19]

Lovejoy's adolescent years, then, seem to have been less turbulent than his earliest ones. Emmeline Lovejoy provided an emotional center for the family that had never really existed before. His father had surmounted the worst of his problems and found in the ministry a calling that assuaged some of the guilt which had oppressed him. Although Wallace was still shadowed by the drug problem, his wife and his work pulled him toward stability. In these years Wallace and his son established a close, if not intimate, relationship, based on mutual respect. In Emmeline, Arthur found the mother he had never known.[20]

The summer of 1891 brought more changes, but ones that could be eagerly anticipated. The family moved to Oakland, California, and Arthur prepared to enter the University of California in nearby Berkeley. In September he applied for admission as a freshman in the classical course of the College of Letters. Like all freshmen applying for admission, Lovejoy had to meet stiff entrance requirements including English, mathematics through advanced algebra and plane geometry, history and geography,

Caesar, Cicero, and Vergil, Latin at sight and in composition, Xenophon's *Anabasis* and Homer's *Iliad* in Greek. Lovejoy passed all of the above with excellent or good grades, except for geometry and Latin composition, which he passed conditionally.[21] His secondary training had prepared him well for the university and provided an early indication of the range of his scholarly interests.

The university Lovejoy entered in the fall of 1891 was a small school chartered in 1868 and still struggling to establish itself on a firm basis. Classes had begun in September 1869. Under the first president, Daniel Coit Gilman, the university held a good deal of promise. Following Gilman's departure for Johns Hopkins in 1875, the school expanded slowly and not without difficulty. The problems were largely overcome by the late eighties, and when Lovejoy entered in the fall of 1891 the enrollment had reached 456. Since the university was completely financed by the legislature, Lovejoy paid no tuition during his four years.[22]

The Berkeley campus had only a few buildings in the 1890s, principally the squat and rectangular North and South Halls, the first structures on the campus. Between them, but set back several hundred feet, was Bacon Hall, the library with its turreted Victorian façade. Behind the campus rose the Berkeley hills and in the other direction one could see San Francisco Bay. Lovejoy lived in Oakland while attending school, commuting on the streetcars that ran regularly from Oakland up Telegraph Avenue to the gates of the university.[23]

His courses ranged widely, but emphasized the humanities. He did well in Latin and Greek, though he continued to have difficulty with Latin composition. His interest in languages, which would continue at Harvard, led him into German and Old English. A smattering of history, economics, science, and literature appeared in Lovejoy's schedule, but his major interest outside of language and classics was philosophy, which he began in 1894, his junior year.[24]

From this beginning, philosophic thought eventually displaced religion at the core of Lovejoy's thinking and became the focus of his academic career. Although he seems to have been attracted to metaphysical ideas almost from the time of his introduction to them, his initial interest was encouraged by a powerful teacher, George Holmes Howison.

Howison was probably more influential as a teacher of philosophy than as a philosopher. His writing, however, placed him in the mainstream of American philosophy during the later half of the nineteenth century, though his particular current cut its own channels. Howison characterized his system as "Personal Idealism." He based his metaphysics on the belief that the freedom vital for human life was impossible if the individual was dependent for existence on any other being, including God. Through a process of self-definition, individuals found themselves related to other similar beings. In this system, God became the ideal standard by which the self-defining existents measured reality. The real world was a body of equals moving toward the Ideal exemplified by the Creator. For Lovejoy, as for most of Howison's students, the details of his professor's system were less important than Howison's ability to encourage philosophic modes of thought.[25]

Howison's emphasis on freedom extended to the classroom, where his main goal was to free his students and set them on a search for truth. Howison wanted to do more than free them from their preconceptions and inhibitions; most of all, he hoped to initiate them gradually into the community of the intellect, where the only criterion for judgment was truth. He used rigorous methods to accomplish this. For one thing, he was a stimulating lecturer; his presentations could hold students from his late afternoon classes well into the evening. Or, on other occasions, he might adopt the stance of a Socratic gadfly. On his lecture desk stood a purple vase filled with marbles to which the names of the class members had been taped. At the beginning of a class, Howison reached into the vase to determine who would be asked one of his piercing questions. After the hesitant reply, Howison considered the answer before rejecting it or approving it. In either case, it provided the basis for that day's discussion.[26]

It is difficult to assess with certainty Howison's impact on Lovejoy. To do so would require much greater knowledge of Lovejoy's beliefs in his first years at Berkeley than is ever likely to be possible. Nonetheless, Howison was a major factor in Lovejoy's decision to undertake philosophical inquiry. Before studying philosophy at Berkeley, Lovejoy had been content with the religious beliefs Wallace had transmitted to his son. Although Howison's teachings, which themselves contained a large religious component, did not lead Lovejoy to reject religion, they, and the philosophical method in general, motivated him to examine more critically his religious beliefs and to begin to develop his own ideas. His father suspected Howison's teachings lay at the basis of Lovejoy's slow turn from religion toward philosophy, but it is more likely that the Berkeley professor awakened in his student tendencies toward independent thought which had thus far lain dormant under the religious instruction of the ministerial parent. Howison's skepticism, rigorous inquiry, and constant pursuit after truth were all present in Lovejoy's own work. However, like so many of Howison's students, Lovejoy soon rejected many of the specific ideas of his teacher, for he discovered that his own path toward truth did not lie in the direction of idealism.[27]

Lovejoy's philosophical interests carried over to his extracurricular activities. He participated in the Inter-Society Debate his junior and senior years and was the senior class historian. He joined the Philosophical Union, which Howison directed, in October of his senior year and was also a member of the Bushnell Union. Composed of students and intellectuals from the entire Bay area, the Philosophical Union each year selected a current topic in philosophy represented by a recent book. The monthly meetings began with a paper on some aspect of the topic and were followed by an open and animated discussion. Here Howison's students had an opportunity to engage their teacher in discussion, something seldom permitted in his ordinary classes. At the end of the year the author was invited to address the Philosophical Union or to participate in a public discussion of the issues.[28]

Journalism was Lovejoy's other major interest at Berkeley. As a senior, he was associate editor of the *Berkeleyan*, the campus paper He was also the first editor of the *University of California Magazine* his last year at Berkeley and published in the April 1895 issue his first historical article. In "James Burnett, Lord Monboddo," Lovejoy briefly reviewed Monboddo's life, discussed his anticipations of evolutionary theory, and described the Scotsman's clashes with Samuel Johnson on scientific issues. The article is interesting primarily because it prefigures both a major intellectual interest of Lovejoy's, the development of evolutionary thought before Darwin, and his historical approach to ideas.[29]

Poetry also attracted Lovejoy's interest at Berkeley and his first published poem, "Rain at Dusk," appeared in the magazine he edited:

A narrow circle of gray sky,
  And misty, pelting sheets of rain
A world of grayness, that the eye
  Still strives to pierce beyond in vain;
Vague, glistening roof-shapes through the veil
  Of rain, and murmuring trees that sway
Their tops, distinct against the pale
  Background of all-enclosing gray.

Here have I seen on other eves
  The soft reflected eastern glow
And, tender lights that sunset leaves
  O'er yonder hills, rain hidden now;—
The summer hills that stretched afar
  All slowly purpling, till at last
The darkness came, and star by star
  The sky to sparkling splendor passed.

O joys of life! O Earth with all
  Thy thousand moods! Now gay, now sad,
Now boisterous joyance, now the pall
  Of melancholy, now the glad
Rejoicing after freshening showers,
  Not less we welcome sad than gay,
Their mood as subtly waken ours
  In purple nightfall as in gray.

Though he would publish two additional poems in the magazine after graduation, Lovejoy later kept this modest talent well hidden, revealing it only to his family and a few friends.[30]

His journalistic endeavors kept him on campus, but his involvement in settlement work took Lovejoy into one of the manufacturing areas of Oakland inhabited largely by Portuguese and Italian immigrants. He had been involved in Boys Club work, at one point helping start a Penny Savings Bank, but was later more directly involved in the formation of a settlement house. In February 1895, the Reverend Frank E. Hinckley and Mary E. B.

Norton established a house in West Oakland called The Manse. Later that spring, a minister Lovejoy knew appointed him to an organizing committee for the settlement. While he complained about the work, he found the reading he did on settlement work interesting.[31]

Lovejoy's religious beliefs, which he had acquired from his father, were a major factor in his decision to perform social service in a settlement house. Wallace Lovejoy believed that Christians must actively practice their faith. They ought to follow the example of Christ by becoming a part of the world and by working to alleviate its problems. Wallace wrote his son that he would rather have him work in a city mission than hug the "thin bosom" of philosophy as his "wet-nurse for milk of human sustenance." Arthur replied that he was much inclined to combine the scholar's life with "an active participation in municipal politics, settlement work, and the like." Teaching, he asserted, was "as legitimate and indispensable a form of service as any other, if done honestly and with reference to its social utility." Settlement work attracted him partly because it offered an opportunity to serve humanity while avoiding any commitment to a particular religious dogma and partly because on this aspect of religious belief, at least, he could agree with his father.[32]

Many of the early settlement workers shared Lovejoy's basically religious motivation. Allen F. Davis has suggested that a "large part of the settlement impulse was religious." Many were apparently motivated by what Jane Addams called the "humanitarian aspects" of Christianity.[33] For Lovejoy, these moral considerations remained important long after theological religion had ceased to play a vital role in his life.

As his college career ended in the spring of 1895, Lovejoy faced the critical problem of whether or not to continue his studies in philosophy, as he wanted, or to bow to his father's wishes and enter the ministry. The dispute with his father involved more than the simple question of what kind of postgraduate training he would receive. While he lived at home he felt a strong obligation to follow his father's wishes and had usually acquiesced to his father's demands. Now, however, he had reached the point where whatever course he took would not only remove him from his father's direct influence but would also largely determine the course of his life and career. Arthur sensed this, and the dispute over his choice of schools was only one battle in a long struggle to establish intellectual, moral, and religious independence from his father.

Lovejoy discovered that philosophy did more than interest him intellectually. As a method of thought it enabled him to perceive more clearly what had dissatisfied him in traditional religious faith. Beyond this, he found it useful as a guide to determine what was "universal and essential in religion, and to establish this, as well as the moral interest in life, by a sane grasp upon reality." He also believed that a firm grounding in philosophy was essential to whatever direction his later career took. In the summer after his graduation from Berkeley, Lovejoy was uncertain what he wanted to pursue. He considered English literature, comparative religion, and the history of moral and religious thought. He knew only that he was interested in the development of thought and that any study he undertook would be along historical lines. For all these reasons, then, Lovejoy decided that the best course was to begin graduate work in philosophy, for that would give him the necessary background for any of his interests.[34]

Resolving to go to graduate school was one problem; deciding where to go was another. Lovejoy seriously considered only three schools, Johns Hopkins, Yale, and Harvard. He preferred Harvard for three reasons: Relatives in Boston and several close friends who would also be attending Harvard would make his stay in Cambridge more pleasant; second, graduate courses there were better than anywhere else; finally, with an eye to the future, Lovejoy knew that a degree from Harvard and the contacts he made there would be very useful in finding a teaching job when he finished.[35]

Lovejoy made up his own mind by early summer that he wanted to attend Harvard in the fall. He had not, however, anticipated the vehemence of his father's opposition. Wallace, probably from the time of his reconversion to Episcopalianism in the late seventies, nourished the fervent hope that his son would become a minister. What Wallace feared most was that Arthur would turn away from religion, as Wallace himself had done by going into medicine. Wallace believed that his own early rejection of religion was the cause of all his subsequent troubles, and he wanted to spare his son a similar fate. Uppermost in Wallace's mind was the knowledge that Arthur's study of philosophy at Berkeley had already begun to wean his son from his faith in Christ; Wallace was certain that more metaphysics would only hasten the process. He employed two arguments against Harvard and philosophy. Primarily, he argued for the necessity of a firm belief in Christ as Savior and faith in Christianity as a whole. He sensed, however, that his son found these arguments less and less compelling. Though he never abandoned the theological approach, Wallace increasingly based his argument on Arthur's filial duty. Wallace asserted that his own experience had made him privy to a "life clue," that parental wishes when sincerely presented should always be followed. Again and again he referred to the disastrous consequences that befell him after ignoring his own father's desires. Still ridden with guilt from his own disobedience and Sara's death, Wallace attempted to compel Arthur's obedience by inculcating in him a sense of guilt concerning the duties of a son toward his father.[36]

Throughout May and June, Arthur and his father debated the issue—Arthur arguing for the primacy of his own interests and Wallace for the necessity of a Christian life and a son's obligation to obey his father. Father and son were determined to defend their respective positions, but, at the same time, neither was totally inflexible. Arthur's own religious impulses were still strong, and he had not completely rejected the ministry as a career at some future date. Further, he respected his father's beliefs and sincerity and hesitated to oppose him directly. Wallace, on the other hand, was reluctant to forbid Arthur to attend Harvard. Rather he hoped that the force of his arguments would persuade his son to make that decision for himself. Arthur finally won his father's grudging assent. He conceded the areas in which he was sympathetic with his father's views and said he was willing, if Wallace insisted, to give up his own plans to follow his father's wishes. Wallace, when the time came, was unable to demand compliance with his own desires. Though he continued to protest Arthur's decision, in the end he did not stand in his son's way. Thus, possessing his father's very reluctant approval and a two-hundred-dollar scholarship from the San Francisco Harvard Club, Lovejoy entered the Harvard Graduate School in the fall of 1895 to study philosophy.[37]

When he left for Cambridge, Lovejoy was uncertain what the

experience would bring. He knew, however, that he had to go forward in his search for some system or method of thought that would help him to make sense of the world. Much as he respected his father and his beliefs, traditional, evangelical Christianity no longer satisfied him. By going to Harvard Lovejoy not only further loosened the already tenuous grip religious dogma had on his beliefs, he also began, in a more overt fashion, breaking his father's constraints on his behavior. Because he felt considerable obligation to his father, the break was neither bitter nor complete. Nonetheless, he clearly established the primacy of his own inclinations in determining his choices. For the younger Lovejoy, Harvard would be a place where he could exercise his new-found independence and begin, in earnest, his inquiry into the universal and the essential.

Harvard in the 1890s had one of the best graduate schools in the nation, and, as Lovejoy recognized, undoubtedly the best philosophy department. Josiah Royce, William James, and George Santayana headed a faculty that also included George Herbert Palmer and Hugo Münsterberg. The department was unusual, not only for the quality of its members, but also for the diversity of their interests. As Palmer acknowledged, it was a diversity encouraged by the members of the department. In this intellectually bracing climate, the student was exposed to some of the best, though often diametrically opposed, philosophical thinking in America. Although each philosopher had his followers, discipleship was not the salient characteristic of a Harvard education. In a situation where James and Royce could repeatedly attack each other philosophically and yet remain good friends, students learned the value of closely reasoned independent thought. The "thick atmosphere" encouraged by James and the other members of the department provided Lovejoy with the perfect setting in which to achieve his intellectual independence from the fetters of traditional belief and to begin to ask basic questions.[38]

Royce and James were the two men who had the greatest impact on the young philosopher. Initially, Lovejoy had a much higher opinion of Royce. Royce's "intellectual subtlety, flexibility, open-mindedness and general breadth of sympathetic understanding" impressed the young scholar. On the basic issue of philosophical ideas, the two Californians did not agree. Even in the first class he took from Royce, metaphysics in 1895–96, Lovejoy dissented from his professor's absolute idealism. Still, Lovejoy respected Royce's skill at "intellectual midwifery" sufficiently to take another course from him on the development of the Hegelian system in his third year at Harvard.[39]

With William James, Lovejoy's opinions of the man and his work changed considerably over the years. Lovejoy took only one course from James, a seminar in his second year on the philosophy of Kant. James, he discovered, was "rather disappointing." Personally congenial, as a teacher and lecturer James left "a good deal to be desired." On the basis of this course James did not seem to "be a thinker of very great insight." Part of Lovejoy's dissatisfaction lay in his belief that James completely misinterpreted Kant, "taking him as a descriptive psychologist rather than as a metaphysician and so making nonsense of the whole system." He admitted, however, that one could probably get more from James in "the independent exposition of his own highly suggestive notions and enthusiasms."[40]

Although Lovejoy's relationship with James during his last year at Harvard is not clear, James's ideas on philosophical issues provided the younger man with vital reinforcement of his own inclinations. Lovejoy would later disagree with many parts of James's philosophy, but by the time of the latter's death in 1910, his estimate of James as a philosopher had changed drastically. Lovejoy praised the "bracing, stimulating, and mind-enlarging influence of his personality" and his "intellectual courage and intellectual candor." Further, he regarded James's most significant contribution to have been his "almost unequaled power of *seeing* these two generic aspects of reality: the uniqueness and inwardly self-authenticating character of concrete individual existences" and "the uniqueness and the primacy of the temporal quality of experience."[41]

Lovejoy also took courses from a number of the other philosophers at Harvard. In his last year he took a course on the historical development of ethical thought in England from G. H. Palmer. He enjoyed Palmer, especially for his literary and biographical, rather than speculative, approach. Lovejoy's classes with Hugo Münsterberg in advanced psychology and George Santayana in Greek philosophy and Plato passed almost unnoticed at the time, though Santayana may have influenced Lovejoy's interest in Platonic thought.[42]

Like so many other students and philosophers, Lovejoy found the diversity of the thinkers at Harvard stimulating. Further, with such a divergence of opinion, he experienced a whole range of ideas that was probably unobtainable anywhere else at the time. Later, he had some second thoughts. He worried that if philosophers working in such close proximity were unable to move toward any consensus it might be impossible for philosophy ever to become a science. Still, for a student beginning his own inquiry into the basic questions of philosophy, the freedom of Harvard imposed few intellectual constraints and reinforced his belief in the necessity of unfettered thought.[43]

While at Harvard, Lovejoy's interests extended beyond philosophy. A major secondary interest, comparative religion, continued into many of his early publications. He took a number of courses from Charles C. Everett, including the psychological basis of religious faith and comparative religion, which examined Vedic religion, Hinduism, Buddhism, Mazdaism, and the Chinese religions. He also studied Hebrew religion with Crawford H. Toy and Sanskrit and some of the sacred Buddhist texts under Charles R. Lanman.[44] Lovejoy enjoyed the religious courses, which seem to have filled a need for him. He was extremely interested in the historical development of religion. As noted earlier, Lovejoy sought in philosophy a method by which he could determine what was universal in religion. In his terms, what was historically determined could not be universal. His investigation of religion was motivated in part by this need to discover what were the essential elements not only of Christianity but also of religion in general.[45]

Lovejoy did not restrict his activities in Cambridge to the academic. However, as at Berkeley, many of his extracurricular pursuits were closely related to his scholarly work. He was a member of the Religious Union, which he described as "an organization of the religiously miscellaneous and undefined." In connection with the Religious Union, he established, in the fall of 1897, a small group to read and study Isaiah. He was also a member of the Graduate Philosophical Society and its secretary during his second year at Harvard. In February 1897, he led a discussion on the problem of evil. In May 1896, he joined and participated in the activities of the Graduate Club of Harvard, a social organization with frequent smokers and monthly meetings to hear talks by prominent speakers. Finally, there was a curious organization called the Cambridge Conferences organized by Mrs. Ole Bull. At the regular Sunday meeting some distinguished individual, including "a due proportion of 'Jews, Turks,' Hindus and other such haythen," lectured on ethics, history, or philosophy. Although Lovejoy was a bit taken aback by the arrangement, he enjoyed the conferences. All these organizations had their social functions, but Lovejoy seemed to enjoy their educational offerings as much, if not more than, their social opportunities.[46]

As he had at Berkeley, Lovejoy participated in settlement work while at Harvard. It was something he had considered doing even before leaving California, but after arriving in Cambridge he waited nearly a year before becoming involved. Early in his second year, he became a student teacher for the Prospect Union, an organization of workers and students and teachers of Harvard. The workers paid a small fee, two dollars in 1899, to join this union. The student and faculty volunteers offered classes in the evenings ranging from elementary subjects through college studies including music and art. In the late nineties the union membership averaged about five hundred workers and around seventy student teachers from Harvard. Lovejoy had anticipated teaching a course in ethics, but in the fall of 1896 was having difficulty recruiting enough students.[47]

The following year, Lovejoy volunteered to work for the Boston Children's Aid Society as a visitor in their Home Library program. The program was designed to inculcate reading habits in children who would not ordinarily have had access to books. Small libraries of twenty or so books were placed in one child's home and the children in the group would meet with the adult visitor once a week to exchange books, discuss their reading, and play games. The children were also encouraged to save by placing their spare change in the care of the visitor. Lovejoy worked with eleven students ranging in age from nine to fourteen. He met with them five or six times a month to talk about their reading and current events, and to participate in other activities, such as street cleaning. The young philosopher enjoyed the work and found that when his students had to correct his results in dividing fractions it made their "collaboration so much the less formal and more exciting." Lovejoy not only worked with the children, but also counseled their parents on how best to deal with a deteriorating neighborhood.[48] With these efforts, he tried to combine the life of the scholar and that of the social activist.

Lovejoy viewed his settlement work in a broader perspective than that of simply meeting a particular religious need of his. He appreciated the fact that Harvard encouraged the development of "public spirit" in its students. The willingness to serve the larger community meant that the university was training its students to be citizens in the broadest sense. Lovejoy believed that cooperation among classes could lead more quickly to a complete solution of the nation's problems. He was not merely reaffirming his earlier position that social service was compatible with scholarship; he now began to suggest a nonreligious motivation—the duties of a citizen toward his nation—as a basis for such activity.[49] Thus, as Lovejoy's own religious impulses waned in the coming years, the call to duty outside the university remained strong.

Lovejoy worked hard at Harvard, both inside the classroom and in his service activities. However, he was not a drudge. He had a circle of close friends, several of whom he had known at Berkeley, and including two of his fellow graduate students, William Pepperell Montague and Ralph Barton Perry. His relatives in Boston provided an easily accessible escape from the rigors of academics. One summer he spent in Montrose, Pennsylvania, with his stepmother's relatives hiking and fishing. Boston was a frequent attraction for plays, or lectures, or just for a walk around Copley Square to enjoy the architecture. Although these activities broke his usual routine, even Lovejoy admitted to his father that "things are getting into a rut with me,—not a wholly bad condition, but probably one not interesting to hear about."[50]

Lovejoy's rut, however, was not without its moments of tension. Although his slow course toward independence from his father was aided considerably by the distance separating them, Wallace still hoped and tried to be a major influence on his son's religious development. In March 1897, Wallace renewed his attempt to convince Arthur to enter the ministry. Believing that everyone must give his life to humanity in the Christian fashion, Wallace urged his son to at least take a year's leave from Harvard to study Christology, the theological interpretation of the life and work of Christ, at Andover Theological Seminary. Arthur immediately protested in a long letter. There were practical difficulties, for Andover seldom admitted students for less than the full course of study. Since it was a denominational seminary, Arthur feared he would be unable to profess a belief in the necessary doctrines. More directly than he had previously, he questioned his father's motives. He suspected that this request of Wallace's was an attempt to force him, through "external means," to accept beliefs which he had already rejected. He further argued that a year at Andover would sidetrack the normal development of his thought. Arthur conceded his father's sincerity and that Wallace had his son's eternal interests in mind, but, as he put it, "you entirely ignore my *will* in the matter." Having made his case as strongly as he could, Arthur became more flexible. As he had in the dispute over going to Harvard, he indicated his willingness to follow the desires of his father should Wallace insist.[51]

When he replied to his son's letter of protest, Wallace modified his position. He admitted knowing little of the conditions at Andover. His wish was not to convert Arthur or to force him into the ministry. He simply hoped that through a close study of Christ his son would come to believe in Jesus as his personal savior. Wallace lamented that while he was on the "heart-tack—the universal tack," Arthur was on the "intellectual tack." In the end, Wallace indicated that he felt less strongly about a year at Andover than Arthur had assumed, especially since it appeared that the seminary was not well suited to his purpose. Arthur's response was also more conciliatory. He admitted that a year at Andover might prove stimulating intellectually and provide the leisure to pursue some special projects. This, of course, was not exactly what Wallace had in mind when he suggested the move. In spite of his greater flexibility, Arthur reiterated his conviction that he would prefer to pursue his studies at Harvard. The matter was left at this stage until Wallace arrived in Boston during the summer of 1897. As had happened earlier, Arthur knew how to win his father's reluctant acquiescence, and he continued at Harvard after having received his M.A. in the spring.[52]

Before receiving the M.A., Lovejoy had talked with Royce about his plans for the future. They decided that he should spend a third year at Harvard and then go to Europe for a year of study. In the spring of 1897, Lovejoy had anticipated that he would finish all the requirements for a Ph.D. by the spring of 1899. However, the M.A. was the only advanced degree that

Lovejoy would receive. William James probably influenced him to change his mind about the higher degree. James opposed the Ph.D., because he felt that the requirements interfered with the development of talent and ideas, fostered academic snobbery, and diverted "the attention of aspiring youth from direct dealing with truth to the passing of examinations." James believed that students could help deemphasize the disproportionate respect accorded those three letters. He argued that every man who refused to take the degree because the "examinations interfere with the free following out of his more immediate intellectual aims" deserved the respect of his country and should not be made to suffer. Letters of recommendation could remedy this deficiency of degree and were, in James's opinion, a better indication of a person's ability. Lovejoy was apparently convinced by James's arguments, for when he wrote David Starr Jordan concerning his first appointment at Stanford his reasons for not having completed the degree were similar to those of James: "I am personally very indifferent about it and regard it as unwise for a man to go at all out of the way of his own philosophical interests in order to conform to the requirements of this exercise."[53] At least in Lovejoy's case, James was right; the lack of the title was to prove no bar to academic success.

The impact of Lovejoy's Harvard experiences on the young philosopher can be only partially assessed here. Nonetheless, it is clear already that Lovejoy's years in Cambridge were vital to his development as an individual. Here Lovejoy achieved much of the personal and intellectual independence he sought. Three thousand miles from home in an intellectual atmosphere that encouraged diversity and freedom of thought, Lovejoy broke more completely the constraints Wallace Lovejoy had imposed. His father could still cause Arthur to consider seriously a more religious course. However, by the time of the dispute about Andover, the father's arguments had lost almost all their coercive force. Arthur still felt a sense of filial responsibility, but it was clear that only this and not Wallace's beliefs could deflect Arthur from his chosen course of intellectual inquiry. In the face of Arthur's self-assured position, Wallace eventually gave way. Thus, when Arthur went to Paris in the fall of 1898 he left America with religious and intellectual debts, but confident that he could face the world alone.

Lovejoy's year in France from September 1898 until August 1899 was initially intended as a research and study trip preparatory to writing a dissertation. Although he did considerable research, no dissertation resulted. Instead, Lovejoy spent the time pursuing his own interests, chiefly a historical approach to comparative religion.

It was the young philosopher's first visit to Europe since his three-year stay in Germany as a child. After a brief stop in England, he journeyed to France, where he intended to study at the Sorbonne. Before the university opened, he rested for several delightful weeks in the small town of Auxerre outside Paris, practicing his French. Later in life he would blame Irving Babbitt, who taught him French at Harvard, for his bad accent. Once in Paris he attended some classes at the Sorbonne. He studied the Book of Psalms with Maurice Vernes and frequently listened to Jean Reville's lectures on the Fourth Gospel on Saturday afternoons. Lovejoy had hoped to take a course in Páli Buddhism from Sylvan Levi, but since Levi was not offering anything that year, the young American occasionally went to the Frenchman's home to read with him some of the sacred texts. Primarily, Lovejoy spent his days in the Bibliothèque Nationale and other libraries pursuing his historical investigations into Jewish and other religious thought. His year of research would only bear fruit in succeeding years when he had time to write several articles based on his discoveries.[54]

Lovejoy went to Europe as a student, but he did not restrict his studies to his books; he was a fascinated observer of European habits and customs. Like his academic work, however, his observations tended to be on religious belief and behavior. Lovejoy was intrigued, repelled, and almost entranced by what was apparently his first real contact with Catholicism. He first encountered the faith in England, where Anglo-Catholicism was creating divisions within the Anglican Church. He viewed the spread of the Catholic movement there as a "melancholy spectacle; one could hardly have expected *a priori* that even any considerable minority of the English race would so far lose its moral virility as to reerect the confessional—not to say anything about the more intellectual side of such a reactionary movement." In France, where Catholicism had not been seriously challenged in centuries, Lovejoy felt that the Church, with its emphasis on the supernatural, was to blame for the nation's political problems. But even this descendant of solid New England and German Protestants could fall, however reluctantly, under the spell of Catholicism. Walking into Notre Dame Cathedral one sunny morning as the multihued light of the eastern rose window shone brilliantly, Lovejoy discovered Mass in progress with not a single worshiper in attendance. He found the elaborate ritual celebrated for itself "extraordinarily impressive" and could understand for the first time the appeal Catholicism had for the "aesthetic sense and the imagination" of man's religious nature. While granting that Catholicism could not be exceeded in its ability to meet certain of man's emotional needs, he nonetheless found its debilitating effect on man's individual will and intellect sufficient cause for condemnation.[55]

As the year in Paris passed, Lovejoy viewed his probable return to Cambridge and the writing of a dissertation without enthusiasm. Then, in March, he received word from his father that a family friend, a Congregational minister in Berkeley, had nominated him for a new position in philosophy at Stanford University. Lovejoy had not expected to be teaching the following year, but the prospect was far more appealing than writing to meet Harvard's Ph.D. requirements. His Harvard professors recommended him highly: Royce described him as "an admirable man, —growing, learned, resolute, ingenious, and sensible," and lacking only teaching experience; C. C. Everett called him "a scholar of a high order" possessed of an "original & interesting mind." When President David Starr Jordan offered him a position in early May, Lovejoy gladly accepted. Since he was the first professional philosopher on the Stanford faculty, he was especially pleased to be able to build a department from the foundation: "Hardly any task could make a greater appeal to one who feels strongly, not merely the interest of the subject itself, but also the significant educational function, at once sobering and fructifying and enlarging, which a properly organized instruction in it [philosophy] ought to perform in the general discipline which a college gives to its students."[56]

In his letter to President Jordan, Lovejoy outlined his proposal for instruction in philosophy. Although he believed "a thorough course in the History of Philosophy should be the basis of all work in the department," he acknowledged that there were difficulties with such a course. He felt that if the teacher was interesting, focused on essentials, and emphasized unity within the diversity of principles, the problems could be overcome. Beyond this basic course, he was willing to offer a class dealing with optimism, pessimism, the problem of evil, and the logic of judgments about existence. He would also teach a course in formal logic if necessary, but preferred that it continue to be taught as a part of rhetoric.[57]

The letter to Jordan is important for what it reveals about the state of Lovejoy's thought. He viewed this appointment as an opportunity to begin to serve the community through his teaching. His wish was not entirely altruistic, for it also enabled him to meet his father's continual criticism of his isolation from the problems of the world. Lovejoy's primary emphasis on a historical approach to philosophy suggests that his historical outlook enunciated when he entered Harvard had been reinforced in the intervening years. Applied in a classroom situation here, historical and genetic analysis would become a hallmark of Lovejoy's investigations into philosophy and ideas. Thus, when he went to Stanford in the fall of 1899, the basic elements of Lovejoy's education were completed. He would continue to learn and to develop, but these processes would, in many ways, simply be an elaboration on a well-established foundation.

CHAPTER II

"TOWARD A RATIONAL THEOLOGY

OF THE FUTURE," 1895–1910

Although he was professor of philosophy at Stanford, Lovejoy's major intellectual interest was the role of religion in modern America. In the "tolerably pagan community" of Stanford, Lovejoy saw an opportunity to lay the foundations of a "restored Christianity and reconstructed Church." He wanted to help establish "a religion which shall be essentially religious and yet absolutely in harmony with the intellectual and social condition and moral ideals of modern life."[1]

As he moved slowly toward the rational deism of his mature years, his course was difficult, for it involved far more than religious belief. Lovejoy had to overcome his strong sense of obligation to his father before he could begin to construct an alternative religious position. Finally, his rational impulse led him to attempt to synthesize ideas about pluralism, time, evolution, and God into an approximation of "the rational theology of the future."[2] Ultimately, Lovejoy failed to merge these ideas into a consistent and useful rational theology, and by the time of the First World War philosophy supplanted religion as the determining factor in his life and thought.

Lovejoy's religious beliefs developed in opposition to his father's. Wallace cared little for the fine points of theology. He repeatedly urged Arthur to "take any view of religion, Bible, XT [Christ], you like, if only you accept him . . . as the divine Son of Man, head and Savior of [the] race, as history shows him." Wallace dismissed all rational, speculative, or historical difficulties; reduced to its essentials, being a Christian meant one was "personally committed to J. XT as leader and Savior." In pressing this view on his son, Wallace also resorted to the doctrine of the "life clue." There was "one clue in life as ineffaceable as Creation, as strong as the heart of God—that of the primary instincts and affections." Filial duty demanded that Arthur follow his father's sincerely expressed wishes. In resisting his father's ideas Lovejoy struggled to determine his own position in religious matters and to ensure that he would be the sole arbiter of what he believed.[3]

His major critique of Christianity centered on the historical basis of religious truth. He rejected the idea that the Biblical events had any compelling force. These mythical events might have exemplary value, but Lovejoy denied the historical validity of miraculous occurrences. He believed religion consisted of universals and that it was absurd to make "historical accident" guard "the gateway of approach to fellowship in spiritual truths which have a universal value."[4] When religious men tied Christianity to a belief in a historical, miraculous Christ they made it difficult for rational men to accept the doctrines of the religion.

Beyond freeing himself from the theological positions of his father, Lovejoy needed to establish the primacy of individual conviction in religious belief. He wrote his father that he had arrived at his convictions with his "eyes open, in the presence of abundant 'influences' of an evangelical sort," and that he could no longer deny that his "native point of view" differed greatly from his father's. Arthur respected his father's beliefs, but they lacked any authority: "The only authority that I know anything about, in religion and morals, is that of inner conviction." Acquiescence to his father's position because of filial duty would have been "a flight from the troublesome stress of living to the vacuity of death, a final giving up of confidence in the soul of man." Lovejoy realized that only by breaking with the past could he be free to follow his own convictions: "However much my ideas may, as I hope they will develop, I certainly do not expect to go back on my tracks; and as the path was not entered upon blindly, I think it is now too late to expect to change it."[5]

While a graduate student, Lovejoy denied the historical justification of Christianity and the religious authority of his father, but he did not completely reject Christianity. The ethical side of the religion he accepted with few qualms. He believed that there was a "loving God" who men may know and who "justifies men's highest endeavors and holiest thoughts." God was "progressively realizing his purpose in the world" and a "true life" aided this process. Finally, one looked to Christ as the perfect embodiment of a moral life in the service of God. Lovejoy accepted Christ's life as an ideal; he rejected, however, any notion of divinity, for that was beyond the bounds of human reason.[6]

Lovejoy's dispute with his father went beyond matters of theology. Since he still professed to be a Christian, the younger man faced the problem of denominational affiliation. While he lived at home, Arthur felt obliged to attend services with his family. However, he never formally joined the congregation. His views, even then, prevented him from subscribing to the statement of belief. In Cambridge, Lovejoy no longer felt any need to maintain a pretense of denominational unity with his family. Still, he desired the religious fellowship that only denominational affiliation offered.[7]

He quickly discovered that it was easier to choose a congenial denomination than to explain his decision to his father. By the fall of his second year at Harvard, Lovejoy decided he would join a Unitarian congregation. As he explained to his father, "the characteristic advantage of Unitarianism, if it be an advantage, is that it refuses to demand that its members shall hold to any specific view, beyond their desire for the religious life and a religious fellowship." Unitarianism attracted Lovejoy for positive as well as negative reasons. He felt that "a man ought to begin to stand for something, to influence the community in his own way and measure, to impart as well as absorb." Active participation in religious fellowship would enable him to follow the moral example of Christ and serve humanity. However, his desires for fellowship were very likely more than simply religious. Belonging to a community of like-minded peers was probably as important as possessing a faith.[8]

As might be expected, his father objected strenuously to Arthur's Unitarian leanings. He argued that his son's intended action was mistaken on three accounts. It removed Arthur from the evangelical tradition of his ancestors, it broke the historical continuity of apostolic succession, and it ran counter to the direction of progress. Since Arthur had already rejected any historically based argument, his father's points had little force.

Although Wallace remained opposed to his son's changed allegiance, he consoled himself with the thought that even an aberrant religious affiliation was better than none at all.[9]

In his years at Harvard, Lovejoy laid the foundations for a more systematic critique of revealed religion. Although his inquiry into religion was rooted in his personal convictions, it quickly developed into a major intellectual problem. The young philosopher was convinced, with Kant, that "religion is a rational necessity of man's intelligent nature & cannot be made to rest in any historical accident." He admitted that religion had a historical aspect, but declared that "a religious truth is not a temporal fact."[10] These statements suggest how far Lovejoy had moved from the positions of his father and the direction his religious studies would take. His reaction against emotion and faith meant that he could accept only rationally coercive religious truth. Lovejoy's awareness of the temporal aspect of the problem, a characteristic of his entire career, suggested to him that rational universals could not be dependent upon changing historical circumstance. The essential elements of any religion, then, would have to be rationally necessary for them to have any compelling force.

Lovejoy continued his inquiry into the historical and rational bases of religion after he left Harvard. He spent most of his year in Paris reading in the subject, but the pressures of teaching forced him to delay writing anything for several years. Thereafter, he published several articles in which he examined the historical basis of Christianity. These essays are important, not only for what they reveal about Lovejoy's religious positions, but also because they are early examples of his work in the history of ideas. As early as 1902, Lovejoy was developing the concept of the "unit-idea," which he would employ so powerfully in *The Great Chain of Being*. So, too, these early articles on religion sketched the history of the ideas of otherworldliness and the self-sufficient good that would be elaborated in his masterful study of the chain of being. In two articles published in 1907, "The Entangling Alliance of Religion and History" and "The Origins of Ethical Inwardness in Jewish Thought," Lovejoy extended his analysis of historical Christianity. The articles focused on the relationship between Jewish historical thought and Christianity.

Largely historical in character, these essays were, nevertheless, addressed to the problem of rejecting a religion of faith and creating a rational religion for the modern world.

"The Origins of Ethical Inwardness in Jewish Thought" was the more explicitly historical of the two articles. Lovejoy argued that the Wisdom Books of the Old Testament contained the basis for Christ's emphasis on the inwardness of virtue. He believed that the Wisdom writers, like Sophists and Socratic philosophers, had sought to "intellectualize morality." This occurred because, at a certain stage in all religions, individuals demanded reasons justifying ethical precepts. Christian thought expanded on this idea of inwardness so that it became the conception of the individual as morally supreme and responsible for his own actions and inner life before God. Lovejoy characterized this idea as one of the contributions of Christianity to "the world's stock of fundamental moral ideas."[11]

Two strains of Lovejoy's thinking are evident in his analysis of Jewish thought. There is, of course, his discovery of the introduction of reason and intellect into religious thought. For him, this was probably one of the most significant developments in the history of thought, for in time it would provide the grounds for eliminating the emotional basis of religion. The notion of individual moral supremacy was equally important. When he began his studies of the Wisdom Books in 1897, he was struggling to establish the primacy of his inner convictions.[12] The writings of these Jewish prophets and the development of their ideas helped Lovejoy to justify his theological independence.

In the other article published in 1907, "The Entangling Alliance of Religion and History," Lovejoy elaborated on the critique of historical Christianity he had sketched ten years earlier in his discussions with his father. He argued that the peculiar Christian emphasis on the eternal aspect of temporal events was a legacy of Jewish prophetism centered on a "religio-ethical and patriotic interpretation of history." Lovejoy believed that Paul had tied Christianity to history by making the whole of the religion depend upon two temporal events, the crucifixion and resurrection of Christ. The seventeenth- and eighteenth-century deists, Lovejoy asserted, began the modern assault on historical Christianity. They argued, much as Lovejoy himself had with his father, that historical truths could be known only to the relatively small number of people within the tradition and thus had none of the universal significance appropriate to a religion. Historical knowledge, especially about ancient events, was only probable and hardly a firm basis for religious truth. Lovejoy felt that while all men might gradually come to hold "the same general beliefs upon the more essential issues of life," agreement on matters of historical fact was probably impossible. Although Christianity should move closer to the temporal order of things, it ought to ignore historical detail.[13] The primacy of reasoned inner conviction on the essential elements of Christian morality and ethics would then be freed from a pseudohistorical mythology so foreign to modern rational minds.

Lovejoy hoped that by tracing both the conjunction of history and Christianity and the ever-increasing reaction against this union he would be able to justify the separation of religious belief from its historical bases. This was not necessary if religious belief was based on faith and emotion, since one may as well believe in the resurrection as in any other miraculous occurrence. However, because he believed that religion constituted "a man's ultimate and definitive intellectual and moral reaction upon his experience" it presupposed "truths valid and significant for all men."[14] For Lovejoy, these truths could be universal only if they were not contingent, that is, if they were rational necessities. By 1907 he believed that he had demonstrated both the historical fallacy of Christianity and the direction in which religious thought must develop.

In the years after his leaving Harvard, religion was more than an intellectual problem for Lovejoy. Just as his disputes with his father shaped his historical work, so his father's teachings on the social aspect of religion helped guide Lovejoy's social activism during his first years as a professor. Teaching at Stanford, Washington University in St. Louis, and briefly at Columbia and the University of Missouri, Lovejoy tried to combine the life of a scholar with that of the humanitarian reformer.

Lovejoy's appointment as the first professor of philosophy at Stanford in 1899 was a mixed blessing. He saw it as an opportunity to practice his beliefs about the social and personal value of philosophical thinking and to combine academics with social service. Others were not so sure that Stanford and its president, David Starr Jordan, would be very receptive either to philosophy or to social reform. George Holmes Howison thought Jordan was so set in his positivistic and materialistic ways that a man of Lovejoy's training and inclination could not even be appointed. Ralph Barton Perry expressed the general attitude of Lovejoy's friends when he wrote of the challenge of "carrying philosophy into the enemy's country."[15]

In spite of Howison's apprehension, Lovejoy's philosophical teachings met little resistance at Stanford. He taught a variety of courses ranging from elementary logic to historical and systematic ethics, the philosophy of religion, and the theory of worth. He also organized a philosophical society along the lines of the one at Harvard. In its first year, E. A. Ross, David Starr Jordan, and Lovejoy, among others, spoke to the group. Lovejoy, unlike some of his friends, was more amused than disturbed by Jordan's materialistic positivism. The enemy was, no doubt, less formidable at close range. In writing to his father he recounted Jordan's comments on philosophy to freshmen: "When you find a student who worries himself about the ultimate destiny of man or the ultimate end of philosophy, you know that what he wants is quinine or something that will act on the liver." Lovejoy admitted that the comment suggested a "certain truth," but it was not "the sort of thing that is calculated to send students flocking into the courses in philosophy." The young professor was probably less hostile to Jordan's views because, in spite of the religious tinge to his philosophy, he was little concerned with ultimate ends. Like Jordan, Lovejoy's interests were focused on earthly reality.[16]

There is little in the record of Lovejoy's first year at Stanford to suggest that he would become a part of one of the most important academic freedom cases in this century. On 11 November 1900 President Jordan accepted the forced resignation of the economist Edward A. Ross, who had long been a controversial figure at Stanford. Ross had supported William Jennings Bryan and free silver in 1896, relatively unpopular positions in academic circles. In succeeding years he had often advocated views guaranteed to upset powerful economic and political interests. Jane Stanford, widow of the founder and sole regent of the university, was especially disturbed by Ross's frequent public statements. For four years after 1896, President Jordan had protected Ross's freedom to speak by placating Mrs. Stanford. In the spring of 1900, Ross spoke publicly against importation of Oriental labor and for public ownership of municipal utilities. Mrs. Stanford demanded that Jordan fire Ross and, when he was unable to negotiate another compromise, the president accepted Ross's resignation. Ross's dismissal quickly became a focal point of debate on academic freedom. Although there is some evidence that Ross attempted to orchestrate the reaction and to exploit the outcry, there can be no doubt that the case powerfully raised the question of the rights of professors to speak and act publicly on social and political issues.[17]

Lovejoy was clearly disturbed by Ross's dismissal, yet apparently held himself aloof from the turmoil for as long as possible. In a situation in which the lines of dispute were sharply drawn, Lovejoy was soon forced to take a clear stand. He recalled that professors were summoned into the office of a senior professor and friend of Jordan's to examine correspondence between the president and Mrs. Stanford regarding the case. The administration expected the faculty, after examining the documents, to sign a "round-robin" that justified the dismissal of Ross, or, at the very least, "to keep silence." Lovejoy resisted seeing the documents for some time, and finally agreed to look at them only after declaring that he retained "complete freedom to take such action afterwards as the circumstances" might require. He concluded that Jordan had fired Ross only under pressure from Mrs. Stanford and that she had specifically objected to Ross's public statements. When the "round-robin" supporting the administration was published in the San Francisco papers, Lovejoy published a statement pointing out that the case involved the principle of academic freedom. At the same time he decided that to remain on the faculty would condone the actions of the administration. In a letter to Jordan on 29 April 1901, he resigned as associate professor of philosophy—"the resignation to take effect either directly or at the end of the semester as you may think best." Somewhat to his surprise, he was ordered to cease all duties immediately. Lovejoy's resignation was not an isolated act; as Mary Furner has noted, "Every professor in the social sciences who could afford the gesture resigned." Others wanted to, but were restrained by their family responsibilities; most of those who resigned were unmarried or without children.[18]

Lovejoy believed that Ross's dismissal threatened the right of scholars to be social and political activists. "Unless the members of our profession show themselves somewhat punctilious in the maintenance of those liberties," he wrote Jordan, "I do not see how either the dignity of the teacher's position or the leadership and social usefulness of the universities in our democratic society can be preserved." If the Ross case had passed unchallenged, academics would have reduced their freedom to use their training and knowledge to advise and lead movements for social and political reform. For Lovejoy, of course, this would have been a severe blow to his longstanding goal of combining scholarship and social service. As a result of his experiences at Stanford, he became convinced that only through united action could university professors ensure their freedom to participate in the affairs of society.[19]

Lovejoy's concern about the freedom of professors to perform public service was widely shared by his colleagues. Many in the Progressive era, including David Starr Jordan, were urging that the university and its faculty become involved in the problems of society. Faced with professors who advocated unpopular positions, the academic community was less sure about the limits of scholarly free speech. To what extent was a professor identified with his university? Could a partisan activist be a nonpartisan educator? How could ideas be tested, if not in the social and political realms? These were only some of the issues that the academic community and society at large confronted.[20] These problems have never been resolved; even Lovejoy, in his long career, would change his views.

In the spring of 1901, however, Lovejoy faced a more immediate problem, finding a position for the coming academic year. He enlisted the aid of his old advisors, including George Holmes Howison, and finally received a letter from W. S. Chaplin, president of Washington University in St. Louis, asking him to come for an interview. When Lovejoy arrived in St. Louis, he discovered that Chaplin had gone to a Minnesota lake on vacation. He followed the president north and, at the resort, found that Chaplin was fishing in the middle of the lake. Rather than wait, Lovejoy rowed another boat out to meet him. The interview was conducted on the water and Lovejoy returned with the position. In many ways it was similar to the one at Stanford; he was the first, and only, professor hired for the new philosophy department, which he was directed to develop as he saw fit. Chaplin offered a salary of up to $2,500 and promised to spend $300 to begin a philosophical library. Lovejoy had some initial misgivings about the school: "Coming from such places as Berkeley and Stanford one feels very much as if one had been washed up into the backwaters of the educational current." In spite of the lack of a library, the antiquated administrative methods, and the absence of student social life, he was optimistic. He viewed it as an opportunity "to get in and stir things up generally—even for the sake of the stir itself."[21]

One philosophy professor could not, of course, remake the school but Lovejoy's activities during his six years in St. Louis reveal a continuing enthusiasm to "stir things up." He continued his intellectual inquiries into religion, participated actively in settlement and other social work, and increasingly turned his attention to the intellectual problems and institutions of academic philosophy. Lovejoy's religious needs were centered more than ever on social religion, but even as late as 1903 he seriously considered an opportunity to teach Unitarian ministers. The value of his work in St. Louis and the problems of philosophy were, however, compelling reasons to stay on the dual course he had chosen for himself.

The temptation to affiliate himself more closely with religion came in the form of an invitation to join the faculty of Meadville Theological Seminary. The offer from the Unitarian seminary north of Pittsburgh was attractive as "a call to a more serious sort of work" in which he could make "more serviceable use" of his education and interests. Lovejoy thought he might influence the Unitarian ministry toward a broader conception of the rational leadership of social reform. His own doubts about taking the position were, however, reinforced by his friends: Ralph Barton Perry, for example, asked if it wouldn't "side track you a little to go to Meadville?" In the end, Lovejoy decided to stay at Washington University because an academic position was less confining.[22]

Even while considering a move to Meadville, Lovejoy actively practiced social religion in St. Louis, where he centered his activities on the North Broadway Social Settlement. Situated in a crowded tenement district, the settlement served a neighborhood of poorly paid Poles, Russians, Italians, and Czechs. The house offered various educational classes ranging from English to music, basketry, and domestic art. Lovejoy served as president of the settlement for at least one year, but resigned "in order to get an energetic young lawyer, with millionaire connections, into the place." During his involvement, Lovejoy participated fully in the affairs of the house, from worrying about finances, to establishing an Inter-Settlement Baseball League, teaching English to Polish immigrants, and writing pamphlets.[23]

In St. Louis, Lovejoy began to deemphasize religion as a basis for social service. He revealed this changing emphasis in a pamphlet he prepared for the settlement in 1902. A social settlement, he wrote, "does not, in the common sense of the term, engage in religious work; for one of its purposes is to serve as a point of contact where men of diverse social conditions, religious convictions and political affiliations may meet as human beings and American citizens . . . and this purpose requires the avoidance of all specifically sectarian and partisan aims." Now he began to view settlement work as "a mission of the trained to the untrained, and an agency for spreading wider and striking deeper through the fabric of society those means to a more enlightened, more interesting, more humane, and better disciplined individual and social life, which education and opportunity have hitherto put into the possession only of certain more highly favored classes in the community." He especially valued four features of the settlement: the settlement identified with the neighborhood and worked within it; the workers emphasized "personal relations and the spirit of sociability"; they cultivated a desire for the benefits of education among the immigrants; and the settlement served as a unifying force in the city. In the last element of settlement work Lovejoy discovered a secular rationale for the movement. He believed that settlements and their workers were "particularly concerned in the task of preventing our society from breaking up into separate classes holding no really vital interests and sympathies in common, possessing no effective sense of social solidarity, and having no good mutual understanding."[24]

As a statement of belief, for Lovejoy and the settlement, this pamphlet suggested a subtle change in the orientation of social service. The movement had always been an expression of the idea of elite stewardship, of the notion that favored persons should lead and uplift the less fortunate. The rise of the natural and social sciences at the end of the nineteenth century slowly altered conceptions of social service. What changed was not the idea of trained leadership—if anything, that became more important. In the religiously and culturally diverse America of the twentieth century the old moral and religious standards were no longer compelling, but available to replace them were the broadly conceived standards of science and education. As Lovejoy argued, it was still a "mission of the trained to the untrained," but now an elite trained in the new rational science would work to mold together the disparate forces threatening to shatter the fabric of American society.[25]

But settlement work and helping children held far greater importance for Lovejoy than his rational arguments suggest. Though he never married and had no children of his own, Lovejoy possessed a special fondness for them, and they in turn warmed to him. At a time when his intellectual pursuits and his religious inquiries had demolished the old certainties but had not yet given him new values, children still gave meaning to his activities. In a very revealing poem published in *The University of California Magazine* in 1902, Lovejoy gave voice to these feelings. He titled it "Ecclesiastes Instructed" and gave it the epigraph, "*Nisi sicut infartes*":

> I thought of the innumerable train
> Of ages gone, and all the heat and stress
> Of myriad lives long lapsed to nothingness,
> To yield, from infinite time, so scant a gain;
> I saw the time to come, a shoreless main
> Where uptost waves of bubbling consciousness
> Shall ever rise and sink in fruitlessness;
> And "Vanity!" I cried, "all toil is vain!"
>
> Then as I walked and mused an eager child,
> With hot and hopeful face, besought my aid
> To show him how some plaything should be made,
> Whereon his ardent heart was set; I smiled,
> Forgot infinity, and with the boy
> Toiled through a happy hour upon a toy.[26]

In spite of its personal importance for him, settlement work and social service never became an integral part of Lovejoy's philosophical thought. Unlike slightly older contemporaries, such as John Dewey and George Herbert Mead, Lovejoy did not develop his epistemology and metaphysics out of his activist concerns.[27] Social service was an outgrowth of Lovejoy's religious upbringing, and though it soon supplanted traditional religion and continued after his religious impulses had largely withered, it always retained a measure of the emotional commitment associated with his father's evangelicalism. To build a philosophy on a foundation of social service was to build with the uncertain bricks of emotion and faith. Lovejoy's entire effort from the mid-nineties had been to build a philosophy on solid rational and logical grounds. Social service met a very important emotional need, but the need for an independent rational philosophy was even stronger.

After 1905 Lovejoy increasingly turned his attention to politics and to legislative remedies for what had once been considered moral problems. He saw reform leadership as the way to "convert the people to 'the right views.' " Holding up Theodore Roosevelt as a model, he argued that the republic could be saved only if the educated classes took the initiative in social legislation. The reformer should center his efforts on the child and on creating a favorable educative atmosphere to counteract the social and economic conditions threatening the child's future and, consequently, that of the state. Lovejoy followed his own advice by working for the Children's Protective Alliance in Missouri to obtain passage of child-labor legislation and compulsory-school-attendance statutes.[28]

Like most other social reformers of the era, Lovejoy's advocacy mixed moralism with social science. He revealed this ambivalence in an article written in 1911, "Christian Ethics and Economic Competition." The "morally significant" type of competition was that between buyers and sellers of labor. Lovejoy characterized as immoral the effort of both labor and management to get as much as possible for as little as possible. Only competition between fellow producers was moral; that between buyer and seller violated Christian ethics. He urged the reduction of this unfair competition by laws which would ensure that "all capital were plainly and unmistakably the product of exceptional skill or energy in the individual possessors of it." His suggested remedy was not, however, a moral one; he advocated social legislation to establish the grounds for fair competition. Lovejoy recognized that such legislation would necessarily involve nationalization of industry and high death taxes. Although he was sympathetic to the views of Christian Socialists, Lovejoy did not wholly endorse their program. Social legislation was the proper method for reducing and eventually eliminating inequities in the distribution of wealth, but, unfortunately, social science and philosophy had not yet devised the means to achieve that goal. Mixing morality and social science, he concluded that "a morally desirable consummation" of the issue "should be appealed to the general reason, and not left to the blind antagonisms of individual desire."[29]

Whereas it had once been almost totally religious in its motivation and expression, Lovejoy's attitude toward social service clearly changed in the years after 1900; now reason, in the guise of social science, began to play a much larger role in his considerations. Christian morality still provided a basis for judgment, but rational leadership using the latest advances in social science should determine the direction of reform. This meant, of course, that reform had to move beyond the personal contact of settlement work to active involvement in the political processes. This development laid the foundations for Lovejoy's own active political participation during both World Wars.

Although Lovejoy devoted a considerable amount of time and effort to social service before going to Johns Hopkins in 1910, he by no means neglected his other role as a scholar and academic. During these years he wrote some twenty articles on philosophy and history, in addition to the religious articles and numerous reviews. He was also involved in the institutions of academics, both in the university and in the discipline.

His interests in these years ranged widely. Aside from the religious articles already discussed, Lovejoy's research centered on pre-Darwinian evolutionary thought, the philosophy of Kant and his predecessors, and pragmatic philosophy. He supported his extensive writing by considerable research, including trips to Europe during the summers of 1905 and 1907. Lovejoy was beginning to be recognized as a powerful critic within the discipline of philosophy. Both William James and C. S. Peirce praised Lovejoy's work in these years. James was especially proud that Harvard had produced a man capable of such good work.[30] Lovejoy also participated in the philosophical associations, serving as secretary-treasurer of the Western Philosophy Association from 1904 until 1906 and president in 1908–9, and reading several papers at the annual meetings.[31]

Lovejoy's interest in the institutions of academics encompassed Washington University, as well as the discipline of philosophy. However, while he was somewhat successful in stirring things up, he was less successful in achieving any substantial changes. There were problems over faculty salaries, tuition costs, declining enrollment, and the relationship of the Correspondence School to the rest of the university. Lovejoy enjoyed agitating, but when it became obvious that little was likely to be accomplished, he began to look for another position.[32]

His opportunity to escape St. Louis came in 1907 when he received an invitation to become a visiting professor at Columbia University. Although it was only a one-year appointment, Lovejoy decided to take a leave of absence from Washington University. He wanted to use the libraries in New York, as well as to teach, and thought that a change at St. Louis would be beneficial for the students. There were some difficulties over the conditions of his leave, but these were resolved and, after a summer in Europe, he went to New York in September 1907.[33]

Columbia was a welcome change from Washington University. As Lovejoy said, "it is a great pleasure and relief to be once more in a real university, where things are organized and looked after, where the machinery is shipshape and smooth running and where there's a library deserving of the name." His light teaching load —a graduate seminar on Kant and an undergraduate logic course —meant that Lovejoy had time for his own research and for the concerts and the theater New York offered.[34]

After his year at Columbia, Lovejoy returned to Missouri, where he accepted a new position at the University of Missouri. During his two years there, he taught such courses as problems in applied ethics, Kant, the conception of evolution, and English philosophy from Hobbes to Hume, each of which was the subject of his own research and writing.[35] Outside the classroom, Lovejoy continued his activism by becoming involved in the dispute surrounding the decision of the Carnegie Foundation to abolish their service-pension system for college professors. He led in the effort to force the foundation to reconsider their action or, at least, to soften the financial blow.[36]

Lovejoy's year in New York had apparently convinced him of the desirability of finding a position at a major university. Early in 1910, he confronted two possibilities: the City College of New York and The Johns Hopkins University. The City College job appealed to him for "two very dissimilar motives—the love of lucre and the missionary—or . . . the settlement-spirit." Lovejoy's salary would have been $4,500, nearly double his Missouri salary of $2,500. Since the students were "largely young East Side Jews, with a sprinkling of Irish" destined to "play a mighty big part in shaping the civilization of the city and the country in the next generation," Lovejoy viewed the job as "a chance to occupy a strategic position in a big and momentous movement of human life." His doubts about City College, however, reveal that the "settlement-spirit" was less important than it once had been. Lovejoy feared that the teaching demands of the primarily undergraduate school would interfere with his "own pet studies and literary projects." The position at Johns Hopkins offered more time for research, but it had other problems. Although it was "an appointment of a good deal more outward distinction and giving opportunity for a more advanced sort of work," Lovejoy was not impressed with Baltimore. Additionally, he worried about the "good deal of pretense and of waste of time about much of the 'graduate work' in our universities."[37]

In February 1910 Lovejoy was invited to Baltimore to give a lecture. The address was well received and Lovejoy returned to Missouri favorably impressed by the university and the city. Similarly, their guest had impressed the Johns Hopkins faculty. Three weeks later, Lovejoy received "a curiously off-hand sort of call from President Remsen to Johns Hopkins: 'Dear Professor Lovejoy: Do you care to consider an invitation to join the forces of Johns Hopkins University as Professor of Philosophy?' " After learning the details of the appointment—his salary would be $3,500, he would teach only graduate courses of his choosing, and sabbaticals could be arranged—Lovejoy was nearly certain he would go to Hopkins. He wrote his father that "if under these conditions I can't write a few things worth while—and also realize some improvements in the organization of graduate study, especially in the history of philosophical ideas and in the correlation of philosophy with other subjects—I shall prove myself a very lazy and inefficient rascal."[38] Before he could begin, however, a professorial dispute had to be resolved. E. F. Buchner, professor of education and philosophy, wrote Lovejoy outlining the courses already arranged for the coming year and suggesting what Lovejoy should offer. Lovejoy was offended by what he interpreted as the condescending tone of the letter and provisionally withdrew his acceptance. Mediation by President Remsen and John B. Watson, the psychologist, persuaded Lovejoy that he would indeed be professor of philosophy with all the prerogatives of the position. In a letter playfully signed "J. Hopkinson Jenks," Lovejoy told his stepmother that he had accepted the appointment to Hopkins.[35]

After arriving at Hopkins in 1910, Lovejoy made a decision that shaped the rest of his career. The missionary spirit of social religion had been declining in importance for some time, and by 1910 Lovejoy wanted to devote more time to his philosophical and historical studies. His waning interest in social religion was accompanied by a slow shift in his intellectual interests as his studies in the problems of pluralism, time, and evolution convinced him that any theology appropriate to the twentieth century would have to be based on rational necessity. The historical arguments discussed earlier had been largely negative; they demonstrated the fallacy of historically based Christianity. At the same time, however, Lovejoy undertook the task of showing the necessity and the possibility of "a rational theology of the future." Once he had completed his journey toward a rational theology, it was but a small step to drop the theology in favor of a rational philosophy.

Lovejoy had begun working toward the elements of a rational religion in several long letters to George Holmes Howison in 1901. Howison had argued, in *The Limits of Evolution*, for a pluralistic theism. The universe was pluralistic because there existed a multiplicity of self-defining, independently existing souls; their "number must be definite as well as vast, though we do not actually know it now." There was also, however, God, in whom "all ideal possibilities, all rational perfections" were "eternally actualised" and "whose very perfection lies in his giving complete recognition to all other spirits, as the complement in terms of which alone his own self-definition is to himself completely thinkable." Furthermore, each member of the "world of minds" must "define himself primarily against the Supreme Instance, and so in terms of God."[40] Lovejoy complained that, although the system was appealing, Howison had left some "very important aspects of reality unrationalized and unaccounted for." He argued that there was no logical necessity for choosing any definite number of souls to compose the total. One number was as good as any other and could be thought without self-contradiction. Further, he was not convinced that Howison had adequately accounted for the existence of beings within the time-process; the failure to do so meant a break in the connection between the "supra-temporal" and reality, and undermined Howison's system. In a second letter, Lovejoy raised the issue of efficient causation. It was easy for him to "conceive that the formal structure of our reason may . . . necessitate the form and universal order of our experience." However, there was something more than this—"a sensuous datum"—which had always been impossible for the self to deduce logically. Howison had argued that *"The created, as well as the Creator, creates"* [Howison's emphasis], and Lovejoy thought this went too far toward pluralism. Without some "preestablished harmony" there could be "no adequate unifying principle in the world." Consequently, the world would present "itself as essentially non-rational, and unintelligible except as a brute fact."[41]

Lovejoy's critique of Howison's position formed the basis of his own positive doctrine. The central factor in his studies was the absolute necessity for an "adequate unifying principle in the world." This principle would, however, have to be both rational and temporal; it must rationally unify and give meaning to the behavior of man within time. Lovejoy's investigations of historical Christianity had suggested that evolutionary thought provided the historical context for the rational introduction of time into the universe. He broadened his historical inquiry into pre-Darwinian evolutionary thought and began his study of Henri Bergson, a prime contemporary exponent of temporalism, in order to provide a firm basis for a rational temporalism adequate to the religious and philosophical needs of modern man.

In ' Religion and the Time-Process," published shortly after the letters to Howison were written, Lovejoy examined the problem that religions have always had with time. Religions have usually defined the supreme Good and the ultimate Worth in otherworldly terms; that is, "in terms of their 'otherness' to the characteristics of the common experience of the life in time and place." The denial of time was understandable, for men had always had difficulty assigning significance to the "external cosmical process." Further, there developed the belief that "the attainment of the good meant the termination of volitional movement." Although Christianity was otherworldly in its orientation, the conjunction of Judeo-Hellenic ideas out of which it arose included a "comprehensive philosophy of history." This idea, which Lovejoy, in anticipation of his concept of the "unit-idea," characterized as a "peculiarly Christian contribution to the Occident's stock of general ideas," contained the seed of temporalism that would eventually undermine the otherworldliness of religion.[42]

The temporalism implicit in a philosophy of history required centuries to become a major factor in man's thought. Lovejoy argued that only since the Renaissance had the worth of fullness and diversity been appreciated and otherworldliness questioned. This process was aided by three movements in thought, the deism of the eighteenth century, the evolutionism so prevalent in the nineteenth, and the development of a new theory of worth in his own time. He believed that the deists had tried to make religion a thing of this world, but that they failed, ultimately, because their definition of the good—"a condition of perfected and stationary equilibrium"—gave no rational meaning to the time process. The rise of evolutionary thought ensured that man could attribute "rationality and spiritual significance to the temporal order of phenomena." Evolutionism, by itself, was still inadequate; it was not completely rational nor did its goal seem of lasting interest to "religious consciousness." However, in the last half of the nineteenth century a new theory of worth arose which gave developmental thought the justification it needed. This was the belief that "the justifying worth of the whole, is, not that the goal should *have been* [Lovejoy's emphasis] reached, but that the game, with all the activity of will and thought and feeling which it calls for, should be played."[43]

The union of evolutionary thought with the new theory of worth permitted Lovejoy to inject rationality into the world, to make it more than a "brute fact." The tendency of the modern religious ideal was "not a wallowing in unorganized emotion, but the strenuous tension of the will." Fixed ends were still necessary, but they were no longer ends in themselves; process, and especially process into the future, was the Good for the modern Christian.[44] Lovejoy hoped that the culmination of these trends in the history of Christianity meant that reason and temporality would make any future religion a thing of this world. Only in this manner could religion speak to his needs and, as he saw it, to the needs of the twentieth century.

The conclusions Lovejoy reached in this essay were far-ranging in their influence, although their full impact was not immediately felt. By rationalizing evolution through valuing process as the highest good, Lovejoy hoped to escape the uncertainties of "unorganized emotion." He did not, however, regard the conclusions of this article as definitive and final; too many problems remained before reason and temporalism could be firmly established as dominant ideas in modern thought. Over the next several years Lovejoy began his careful historical studies of the Enlightenment, deism, and evolutionary thought that contributed so much to the rationalistic and temporalistic character of modern thinking. At the same time, he initiated his critical studies of the two contemporary philosophies—the temporalism of Bergson and pragmatism—which seemed to possess at least some elements of the rational temporalism Lovejoy sought to develop.

When he finished "Religion and the Time-Process" in 1902, Lovejoy knew what problems he confronted if he wanted to establish the foundation for a rational theology. The history of modern thought had provided the elements for developing such a position, but they had not yet been molded into a consistent theology. Lovejoy, in three articles written later in the decade, tried to outline the characteristics of the new religion. He advocated a religion of this world in which the moment of decision making was crucial and in which reason became the basis for ethical behavior no longer dependent upon transcendent ends for justification.

"The Desires of the Self-Conscious" was Lovejoy's first attempt to develop a rational ethics consistent with man's psychological drives. He assumed that "the capacity for morality depends upon self-consciousness." As he put it, "The fabric of ordinary moral experience is obviously made up of mental processes and mental contents which are simply special consequences of the power of self-representation." Only "a conscious agent not constitutionally incapable of such things as self-criticism" could be constrained by moral imperatives. The problem for the moralist, then, was to account for rational man's capacity to be "controlled by self-referring motives." The psychological element must not be ignored, but the ethical theorist must ask, "How does self-consciousness affect or transform desire and impulse?"[45]

The rise of self-consciousness in man made possible the conception of the self "as a sum of interests, as a possessor of potential goods, distinct from the interests and the goods of other selves." Lovejoy distinguished this "objectified self" from the "actual 'subjective self' of our successive moments of consciousness." The objectified self was an "abstract artefact" of our thought whereas the subjective self was the sum of the attitudes and feelings of man at any time in consciousness. The two were connected, for the subjective self has an active interest in "the objectified self as an object of approbation or disapprobation, as a subject of favorable or unfavorable predicates." He thought that the modern moralist must use this link to unite the psychological desires of the subjective self with the rational self-consciousness of the objectified self.[46]

The emergence of the objectified self was accompanied by the appearance of the " 'approbative' type of interest." Lovejoy argued that just as the subjective self could conceive the self as an object of thought, the self could also be so conceived by others. Since we make judgments about our selves, it was reasonable to assume that our objectified self was judged by others. Self-conscious man was very desirous that he be well thought of by others. Lovejoy believed that this impulse was not simply the desire for fame: "The desire involved is not the desire that the objectified self shall *get* anything in the future; it is due entirely to the interestingness of the idea of the self as *being*, at the conceived moment of action, *describable in certain terms* implying certain attitudes on the part of other selves [Lovejoy's emphasis]."[47]

Lovejoy believed that the concept of objectified and subjective self and the judgmental attitudes were acquired by all self-conscious men. Consequently, "a self, as actually thought about, is usually thought, and is always potentially thought, as the proper logical subject of some kind of descriptive adjectives or epithets which carry with them favorable or unfavorable connotations." The subjective self is pained when the objectified self is thought ill of and pleased by approval. Lovejoy thought that the process of judgment was a continual one: we always desire to be something, and "this desire is manifestly capable of controlling volition in our most completely self-conscious moments." He argued that what "chiefly influences deliberate human action is not the will for life or for pleasure or for power (except in so far as these are involved in the other), but the will for the good predicate for one's objectified self." "The chief end of man," he believed, "is an adjective; the ruling passion of the self-conscious animal is the pursuit of the good predicate for his acting self—the pursuit not, indeed, of 'praise' (in the terminology of Adam Smith) but of 'praiseworthiness.' "[48]

So far, Lovejoy had avoided discussion of an "ought" in his ethical theory. He believed that an "ought" was possible only because there were two types of desire that determined man's deliberate choice: "(a) the direct or spontaneous interest in a conceived future situation that may result from one's action; (b) interest in having the self *in* action the subject of approved predicates." Lovejoy argued that the first was not really ethical since there was "no means of effectually appealing from the facts of desire to any 'ought.' " The second, of course, involved approbative interest. Lovejoy thought it was possible to determine how men ought to behave if they want to receive the approval of their subjective self and of others. He concluded that "the rational agent is not primarily a chooser of ends at all, but a chooser (or avoider) of personal attributes or adjectives; that all ethical dialectic necessarily presupposes and appeals to such an interest in the predicates of the represented self; and that the notion 'ought' has no pertinency whatever to ends, except in so far as the choice of some end is conceived as the ground of the application of some adjective by the self to the self."[49]

In this essay Lovejoy brought together several strains of his thought. His assumptions about man's rational nature are very evident, but he was aware that feelings and desires were controlling factors in our behavior. Man could placate his subjective desires for approval only by rationally choosing to act in a way that would win such approval for the objectified self. Temporalism, too, played an important role in this ethics. What was important for Lovejoy was, not an ultimate end, but choices within the flow of time. Rational man considers how he will be thought of when he makes his decisions, not in reference to some distant end. Developing the idea of rational, ethical decision making in the time process was, however, only the first step toward outlining a rational theology.

The following year, Lovejoy returned to the question of a temporally based religion. "Pragmatism and Theology" was largely a critique of pragmatic epistemology, especially its theory about the meaning of propositions as it applied to theology. He concluded that pragmatic epistemology was useless, thus clearing the ground and making it possible to recognize a pragmatic metaphysical insight of James vitally important for any rational theology. James had often argued that the central event in any life was "the moment of voluntary choice—the moment in which, in the presence of alternative real possibilities, and with the full consciousness that some actual content of the future now truly hangs trembling in the balances of volition, the mind somehow reaches its fiat and, by the 'dumb turning of the will,' performs the daily miracle of excluding one of those real possibilities thereafter and eternally *from* reality." The metaphysical and quasi-epistemological principle which lay behind this belief was the idea that "no proposition is to be accepted as legitimate which, directly or by implication, *denies to the future the genuine character of futurity and contradicts the reality of open possibilities* [Lovejoy's emphasis] at any present moment of conscious choice between alternatives."[50]

Lovejoy was certain that this idea of the possibility of choice had revolutionary implications for theology. The monistic and eternalistic theology so characteristic of religion had always denied any "real, determinative responsibility" on the part of man, for all his actions were subsumed under some absolute. The pragmatic view, however, assumed that the future was open, that man could and did make choices which contributed to the making of future reality; man, in this sense, was as much the creator of the world as God. Liberating as this doctrine was, it was not without its dangers. Because it was a doctrine of process, there was no assurance that the result would be the perfection of the world. Even though God must now be conceived as a "God having an existence in the temporal world which alone is real to us," Lovejoy argued, recalling Howison, that there was still reason to believe that our rational cooperation with the God of this world resulted in progress toward increasing perfection.[51]

The pragmatic philosophy of James provided Lovejoy with the metaphysical basis for a theology of choice. Choice became a real event that could determine the direction of the time-process and the shape of the future. In this framework, the act of making a decision took on a great deal of significance, for every choice made a difference and could no longer be left to the caprice of human emotion. Lovejoy's rationalistic ethics gave him the means by which choices could be made that were both rational and moral. Confronted by a choice, the self-conscious man rationally chose that alternative that would win the approval of his subjective self and of others.

Although Lovejoy had already suggested that ideas about the eternal were useless in the modern world, he took up the question again in "The Obsolescence of the Eternal." He wanted "to determine whether a belief in the eternal character of 'ultimate' reality, or of any reality at all, is reconcilable with a belief in the actuality of evolution, in the most general sense." He defined evolution as "real temporal Becoming" that included the appearance of completely new items of existence that increased the total content of the universe. Eternity, on the other hand, meant "timeless existence." Examining possible eternals, he found both the constant of physical science and neo-Kantian idealism deficient. With regard to the first, he argued "that a world in which qualitative evolution is supposed to take place is one in which, as a total, quantitative constancy cannot be said to subsist." Second, he asserted that, contrary to the hopes of the absolute idealists, the eternal cannot contain the temporal: "For the eternal to enter into relations with aught that becomes or changes is *ipso facto* to lose its eternity." Lovejoy concluded that "the idea of eternity is an idea which cannot be positively thought, under the conditions involved in all our thinking as beings in time. It is a self-contradictory, and therefore wholly empty notion."[52]

With the denial of the eternal, Lovejoy completed his attempt to outline a "rational theology of the future." He believed that he had convincingly shown how religion must become a thing of this world. Not only had he demonstrated to his own satisfaction the self-contradictions of the eternal, in pragmatic metaphysics and rationalistic ethics he thought he had also provided a viable rational and temporally based alternative to the empty theology of eternalism. Further, he believed that he had escaped the uncertainties of a religion based on faith and emotion. True, the new theology was based on the possibility of real choice, but Lovejoy thought that modern self-conscious man would make rational and moral choices out of his desire to be praised. What Lovejoy seems not to have realized is that he had smuggled capricious emotion in through a back door. Man's desire for approbation is not wholly rational and, thus, not wholly uniform. By resting rational choice on the subjective desire for approval (or fear of disapproval) Lovejoy based his rational evolutionary order on the very uncertainties he feared. Establishing rational certainties would be more difficult than even Lovejoy anticipated.

Lovejoy's religious ideas developed considerably from the evangelical views to which he was exposed as a child. Although neither he nor his father seems to have fully realized it, by 1910 Lovejoy was on the verge of abandoning religion as a significant factor in his life. Even in the area of social service Lovejoy's attitudes had been largely secularized. He would continue, for some time, to be involved in settlement-type activities, but, more and more, his attention turned to political problems, especially the problem of ensuring the survival of freedom and democracy. Theologically, as well, the development of his views had taken him to the very edge of religious belief. His rational theology had eliminated the eternal and ultimate ends and had reduced God to the status of a partner with man in the creation of the universe. With theology diminished nearly to the point of invisibility, metaphysics and the problems of creating a rational philosophy became the focus of Lovejoy's quest for order in a pluralistic universe.

CHAPTER III

IDEALISM, PRAGMATISM, AND

TEMPORALISM

In February 1910 an unsigned review of Hugo Münsterberg's new book, *The Eternal Values*, appeared in *The Nation*. The reviewer noted that Münsterberg's philosophy was "interesting, impressive, and highly edifying" but that Münsterberg had not "philosophized with the philosophizing of his time"; the Harvard idealist had attempted to resurrect the systems of Fichte and Hegel without considering recent criticisms of those philosophies. William James thought he knew the author of the review and wrote Lovejoy hoping to confirm his suspicion. Lovejoy replied that though he had some "qualms about the rather personal and pointed character of the criticism, I can't say, like the man who wrote 'The Purple Cow,' that 'I'm sorry now I wrote it'—since you liked it and think it just." Lovejoy was most disturbed by Münsterberg's disregard for contemporary questions and current issues in philosophy. He wrote James that philosophers in general were "under some professional obligations to try to keep honestly in the contemporary game—and not go off in a corner, put in a thumb into the cosmic pie, pull out a plum for private gustation,—and say 'What a smart boy am I!' "[1]

As both his review of Münsterberg and his letter to James implied, Lovejoy believed himself to be a philosopher who dealt with contemporary issues and problems. Although trained as a philosopher at Harvard, questions of religious belief and social service had engaged Lovejoy most fully in the years after 1898. Not until 1908 did he begin to philosophize systematically and to participate extensively in contemporary philosophical debates.

Thereafter and for the next forty years Lovejoy's powerful critical voice could be ignored only at one's peril.

Lovejoy's philosophy was not fully formed when he entered the philosophical lists in the first decade of this century. His ideas developed through comparison with and criticism of other philosophers, and through criticism he eliminated untenable positions, thus leaving the irreducible elements of a consistent philosophy. Since even his major philosophic work, *The Revolt Against Dualism*, is largely a criticism of his opponents, one can examine the development of Lovejoy's ideas and the exposition of his philosophic position only by tracing his thought from his early skepticism about idealism to the pragmatic, temporalistic, rational, and dualistic philosophy of *The Revolt Against Dualism*.

In the philosophies of George Holmes Howison and Josiah Royce, Lovejoy confronted two very different forms of idealism. Howison was beginning in the nineties to develop more clearly his pluralistic idealism in which the entities of the temporal world had an identity separate from that of God and created the world with God. Royce, in the classroom and in his writing, was postulating and defending a monistic idealism in which all entities and experiences were somehow contained in the Absolute Experience. When Lovejoy, still a graduate student, began to write on philosophy in the late nineties, he had already reached the position of a skeptical idealist. His earliest papers reveal a young man struggling with problems he saw in the philosophies of both Royce and Howison, and with idealism in general. The monistic idealism of Royce seemed to account for error, but Lovejoy wondered whether the Absolute could be directly related to temporal reality without contradiction. Howison's pluralism solved the problem of the independent existence of entities in the temporal flow, but, initially at least, this philosophy seemed so pluralistic that it lacked any attributes capable of unifying the brute facts of existence. Lovejoy's early efforts in philosophy attempted to resolve these problems and to resolve his doubts concerning idealism.

Lovejoy first took up these problems of idealism in two closely related essays that he wrote for Josiah Royce in the spring of 1896. Philosophical inquiry developed, according to Lovejoy, when man began to ask, "What, upon analysis, does it turn out that we mean by the word 'real' and its opposite?" Central to any metaphysical inquiry was the notion of "self-subsistence," the idea that there is "some *thing* which has the character that it has in its own right, which maintains its character permanently, to which my concepts can correspond or fail to correspond, and which, therefore, above all, is independent of my way of regarding it." From these considerations Lovejoy deduced two "requirements" he would employ in attempting to answer the question of what was meant by the "real." "The ultimate reality," he wrote, "should stand in some intelligible relation to the relative realities of ordinary human experience." A satisfactory answer to the metaphysical question would allow us "to conceive ordinary experience as in some sense real, and as grounding whatever of reality it possesses in the ultimate reality." Second, "the ultimate reality, as conceived, must provide some ground for the distinction between truth and error . . . and furthermore, that distinction must be other than the distinction between partial and complete analysis of presentations."[2]

Using these criteria Lovejoy then criticized the positivist, thing-in-itself, and Absolute Experience conceptions of reality. He defined positivism as the belief that the "absolutely real is the immediate experience as it comes," and faulted it for failing to meet either of his criteria. The first criterion could not even be applied, for it presupposed that "the immediate of ordinary experience, while somehow real, is not the only, or the genuinely self-subsistingly, real." When he turned to positivist conceptions of truth and error Lovejoy discovered that here too this philosophy did not satisfy the criterion: "positivism, so far as it meets the second requirement, has ceased to be positivism; so far as it does not meet that requirement, it is unintelligible."[3]

The thing-in-itself conception, according to Lovejoy, held that "the absolutely real is that unrelated and indivisible Thing which exists in and for itself, apart from all phenomena." This view divided the world in two; "on the one side lies the Thing-in-itself, absolutely real, and on the other side, phenomena, absolutely unreal." As Lovejoy noted, "our first requirement fares ill here." Since the thing-in-itself is self-contained, and the only real, with no relations to any other thing, it is incapable of serving as the ground of relative realities. With regard to the second criterion of truth and error, this doctrine also fails. Absolute truth resides in the thing-in-itself, while error is a property of the relative world. Since there are no real relations between the two

worlds, "the truth and the error lie in entirely different worlds.
. . . The two being different in kind, the error can never be compared with the truth, nor can the truth stand out against a background of error." Lovejoy dismissed the thing-in-itself conception
because, like the positivist conception, it failed to satisfy his two
criteria.[4]

The conception of an Absolute Experience had more appeal
for Lovejoy, but even here he found difficulties. This conception
seemed to meet the first requirement, for "everything known belongs to the absolute reality, and stands to it in the relation of
partial to total experience." Lovejoy saw a potential problem if
there existed any phenomena that could not be "regarded as a
part of the immediate experience of the Absolute"; in that case,
the conception failed the first requirement. The phenomena Lovejoy had in mind were "the partial experience of self-conscious
individuals." He doubted that these "individual, self-conscious
experiences" existed "*as parts* of the Absolute Experience." His
second question concerning Absolute Experience involved the
problem of truth and error. Under this system all error was partial truth, but Lovejoy believed that "for ordinary experience all
error is not partial truth." This suggested a problem with his
second criterion, but he lacked the space to expand his criticism
and deferred a detailed critique of Absolute Experience to his
next essay.[5]

Lovejoy renewed his criticism of the Absolute Experience in
his final essay for Royce's course on metaphysics. He began with
"the hardly incontrovertible idealistic assumption that whatever
is real must be some sort of experience." The course had focused
on F. H. Bradley's *Appearance and Reality*, which would provide
Lovejoy with his target in this essay. He distinguished two characteristics of this conception of the universe: "1) the Absolute
Experience is complete; 2) its relation to the appearances whose
ground it is, is the relation of whole to part." Since Bradley emphasized the "quantitative category of totality," Lovejoy dubbed
the English philosopher's conception "totalistic idealism." He
proposed to expand his earlier critique and to indicate what
seemed to him the "one central and inevitable fault in the system so far as it professes to be a final account of the nature of
reality."[6]

Before beginning his critique, Lovejoy laid down "the conditions and guiding principles of metaphysical inquiry." "How," he asked, "does one come to look for an absolute or ultimate reality at all, and what precisely is one seeking when one looks for it?" Lovejoy discerned "two obvious but significant aspects of ordinary experience" that motivated the search and shaped its results. "In the first place, one has a universe of some sort on one's hands. However one define it, there it is, as an immediate fact—something actually exists. And this something, moreover, has parts, diversities, various content." The existence of the world and its diversity could not, Lovejoy believed, "be stated in ideal terms—there is no assignable reason why there should be any world, or why the world shouldn't be all one; but the diversified actuality is a brute fact" that could not be ignored. Any metaphysician, then, had to begin with the "first fact" that "there is actuality, and that actuality is diversified." Lovejoy's second basic fact derived from the first: "an actual world given as diverse is a world full of differences requiring to be united and harmonized; it is a world demanding to be made intelligible." Since the harmony was not immediately given, it must be sought. A diverse world meant a world of relations, but relations, by themselves, were incapable of providing intelligibility. Man's desire for intelligibility soon led him on a "search after a self-subsistent, an absolute, a something capable of explaining (i.e., of making coherent) the certain but otherwise inexplicable existence of the rest of the world, as immediately given." For Lovejoy, the self-subsistent and the actual were inextricably linked: "the actual diverse world is nothing except as implying a self-subsistent, and on the other hand, . . . a self-subsistent is nothing except as we find it implied in the actuality."[7]

In applying these criteria to Bradley's account of the world, Lovejoy encountered several problems, though he conceded that Bradley had recognized the need to construct an absolute that was connected to the actual world. Lovejoy's major difficulty came with Bradley's attempt to unite the "comprehensiveness of the ultimate reality and its absoluteness." Bradley relied on the idea of totality—"the relation of whole to part"—as the basis for his absolute. This reasoning disturbed Lovejoy, for he doubted that "ultimate reality" could ever "be adequately described in terms of bare totality." The problem lay in the relationship of the actual world to the ultimate reality. If the actual were somehow subsumed into the absolute, what was the nature of the parts in the whole? Did the entities and experiences of the actual world maintain their independent character as part of the absolute, or were they harmonized, becoming simply another element in the undifferentiated mass of Absolute Experience? If the absolute were to maintain actual distinctions, in at least some form, it must think, which Bradley claimed his absolute did. This was a key point for Lovejoy, because if Bradley's conception did not maintain the distinctiveness and diversity of the actual world, it would fail as a metaphysical system.[8]

Taking as a given the idea that the absolute thinks, Lovejoy raised several questions implied by that conception. If the Absolute Experience was complex, did that not imply that it was "quantitatively limited?" If so, then it must "experience itself as a whole in distinction from its parts." And, if it must think itself, could it "still possess the character of absoluteness?" Finally, given these considerations, was there any way the absolute could be described as "non-personal," as Bradley had? The answers, for Lovejoy, were not encouraging. The absolute must be a "real complex" and "as complex it must be in some sense quantitative." It was also "a complete experience." That being the case, "it must be also finite," for all other forms of actuality that were complex and complete were also finite. But here was the problem, for "if the 'Comprehensive Experience' is finite, it seems difficult to see how it can be Absolute."[9]

Facing these difficulties in Bradley's system, Lovejoy sought relief in a formulation of Josiah Royce, only to be disappointed in the result. Royce had postulated the idea of "a moment of arrest" in the Absolute Experience as a way of meeting the problems of complexity and limitation. Royce held that "the Absolute has present to it a veritable infinity of possible experiences, of conceivable alternatives; but out of these possibilities it gives, by an (eternal) act analogous to our own rational arrest of attention, concrete reality only to a limited number or quantum." Lovejoy found this conception "far more consistent and intelligible, as well as more elaborate" than Bradley's formulations. But, did it really solve the difficulties in the Englishman's system? Lovejoy saw two problems. First, the idea of the arrest of attention implied selection, and selection implied a will that selected. A will, however, required a personality, while Bradley had explicitly denied that a personality could be an absolute. Royce's conception might meet some general problems of idealism, but it appeared incapable of rescuing Bradley's version. The second way of dealing with imitation was to postulate that it was capricious. Capriciousness, however, was incompatible with the absolute as conceived by Bradley. The failure of these two attempts to resuscitate Bradley's metaphysics—whatever their implications for idealism in general—meant that "mere totality does not give us an Absolute, because totality means quantitative limitation, and limitation means determination by an Other." Lovejoy could find no way whereby Bradley's absolute could be absolute and at the same time the ground of all actual reality.[10]

Lovejoy conceded that the result he reached was "purely negative." He felt that he had been unable "as yet to accomplish anything very satisfactory to myself beyond clearing the ground and getting a general notion of the points of the compass in the metaphysical country." He feared he might have "to take shelter from the resulting glare of contradictions in the Kantian cave of agnosticism, denying the possibility of conceiving of an Absolute, and finding the ideas of reason only relatively useful as guiding principles within the phenomenal sphere." He had not, however, given up all hope of successful "metaphysical construction." Self-consciousness, he thought, held promise for future exploration: "Real, perhaps, is the process in which the One and the Other mutually determine each other, in which reciprocity the thinking process gives form to the whole diverse content of the world."[11] This path of future exploration followed one already established by George Holmes Howison.

By the end of his first year as a graduate student Lovejoy had laid down his criteria for a successful metaphysical system and had identified the chief sticking point in absolute idealism. Metaphysical inquiry demonstrated the need for a self-subsistent, but this self-subsistent must meet certain requirements if it was to be acceptable as a foundation for metaphysical thought. Any successful formulation had to recognize and maintain the diversity and variety of the actual world, to render that actual world intelligible, and to account for truth and error. Lovejoy's critique of Bradley's system demonstrated to his satisfaction that the Englishman's totalistic idealism could not maintain the diversity of the actual world in the absolute and still remain an absolute.

This critique revealed the weakness of all absolute idealisms in the relationship of the actual diverse world and the absolute. If the absolute could not maintain a real relationship to the actual world without contradiction, then it was a failure as a metaphysical system. Lovejoy was not prepared to go so far in 1896, for he still required a self-subsistent and thought that it was most probably an absolute, though he was unsure of its form or its relation to the actual world. During his struggles with the monistic idealisms of Bradley and Royce, the pluralistic idealism of Howison offered an attractive alternative, for it seemed to maintain more successfully the diversified character of the actual world.

Howison's pluralism had been a major weapon in the arsenal of the opponents of monism among Harvard graduate students, but it, too, had its weaknesses. Lovejoy recalled that in the winter of 1897–98, "the more advanced students whose philosophical interests had not been corrupted by the laboratory habit" had frequently engaged in "a great deal of very free and lively discussion over the general metaphysical questions—both in private and in the semi-public conferences at Professor Royce's." The young pluralists, including Lovejoy, found Howison's arguments useful in attacking Royce's variety of monism: "So long as one kept the offensive for pluralism all went well; it was not very hard to prove both that the monistic conception of the Absolute was religiously inadequate, and that it was logically inconsistent and impossible." The problem came when the pluralists had to defend their view, for "it was not so much the 'necessity' as the possibility of the pluralistic conception that offered difficulties to those of us, even, who were in the main disposed to profess and call themselves pluralists."[12]

Lovejoy's dissatisfaction with the idealism of Royce had deepened in the two years since his class in metaphysics. He found Royce's "reconstruction of natural theology . . . absolutely lacking in religious or moral value." It was incomprehensible to him how God could be pictured as "finding his bliss in exploiting the sufferings and sins of his unfree, but (unhappily) self-conscious members for his own greater glory." He also thought that there were "aspects of finite experience which it is inconceivable that an absolute experience could ever embrace *as* experience—though it might know them as facts." This suggested to Lovejoy that there were "outlying bits of reality which can't be taken up into the pretended inclusive whole." He returned to his early doubts concerning self-consciousness, for it remained "hard to see how the peculiarities of empirical self-consciousness can be taken up into the divine consciousness without alteration or abatement of their special character."[13] Pluralism was useful in attacking these weaknesses, but when the monists counterattacked, pluralism revealed its own weaknesses.

Writing to Howison, Lovejoy pointed out his difficulties with pluralism. He was uncertain how "truly separate and independent" monads could be related. And if they were related, did that not make them, "in effect, only parts of a larger whole?" Howison had postulated a "preëstablished harmony" to explain the relation, but Lovejoy failed to see how that solved the problem, or avoided the problems inherent in a monistic account. His second question concerned "the arithmetical aspect of reality." If there was more than "one absolute or self-active consciousness," what determined how many there were? Here absolute idealism had a real advantage, for if "the whole of reality is describable only as the content of a single consciousness," then "the whole of reality is also conceivable as throughout rational and intelligible." But, under pluralism, with its finite and unknowable number of souls, there appeared to be no rational reason for declaring how many souls there were, thus leaving an important aspect of the system "irrational and fortuitous." This second question led to a third; What was "the real function of a deity in a consistently pluralistic scheme of the universe?" One possibility, he thought, was to conceive of God as "the idea of an archetypal Knower of facts and values—an inclusive knowledge (not an inclusive experience)—and thereby also a perfect Will—so that the essence of the cognitive and moral life of all human souls would consist in bringing their conceptions of truth & their effective judgments of value into conformity with this adequate Truth and universal Will." Unsure how close this was to Howison's conception, Lovejoy believed it the only possible God consistent with pluralism. Otherwise, he wrote, "it is not plain to me why the conception of God is not—to put it frankly—*theoretically* superfluous in a thorough-going pluralism, however naturally our religious instincts may lead us to introduce it." Lovejoy believed these problems weakened pluralism, though not fatally, and he concluded by urging Howison in his writing to address the "conceivability and consistency of pluralism as a positive and constructive doctrine."[14]

Lovejoy returned to the difficulties with pluralism in two very long letters to Howison following the publication of Howison's *The Limits of Evolution* in 1901. He admitted that Howison's system appeared "singularly persuasive and satisfying" so long as one looked at it "only with the eye of the philosophical imagination." When, however, he descended to "the dull levels of analytical understanding," the system still gave him "a good deal of difficulty." Howison's new exposition had not satisfactorily resolved the problem of the arithmetical aspect of reality. He had failed to explain to Lovejoy's satisfaction why the universe, though finite, must be composed of a particular number of souls. There seemed to be no rational reason for choosing any particular number. If there was no reason, then there was a "very important aspect of things which is real and yet has no rational ground." Lovejoy also failed to understand why there must be "a soul representing every possible degree in the scale of perfection," as Howison had argued. These numerical questions were also implicit in Lovejoy's reading of Howison's thesis that there was a series of monads approximating and approaching the divine perfection. Lovejoy was unable to determine whether that series was infinite or finite, and in either case there were unresolved difficulties.[15]

In the second letter Lovejoy attempted to pinpoint more precisely his difficulties with pluralism. He admitted at the outset that none of the difficulties, even if they proved insuperable, affected the main principle of pluralism, "the doctrine that there can be no single possessor of *all* the content of actual experience, no single self in which the personality and life and inalienably unique inner experience of other selves can be absorbed, and no single real agent in the events occurring in the time-process." Lovejoy's first set of difficulties resulted from Howison's attempt "to rule out the possibility of any central efficient cause either of the existence, or of any factor in the experience, of the . . . individual minds." The problem he saw in "denying the efficient causation of God" was that it removed "an element, lacking which the world cannot be conceived to be rational, ideal or philosophically intelligible at all." Without an efficient cause, Lovejoy saw no way to resolve his earlier dilemma of the number of souls, and nothing in Howison's book provided solid evidence for a resolution.[16]

The lack of a single efficient cause also posed difficulties in explaining ' the contingent element in our experience." Howison had proposed " 'to explain Nature *wholly* from the resources of the individual mind.' " Lovejoy conceded that "the formal structure of our reason may . . . necessitate the form and universal order of our experience." What he could not understand was how the ' generic nature of the individual conscious self" could be expected "to evolve all the choir of heaven and furniture of earth." Unless there existed "the efficient causation of one monad, or of God," one could not even speak of a "preëstablished harmony; for there is, by hypothesis, nothing that is competent to preëstablish it." Such a conclusion was unacceptable to Lovejoy because it left "no adequate unifying principle in the world; and the world thereupon presents itself as essentially non-rational, and unintelligible except as a brute fact."[17]

In the summer of 1901 Lovejoy was still a metaphysician in an idealistic mold, but increasingly skeptical of contemporary formulations. The pluralistic idealism of Howison had given him the weapons to attack the monistic idealism of Royce, though the rational intelligibility of an absolute world still beckoned. Howison's pluralism, though it recognized and maintained the real diversity of the actual world, proved to be too pluralistic, for it lacked any efficient cause that could give meaning to the universe. Here, then, was Lovejoy's metaphysical dilemma, to construct a system that maintained the real diversity and temporal flux of actuality *and* provided some ground for making that actuality intelligible. When he began to publish philosophical essays in 1908–9, epistemological questions took precedence over metaphysical ones. But if the questions changed, his object remained the same. He believed that an adequate account of knowledge in a diverse and temporalistic universe was essential to intelligibility. As epistemological problems came to dominate his thought, the absolute receded from his thinking to such an extent that in 1909 he concluded the eternal was now obsolete.

Between 1901 and 1908 Lovejoy devoted considerable effort to the development of a rational theology. Beginning in 1908 he turned his attention increasingly to philosophical problems, especially to pragmatism and temporalism. As the religious impulse waned, philosophy grew in importance as the potential source of rational intelligibility in the universe. But in 1908 Lovejoy's developing philosophy provided more questions than answers. The world seemed to be pluralistic in character, but what made it intelligible, what kept chaos at bay? So, too, the universe seemed basically temporalistic, but was there anything that directed change and our behavior as beings in time? Was it possible to construct a consistent philosophy that contained both ideas and real, self-subsisting external objects? If that was possible, what was the basis of knowledge in such a world?

Lovejoy started his critical work in philosophy by examining pragmatism. A superficial reading of his articles on pragmatism can easily lead to the conclusion that he was a confirmed and unalterable opponent of that philosophy.[18] However, while Lovejoy was a severe critic of what he considered to be the errant views of most pragmatists, he was basically sympathetic to certain aspects of the philosophy, and much of his criticism was directed toward convincing "all loyal retainers to return to their true allegiance."[19]

Lovejoy was attracted to several of the doctrines of pragmatism because they were consistent with a pluralistic and temporalistic universe while suggesting ways to make such a world intelligible. He wrote William James that "like the colored gentleman of the popular song, 'way down in my heart, I got a feeling for' pragmatism." More seriously, he told James that while pragmatism as a whole had a very tenuous existence, there were, nonetheless, several distinct ideas that bore the label: "Of these opinions, I think some true and important; others I suppose true but of no great importance; others I can only regard as erroneous." He strongly sympathized with "the doctrine of the *devenir réel*; the negation of the 'necessity' of some (not all) of the 'necessary truths' alleged by the rationalist; and the voluntaristic doctrine of the legitimacy and practical indispensability of postulation in certain situations."[20] The doctrine of the *devenir réel* supported Lovejoy's own temporalism and was consistent with the evolutionary pluralism he found congenial. The voluntaristic beliefs formed a basis for the development of a rational religion and the possibility of rational choice in a pluralistic universe.

If Lovejoy can be legitimately called a pragmatic sympathizer, he was by no means an always friendly one. Even James was hard pressed, in the particular instance of "The Thirteen Pragmatisms," to detect Lovejoy's sympathy. He complained that the "reader doesn't know whether you are condemning or developing" pragmatism. Lovejoy replied: "I personally do not care a hang which I am doing; no question could seem to be more irrelevant."[21] It was far more important for the younger man to distinguish those beliefs that had been labeled pragmatic and then to determine which of those philosophical positions were internally coherent and consistent with a rational, pluralistic, and temporalistic philosophy. In this fashion that amorphous object called pragmatism might be reduced to several meaningful and valid beliefs.

Lovejoy's critique of pragmatism centered on five elements; the tendency toward antiintellectualism, the confusion of theories of meaning and truth, the belief in direct realism, the contradictions inherent in epistemological monism, and the frequent disregard of relevant temporal considerations. Lovejoy preferred to discuss the positions of particular philosophers, with William James and John Dewey the most frequent victims of his attacks. He was continually disappointed that philosophers of such stature should so often be confused and, as he saw it, wrong.

Unlike many of the idealistic systems, pragmatism, at least as advanced by James, was a philosophy of change and flux, of becoming. The universe was not rationally conceived a priori but evolved through the choices and decisions made within the world. This aspect of pragmatism appealed to Lovejoy, for it made time, which he regarded as an irreducible factor of experience, a central element of philosophy. However, a temporalistic and pluralistic philosophy such as pragmatism possessed an antiintellectual tendency that was anathema to Lovejoy. If time was one of the rocks upon which he built his philosophy, reason was the other. When he discovered the antiintellectual tendencies evident in pragmatist thought, his criticism was quick and severe.

William James bore the brunt of Lovejoy's attack on these tendencies. The occasion of the criticism was the appearance in 1909 of *A Pluralistic Universe*. Lovejoy went "along with most of the argument with conviction and enthusiasm." However, as he wrote James, "I balk seriously only at one point—but that one is perhaps to your thinking the most important of all, the dark Jordan that must be swum through before your Celestial City can be entered—I mean the extreme of anti-rationalism to which the book gives expression."[22] James had argued that "reality, life, experience, concreteness, immediacy, use what word you will, exceeds our logic, overflows and surrounds it. . . . I prefer bluntly to call reality if not irrational then at least non-rational in its constitution,—and by reality here I mean reality where things *happen*, all temporal reality without exception." The Harvard pragmatist thought that intellectualism derived from our power of "translating the crude flux of our merely feeling-experience into a conceptual order." "One of the sublimest of our human prerogatives," this faculty had often been abused. Philosophers often treated man-made concepts as "a superior type of being, bright, changeless, true, divine and utterly opposed in nature to the turbid, restless lower world." The result of this process was that "concepts, first employed to make things intelligible, are clung to even when they make them unintelligible." James concluded that in the world of flux, contradiction and logical distinction were not important: "contradiction results only from the conceptual or discursive form being substituted for the real form." As he put it in a letter to Lovejoy, "if continuity & flow mean logical self-contradiction, then logic must go."[23]

Lovejoy agreed with James that the flux was "alien to certain intellectual processes." However, he could not accept James's conclusion that reason and logic must thereby be discarded:

> That the concrete flux of temporal existence is a thing ultimately alogical, incapable of exhaustive definition, always transcendent of the concepts that seek to express it; that analytic thought is a thing secondary and derivative, and instrumental to ends to which it is, by itself, incapable of giving any meaning or value:—these propositions seem to me true. But do they amount to saying that concrete experience is literally self-contradictory—it and all its elements and aspects—and that reason is irrelevant, even so far as it goes? I do not see it so.

Lovejoy went on to argue that the continuity of change was not a contradiction, "though it undeniably baffles the craving of the intellect for fixed, permanent and chopped-off identities." He believed that the flux "never *is* a mere flux; it is made up of qualities of meanings and relations; and these can be what they are—and thus the flux can be what it really is—only by being conceived as distinct from one another, as of a fixed import, as having significances and connections other than that of mere successive presentation and independent of that succession."[24] Since reason assigned these "meanings and relations" to the flux, rationality was essential.

Three years after this letter was written, Lovejoy returned to the issue of James's antiintellectualism. He conceded that because reality was temporal it contained "an alogical factor" and that "the universe is not wholly reducible to a system of intelligible conceptual necessities." He defined antiintellectualism more narrowly as the belief that "reality is illogical, that entities may exist, and are known to exist, which are not merely undeducible from, but are in conflict with, the supposed requirements of conceptual thought—which, in a word, are incongruous with the principle of contradiction as well as the principle of sufficient reason."[25] Lovejoy then reiterated his criticism of James's antiintellectualism, but in the intervening years a closer reading of *A Pluralistic Universe* and of James's *Some Problems of Philosophy* (1911) convinced him that his former professor had drawn back from the abyss of antirationalism. James had also argued that contradictions in change could be avoided by regarding "change no longer as being continuous, but as taking place by finite not infinitesimal steps." Lovejoy thought this conceptualization of the flux showed us that there is "a reality entirely harmonious with the requirements of logic."[26] When he conceived the flux in this fashion James used reason to order the real world. By doing so and by conceiving an order consistent with logic, the Harvard pragmatist had stepped back from the antiintellectualism Lovejoy found so disturbing.

Although James seemed to have returned to "the true way of temporalism," Lovejoy's critique of the antiintellectual tendencies of temporalistic pragmatism still stood. He advocated a middle course between the extremes of rationality and irrationality. He admitted that the "concrete flux of temporal existence" was "ultimately alogical." To impose a priori rational constructs on this world of lived experience only trapped one in useless contradiction. Still, there were certain rational concepts that existed and enabled man to ascribe meaning and relation to his experience:

"Presence" *does* "exclude absence," when the thing present and that to which it is present have been properly defined—every such definition involving, indeed, as even Royce has shown, an extra-intellectual, but not necessarily illogical factor. Time *does* exclude space, *etc.*; to say otherwise, and to imply the general deliquescence of all conceptual distinctions of meaning, is to open the door wide to every form of hocus-pocus. . . . Experience has, so to say, more than one dimension; and in some of them "absolute cuts" and thorough-going reciprocal exclusions of elements are essential.[27]

These basic principles of contradiction and sufficient reason had to be maintained if man was successfully to order and conceptualize the world in which he lived. In so arguing, Lovejoy ensured that the foundation of reason which he required, both philosophically and temperamentally, remained intact.

For Lovejoy, even more basic than the antiintellectual tendencies of some pragmatists, were problems involving pragmatic theories of meaning and theories of truth. When he examined the doctrines of pragmatism closely, Lovejoy discovered that several pragmatists were prone to blur the distinction between the two theories. Although he credited James with being the one pragmatist who most consistently maintained the distinction, he also criticized his former professor for confusing the theories. In a letter written to James after the appearance of *Pragmatism*, he criticized both James's theory of meaning and his theory of truth. James held that the meaning of a proposition lies in the "future consequences in experience of the proposition's being true." Lovejoy thought this was ambiguous: it might mean "(a) the future experiences which the proposition predicts will occur *no matter whether it is believed or not*; or (b) the future experiences which will follow *provided the proposition be believed.*" Since James seemed to incline toward a belief in the second of these propositions, Lovejoy directed his further criticism to that formula, but he thought this formula was *"incapable of any application*—it cannot show any proposition or belief that anybody actually holds to be meaningless." Any belief that is held into the future will have pragmatic consequences and will thereby be meaningful. Without "gradations of pragmatic significance," this doctrine was useless in "the quashing of controversy."[28]

When Lovejoy again turned to these problems, he did so in one of his best-known articles, "The Thirteen Pragmatisms." It is unnecessary here to reiterate the thirteen varieties of pragmatism; those readers curious about the "baker's dozen of contentions" can turn to the readily accessible essay itself.[29] The key element of Lovejoy's critique was that these separate doctrines were not merely discriminable, they were also "logically independent, so that you may without inconsistency accept any one and reject all the others, or refute one and leave the philosophical standing of the others unimpugned." Lovejoy hoped his article would be a first step toward a "clarification of its [pragmatism's] formulas and a discrimination of certain sound and important ideas lying behind it from certain other ideas that are sound but not important, and certain that would be important if only they were not unsound."[30]

The discriminations of "The Thirteen Pragmatisms" muted Lovejoy's criticism, but his opinions are evident nonetheless. He found the pragmatic theories of meaning and truth, and some of the theories of knowledge, to be unsound. He argued that, as a first step, pragmatists must clearly separate the theories of meaning and truth. Once the logical distinctiveness of these doctrines was accepted, they could then be examined separately.

The pragmatic theory of meaning held that the meaning of any judgment consists, in some sense, of the future experiences of it or consequences of believing in it. Lovejoy argued that if judgments have meaning only when applied to "future experiences" then, paradoxically, many issues man considered important were excluded from "the field of legitimate consideration." If, however, meaning attached only to those judgments which consist of having future consequences of a belief in the judgment, there was "no paradox at all, but the mildest of truisms." He concluded that "all the charm and impressiveness of the theory [of meaning] arises out of the confusion of its alternative interpretations. It gets its appearance of novelty and of practical serviceableness in the settlement of controversies from its one meaning; and it gets its plausibility entirely from the other."[31]

If the pragmatic theories of meaning were unsound or mildly

truistic, its theories of truth and validity did not fare much better. Lovejoy first took up James's contention that "truth *happens* to an idea. It *becomes* true, is *made* true by events. Its verity *is* . . . the process . . . of its verifying itself." Lovejoy noted that this theory of truth was "not at the same time functionally serviceable as a theory of knowledge." Furthermore, "judgments are not known to be true until they become true, and until they become true they have no use or importance." However, once it becomes true, the proposition belongs to the "dead past" and, properly speaking, would have no pragmatic meaning. He characterized this theory as "epistemologically functionless." [32]

Lovejoy was also dissatisfied with most of the pragmatic theories of validity. These argued, in general, that those propositions were valid which were true in the past, were biologically serviceable, or were in some sense satisfying. The first derived its "plausibility from its resemblance to the ordinary empirical doctrine" that things are true which have been "realized in past experience." There was little here that was distinctively pragmatic. On the second aspect, Lovejoy contended that many beliefs which were biologically serviceable (his example was the Jewish belief in the imminent return of the Messiah) predict nothing or "predict what is not going to occur." He found it paradoxical that a proposition which predicted nothing in a predictive theory of truth could be regarded as true. Finally, in taking up the propositions that valid judgments were in some sense satisfying, he argued that they were either sound but unimportant truisms or that to a "maker of rational judgments" satisfaction was an unacceptable criterion of validity. [33]

Lovejoy's discriminatory exercise was not, however, wholly critical; a few of the doctrines he regarded as sound and even valuable. The pragmatic ontological theory was the most important of these. This was "the doctrine of the 'open-ness' of the future, and of the determinative or 'creative' efficacy of each 'present' moment in the ever-transient process of conscious judgment, choice, and action." This metaphysics appeared "to imply the partial contingency and (from the standpoint of any 'present' knowledge) indeterminateness of the future content of reality." Nonetheless, there was nothing in this temporalism that justified "the denial of the possibility of the making of 'true' judgments about contemporaneous or past (but not yet consciously verified) realities."[34] This, of course, was very close to Lovejoy's own pluralism and temporalism, and he used it in support of the possibility and necessity of rational choice in a pluralistic universe.

The second aspect of pragmatism which Lovejoy regarded as sound were two closely related doctrines dealing with the legitimacy and limitations of postulation. The first of these was James's view that "our ready-made ideal framework for all sorts of possible objects follows from the very structure of our thinking." Lovejoy described this as "the doctrine that axioms are necessities and that the action of voluntary choice in belief is always limited by a permanent system of a priori principles of possibility and impossibility inhering in the nature of intellect." Related to this was the "assertion of the *equal* legitimacy of those postulates . . . which appear indispensable as presuppositions for effective dealing with the world of our physical experience, and of those which, though lacking this sort of 'physical' necessity as completely as they do the logical sort, yet seem demanded in order to give meaning to, or encouragement in, men's moral strivings, or to satisfy the emotional or esthetic cravings of our complex nature." Lovejoy thought this theory best deserved the name of pragmatist epistemology.[35]

Lovejoy judged sound those pragmatic doctrines that were consistent with his developing philosophical views. The open, pluralistic universe of James lent support to Lovejoy's efforts to demonstrate the necessity of pluralism.[36] The equal legitimacy of physical and rational necessities within their proper spheres provided a justification of Lovejoy's growing realism and his rationalism; both were necessary to make a pluralistic universe intelligible. Although some varieties of pragmatism were flawed, those that were sound helped Lovejoy toward a philosophy that was pluralistic and that dispensed with the Absolute.

"The Thirteen Pragmatisms" was only the opening shot in an extended campaign against the erring habits of the pragmatists. Following a series of varied essays on pragmatism, Lovejoy summarized his major criticisms of the philosophy in "Pragmatism *Versus* the Pragmatists," his contribution to *Essays in Critical Realism*. Focusing on the philosophy of John Dewey, he criticized what he regarded as Dewey's aberrations: the confusion of realism and idealism, the problems of epistemological monism, and the difficulties concerning intertemporal cognition.

"Pragmatism *Versus* the Pragmatist" is a difficult article, because Lovejoy had a serious problem in deciding which of Dewey's seemingly contradictory pronouncements on the issues were to be taken as definitive. The discussion of realism, idealism, and epistemological monism or dualism is especially confusing; Lovejoy found Dewey wavering between a realistic and idealistic view of the world and, as a result, the consequences for epistemology were often in doubt.[37]

According to Lovejoy, a consistent pragmatist could not be a realist and an epistemological monist. A pragmatist could not deny the existence of mental entities, since "he is insistent upon the reality of 'aims' and 'ideal contents' in their true character as genuinely external to their objectives and fulfillments"; he could, however, "reject the hypothesis of an independent physical world altogether, in which case he is left with *nothing but* mental—i.e., sensibly experienced—entities in his universe." The true pragmatist was thus restricted to "*either* idealism or else dualism, both in the psychophysical and the epistemological sense of the latter term." Lovejoy thought that this conclusion was implied in the pragmatist's "most indispensable premise—namely, that we have thoughts of the future—as soon as it is recognized that (as Mr. Dewey justly insists) these thoughts include contents which are present-as-absent, and that such contents (as he does not appear to note) are necessarily nonphysical."[38]

Dewey was unconvinced by most of Lovejoy's arguments,[39] but the positive implications of Lovejoy's criticism are more important here in any case. By concluding that a consistent realistic pragmatism was necessarily epistemologically dualistic, Lovejoy closed the gap between his own philosophical positions and those of what he regarded as a consistent pragmatism. To be sure, this congruence of doctrine does not make Lovejoy a pragmatist, but, at the very least, his own fundamental positions were not, as he saw it, contradictory to a pragmatic philosophy.

Lovejoy turned next to the epistemological problems inherent in Dewey's accounts of intertemporal cognition. Pragmatists had argued against retrospective knowledge since the " 'truth' of a retrospective belief, in the sense of some sort of present correspondence of present data with past data" was impossible. Lovejoy believed that what trapped the pragmatist in the paradox of denying retrospective knowledge was "his unwillingness to concede that a belief can ever be adequately validated indirectly, i.e., without the fulfillment of the belief's meaning in actual experience, the presentation as immediate data of the matters to which it relates." Lovejoy thought that a "faithful analysis" of the "moment of practical reflection" would include "an enumeration of the not-immediately-given things which it is *needful for the effective agent, at that moment, to believe or assume.*" The pragmatist was required to believe some unverifiable things about the future; for example, he must assume "that there is to *be* a future for him to act in." He must also assume that "knowledge about the past is equivalent, within limits, to prediction about the future." Since the pragmatist was willing to accept prediction that was not immediately verifiable, he had no justification for denying verifiability to past knowledge on the grounds that it could only be indirect. Lovejoy concluded that "all strictly 'pragmatic' verification is indirect verification, based either on instinctive assumptions or upon inference from explicit postulates; for only such verification is attainable within the limits of the moment of practical reflection."[40]

Although his argument had focused on the particular instance of prospective and retrospective knowledge, Lovejoy believed his conclusions about pragmatic reliance on indirect verification had other implications. He argued that in an epistemological sense knowledge of the past was "analogous to a knowledge of transempirical realities" since in neither case can the object of representation ever be directly experienced and thus compared directly with the idea of it. The pragmatist, at least by Lovejoy's reasoning, was forced to admit the validity of retrospective knowledge, which was, of course, indirect. This being the case, he concluded that "if we can have meaningful and legitimate beliefs about past (or future) events now inaccessible to direct experience, we may conceivably hold meaningful and legitimate beliefs about contemporaneous existents inaccessible to direct experience."[41] There was nothing, in other words, about a pragmatic philosophy that debarred a consistent and thoroughgoing dualistic epistemology. Indeed, if Lovejoy was correct, such a view of knowledge was the only one a consistent pragmatist could hold.

Lovejoy presented his conclusions about pragmatic epistemology in a separate section in which he enunciated the principles of a consistent, realistic pragmatist. He wrote that a consistent pragmatist must accept:

> a. That all "instrumental" knowledge is, or at least includes and requires, "presentative" knowledge, a representation of not-present existents by present data;

> b. That, pragmatically considered, knowledge is thus necessarily and constantly conversant with entities which are existentially "transcendent" of the knowing experience, and frequently with entities which transcend the total experience of the knower;

> c. That is, if a real physical world having the characteristics set forth by natural science is assumed, certain of the contents of experience, and specifically the contents of anticipation and retrospection, cannot be assigned to that world, and must therefore be called "psychical" (i.e., experienced but not physical) entities;

> d. That knowledge is mediated through such psychical existences and would be impossible without them.[42]

The position Lovejoy outlined here, epistemological and psychophysical dualism, he would develop and justify at greater length in "The Anomaly of Knowledge" and *The Revolt Against Dualism*.

In the concluding section of the essay, "The True Pragmatism and the False," Lovejoy provided further clues to what he regarded as a sound and valuable pragmatic philosophy. He described pragmatism as a *"philosophy of man as agent, and as reflective agent, in a physical and social environment."* The "deepest-lying premises" of this philosophy were that "knowing is 'functional,' that it 'makes a difference' and does so by virtue of those characteristics which are distinctive of it *as* knowing." Lovejoy's problem in dealing with pragmatism was to unite these propositions about the nature of man in his environment with epistemological and psychophysical dualism. Pragmatic philosophy, for all its aberrations, emphasized the plural, open character of the universe, in which development was the crucial process, and in which man stood as a creative, reflective agent. Pragmatic voluntarism thus supported his belief that man, as a rational maker of choices, had a real role in the creation of an intelligible universe.[43]

Lovejoy found pragmatism congenial, in part, because time and succession were central elements in the philosophy. Until he began his inquiries into the philosophy of James, Lovejoy had considered temporal problems almost solely in connection with his studies of religion. Starting in 1909 with "The Obsolescence of the Eternal," which mingled religious and philosophical considerations, Lovejoy took up the philosophical implications of temporalism. Much of Lovejoy's writing on the subject concerned the French philosopher Henri Bergson, a leading exponent of temporalistic philosophy. Lovejoy objected to certain aspects of Bergson's philosophy, especially his antiintellectualism, and the American's temporalism was developed in respectful antagonism to that of his European contemporary.

Lovejoy set out, in "The Obsolescence of the Eternal," to answer two questions: whether "real evolution and real eternity can be congruous in the realm of concrete existences" and whether the "eternal can conceivably be correlated in any logically consistent or practically pertinent way with the empirically undeniable existence of the temporal and the evolving." On the first problem he concluded that "a world in which qualitative evolution is supposed to take place is one in which, as a total, quantitative constancy cannot be said to subsist." In other words, assuming the existence of "real evolution," which Lovejoy did, "real eternity" was a contradiction and could not, therefore, exist. When he turned to the second question, his conclusions were equally damaging to the eternal. The "assertion of a real relation between an eternal and a temporal," he argued, "reduces the eternal to the temporal." Furthermore, there was still another principle, "a temporal form of the law of the excluded middle": "It appears to me to be impossible for us to conceive any concrete thing save as either *now* existing or not now existing,—as other than past or present or future." Since an eternal could not either be or not be, for the one temporalized it and the other denied its existence, Lovejoy concluded that "the idea of eternity is an idea which cannot be positively thought, under the conditions involved in all our thinking as beings in time. It is a self-contradictory, and therefore wholly empty notion."[44] Some thirteen years after he had first expressed doubts about the absolutes of Bradley and Royce, the earlier skepticism had become fixed conviction; an absolute was neither necessary nor possible.

Having disposed of the eternal and the absolute, Lovejoy soon turned to developing a consistent temporalism. He defined temporalism as that philosophy which maintained the following four positions:

> first, that time is not "ideal" in the sense that it can be
> regarded as unreal, as an illusion or a "false appearance"
> of something non-temporal; second, that temporal suc-
> cession and duration constitute a qualitatively unique
> mode of reality, which can not, without falsification,
> either be reduced to any other type of serial ordering or
> be conceived as forming part of any whole which, as a
> whole, is non-successive or changeless; third, that, since
> the experience of temporal succession involves an essen-
> tial distinction between the givenness of past content of
> experience and the unrealized character of the future,
> the reality of the time-experience proves that reality as a
> whole can at no moment be truly called complete, self-
> contained, an organic unity; fourth, that the reality of
> the time-experience likewise shows that the total sum of
> given reality receives from moment to moment an in-
> crease in *some* sort of content, and that, therefore the
> notion of becoming or process is fundamental in the
> description of the general nature of reality.

Lovejoy recognized and accepted the fact that temporalism was "incompatible with the more extreme sort of rationalism in metaphysics—*i.e.*, with the assertion that all that is real is rational and all that is rational is real." The problem with a wholly rational system was that in it "all the parts or elements must obviously be realized all at once and eternally."[45] Although seemingly confronted with a temporal excluded middle—things were either temporal and nonrational or eternal and rational—he believed that such was not the case. He steadfastly maintained that while our reason did not create the universe, rationality was necessary if we were to order, in any sense, our perception of the temporal flux. We did not experience time and succession directly and it was man's reason that ordered and mediated our experience of the temporal. It was on this subject of the nature of our experience of time and the role of reason that Lovejoy differed most notably from the other temporalists of his generation, especially Bergson.

As with the philosophy of James and pragmatism in general, Lovejoy sympathized with elements of Bergson's philosophy. The American temporalist wrote to his French counterpart that "to your skilful and impressive and admirably radical expression of the fundamentals of that doctrine, I, like many of my contemporaries, owe the greatest incitement and instruction." "The conception of evolution as a *d'evinir reel* [sic]" was, Lovejoy thought, "a contribution of the utmost importance to metaphysics; . . . we all have to thank you for its clearest and most vigorous formulation."[46] However, when he began to grapple with the details of Bergson's formulations, Lovejoy discovered serious problems.

The sticking point for Lovejoy about Bergson's philosophy was the Frenchman's antiintellectualism. This arose, he believed, from Bergson's "paradoxical conception of the nature of real time." Bergson held that "'real duration,' the time that is an immediately certain reality, the actual succession of inner experience . . . is not subject to the categories of number or quantity." Real duration did not consist of separate, definable quantities that could be aggregated into a whole. To do so would be to "spatialize" time, since magnitude and quantity applied only to space and, thus, falsified the nature of time. "A mind which had the idea or the experience *only* of time, and was wholly ignorant of space, would necessarily represent duration as 'at once self identical and changing,' 'as a succession without distinction,' as a 'solidarity.' " Bergson admitted that time implied succession, but denied that "succession presents itself primarily as the distinction of a juxtaposed 'before' and 'after.' " Intellect applied concepts such as succession and quantity to the time experience. Bergson held that reality was "pure duration" and could not be understood in such rational terms. In the end, then, Bergson's doctrine implied that "reality in its true nature is self-contradictory," or, in other words, irrational.[47]

When Lovejoy examined Bergson's philosophy he discovered that the case against the intellect was less convincing than Bergson thought. Lovejoy's critique had two central theses: logical, conceptual thought *about* time did not violate the alogical character of the reality of time; and Bergson's account of the perception of time was psychologically unsound.

Lovejoy argued that Bergson had confused the idea of "representing simultaneously" with the idea of "representing as simultaneous." Bergson's theory held that representation of a whole of parts involves summation of the individual units, which is impossible "through a *purely* successive apprehension of the units." The units added must be represented simultaneously. Further, "to represent two or more units simultaneously means to think of them as simultaneously juxtaposed in space." This representation in space was, for Bergson, totally incompatible with the idea of duration, thus duration could not be composed of a numerical sum. Lovejoy thought that in "a single specious present" he was "capable of thinking *about* two or more non-present moments, and of distinguishing them as temporally earlier and later." For him, the "coexistence, in the mind, of two ideas of objects or events" was "not necessarily identical with the idea of the coexistence of the two objects or events." If we could think about succession by aggregating the sequence in our minds, that implied nothing about the disaggregate character of the actually existing flux. The way we rationally ordered our experience of time left the irrational quality of real temporal succession unchanged. Remove Bergson's confusion, argued Lovejoy, and one discovers not a contradiction but a distinction we "make with entire clearness and logical efficiency every hour of our waking lives."[48]

Lovejoy's second rational critique of Bergson attacked the French philosopher's argument from "the continuity of time to its logical inconceivability." Bergson believed that if "duration is a continuum, the passage from any given moment to any subsequent moment would involve the summation of an infinite series." Since this was impossible, one could never pass from one moment in time to another. As Lovejoy pointed out, this argument against the logical conceivability of time rested on the assumption that "if time were a quantity at all, it would necessarily be a continuous, infinitely divisible quantity." Since he found no arguments in Bergson to justify such an assumption, he proposed a contrary postulate: "the succession of our actual experience is not a true continuum, but rather a series of discrete, internally stable states, each of them containing a peculiarly temporal sort of backward and forward 'pointing.' "[49] This position, Lovejoy believed, was consistent with reason and closer to our actual perceptual experience.

Lovejoy's most basic critique was that Bergson had misapprehended what actually happens in our perception of succession. Using the example of the apprehension of a melody, Bergson argued that in experiencing the melody its elements were "not separately apprehended at the successive moments of their occurrence. They are given only as organized into an indivisible but qualitatively definite unity." Lovejoy, however, thought that, even if this is how we perceive such things as melody, Bergson's example had failed to prove his point about the indivisibility of succession. He argued that the recognition of the melody as a whole was "*not* an experience of succession or duration. It is simply a case where a series of stimuli which objectively considered—from the point of view, for example, of the psychologist conducting the experiment—are successive, has finally produced in the consciousness of the subject an instantaneous apprehension of a certain definitely qualified content, *not* apprehended as a numerical aggregate nor as a succession." For Lovejoy, the "definitely qualified content" of an apprehended melody stood outside the experience of succession: the successive notes were not the melody, nor was the melody the succession of notes. This lack of perceptual connection led him to conclude that Bergson's account was faulty.[50]

Lovejoy also attacked Bergson's contention that time was no more "a quantity composed of moments" than motion was "a quantity composed of positions." Initially skeptical that the assertion could prove what it was supposed to, Lovejoy argued that even if valid, it showed "only that a duration is not a quantity composed of states; it does not show that a duration is not a quantity at all." He was willing to grant, for the sake of argument, Bergson's notion that if time were composed of separate divisible moments, none of those moments would contain any experience of succession. He countered with a question: "What reason is there for maintaining that we have any direct experience of transition as such?" On this point, Lovejoy could find no place where Bergson had provided a convincing argument. Transition was baffling to the intellect, as Lovejoy willingly conceded, but that in itself was no reason to accept the indivisible and, thus, paradoxical character of time.[51]

Bergson found Lovejoy's critique of his philosophy interesting and suggestive, but the American's attacks did little to change the Frenchman's ideas.[52] Lovejoy, for his part, remained totally unconvinced that Bergson's temporalism was either accurate or consistent. Near the end of his life, Lovejoy published another consideration of Bergson's philosophy, "Bergson on 'Real Duration.'" He returned to the critique he had developed before World War I, when Bergson enjoyed his greatest vogue, and again pointed out Bergson's confusion of a "succession of perceptions" and "the perception of succession." So, also, he challenged anew Bergson's account of the perception of succession. When Lovejoy heard a melody, he heard a sequence of notes which were a part of some whole. Because a melody could stop at any point, it seemed clear that a succession such as a melody was not a "temporally 'indivisible' unity": "a temporally 'indivisible' unity would have all its elements present at once, and there could be no question of stopping or not stopping." Lovejoy also relied on an argument from memory to counter Bergson. He thought that any "moment of consciousness which has any temporal character whatever" contained three components: first, the "especially vivid content, usually sensory or affective, which *feels* 'new,' and thus serves to identify the moment as 'now'; second, imagery, vague or clear, or fading sense-content, which is *not* felt as simply 'new'; and third, . . . a conceived pattern or *schema* of relations of before-and-after, in which all the other elements of content, including the 'now' itself, are thought as having relative positions, or dates of existence."[53] This account of memory consistent with his epistemological dualism allowed Lovejoy to explain Bergson's paradox. When we experience a succession such as a melody we are able to hold within our consciousness both the fading memory of the initial notes, the experience of their passage through time, and the apprehension of the succession as a whole. This account violated neither perceptual experience, the logic of conceptual thought, nor the flux of real time.

Implicit throughout Lovejoy's critique of Bergson were the elements of his own consistent philosophy. Lovejoy began, as he later recalled, by applying one "touch-stone" about the character of reality or knowledge: he felt that the "most indubitable fact

Lovejoy confronting the pluralistic universe
(Special Collections: The Johns Hopkins University)

of our experience" was that "experience itself is temporal." He qualified this statement slightly by arguing that a temporalist philosophy "would not necessarily assert that all that is is temporal; but it would insist that whatever empirically *is* temporal is so irretrievably."[54] From this beginning he developed a philosophy of temporalism which was consistent with the four-part definition of that term, the logic of human thought, and the reality of time.

Assuming that time was a real and irreducible fact of our experience, Lovejoy's problem, and that of the other temporalists, was the question of how man perceives and orders that experience without violating its nature as real flux. Lovejoy, of course, had the additional requirement that any account of temporal succession and experience must not contradict the principles of reason. Unlike Bergson, who postulated that time was an indivisible continuum, he thought that "the sequence of changes in consciousness which constitutes the perceptual flux and grounds our ideas of time, is a discrete sequence." To quote James, as he did, "time itself comes in drops." This idea seemed to be a more accurate account of the perception of time and to avoid the Zenonian paradox inherent in the conception of time as a continuum.[55] Furthermore, it suggested ways in which Bergson's confusions regarding a perception of succession and a succession of perceptions might be avoided. In this Lovejoy enlisted the aid of memory. He argued that at each new moment in time our consciousness contains not only the vivid experience of that moment, but also the fading memory image of past moments, and the idea of the progression of successive moments. He thought that this account maintained the successive character of time because we never directly had before us more than one moment in time. The other moments contained in the apprehension of the larger unit were, in a phrase of Dewey's, "present-as-absent"; that is, we possessed the idea, the memory, if you will, of their past existence, though they no longer existed. This conception of the capacity to know things which were not directly and immediately present in our consciousness presented serious philosophical problems. They, however, appeared solvable with the adoption of a dualistic epistemology enabling Lovejoy to know things which did not, at the moment of their knowing, exist.[56]

CHAPTER IV

CRITICAL REALISM AND THE DUALISMS

Lovejoy's early work in philosophy was largely critical; he attacked the idealism of Royce and Howison, the pragmatism of James and Dewey, and the temporalism of Bergson. His criticism of these philosophers was not unfocused; he was consistent in the points he made and the positions he defended. Implicit throughout Lovejoy's critiques were strong beliefs in the temporal character of existence, in the necessity of basic laws of thought, in the independence of objects external to man's consciousness, and, finally, in man's ability to obtain knowledge in such a pluralistic universe and, thus, to make the world rationally intelligible. To the philosophic community of the early twentieth century, however, these positions were by no means self-evident.

The crux of Lovejoy's problem was not his adherence to any one of these beliefs. By themselves they were fairly common in contemporary philosophical discourse. His most serious problem was an epistemological one: how do we know what we know in a universe composed of such elements, indeed, how can we know anything at all? The acceptance of a pluralistic and temporalistic universe implied, as Lovejoy well knew, the acceptance of epistemological dualism.[1] In the contentious world of twentieth-century philosophy, such a basic position could not simply be accepted, it had to be defended systematically.

Lovejoy's systematic philosophizing was entwined in an important facet of his thinking. He was totally convinced that philosophy was a rational discipline and that philosophical issues could only be settled, if at all, through rational discourse among philosophers. There was considerable feeling in the philosophical profession before World War I that the wisest course for the discipline would be to establish some guidelines to philosophizing in hopes of resolving outstanding issues, instead of continually creating new problems. Lovejoy's presidential address to the American Philosophical Association in 1916, "On Some Conditions of Progress in Philosophical Inquiry," is a classic exposition of this approach to philosophy. An understanding of this attempt to establish a rational and scientific method in philosophy is essential to understanding Lovejoy's cooperation with the critical realists and his exposition of a dualistic epistemology.

The formation of the American Philosophical Association (APA) in 1901 was, in part, the response of academic philosophers to the professionalization and specialization increasingly characteristic of the academic disciplines in America. In his address as the first president of the APA, James Edwin Creighton urged his colleagues to engage in cooperative scientific inquiry, for it was the surest path to the attainment of "real results in the search for truth." The development of "intellectual fellowship and coöperation" was the "most hopeful sign of all scientific work" and "the source of the inspiration which animates all modern investigation and scholarship."[2] Creighton's advocacy of scientific cooperation as a response to the challenge of the sciences became an important issue in the early years of the APA. Did philosophy have its own method and standpoint, perhaps less scientific than the other disciplines, but no less valuable, or should philosophy try to become another scientific discipline dealing with a clearly recognized body of special problems?

Lovejoy played an important part in the disputes over this problem, which lasted, with varying degrees of intensity, from 1901 until the early 1920s. Much of the debate on cooperation and scientific inquiry focused on the organization of philosophical discussion within the APA and at the annual meetings. Some philosophers hoped that the organized discussions held at the annual meetings would introduce greater scientific rigor to the discipline. Although at least ten of the first sixteen meetings had such discussions, they ushered in neither a rapid increase in philosophic progress nor the comforts of scholarly comradeship. By 1910 it was clear to the advocates of a more scientific philosophy, including Lovejoy, that the annual debates, while interesting, were doing little to meet the challenge of the other sciences. During the Tenth Annual Meeting, Lovejoy suggested that mutual understanding would be helped by a closer adherence to definitions and urged the appointment of a committee "to define the fundamental terms" for the next discussion. The APA acted on his suggestion and appointed a Committee on Definitions, chaired by F. J. E. Woodbridge and including Lovejoy and W. P. Montague among its members.[3] In choosing "The Relation of Consciousness and Object in Sense-Perception" as the topic for the 1911 meeting, the Committee went beyond a simple definition of terms. They attempted to "formulate somewhat precisely the issues involved and to indicate what appears . . . to be, at the present juncture in philosophical discussion, the most promising mode of approach to those issues." The Committee felt that, whatever the success or failure of this first effort at organized "cooperative philosophical inquiry," the promise of such inquiry had "important possibilities for the future of philosophical study."[4]

The December 1911 meeting at Harvard was only a qualified success The immediate debate, which one observer called a "riot of philosophic anarchy," focused more on what "ought to have been but was not" than on the ostensible subject. In spite of these problems, there remained "the unmistakable promise of a new type of accomplishment at future sessions," and by the end there seemed to be a general consensus that "the method of debating a clearly formulated issue should by all means be continued as by far the most profitable mode of philosophic discussion." Promise there was, but there were also problems, some of which Josiah Royce raised after the meeting. He worried that the organization of highly structured discussion risked excluding a fair number of philosophers. Royce hoped the discussions would continue, but that they would be open to "anybody whose views are seriously represented in classic or current philosophical discussion."[5]

The following year, 1912, the APA, through its newly renamed Committee on Discussions, decided to confront directly the problem of agreement and progress in philosophy. The Committee, again including Lovejoy, proposed the question: "*Is a continuous progress towards unanimity among philosophers on the more fundamental issues* (a) Desirable? (b) Attainable?" They wanted participants who thought unanimity undesirable or unattainable to consider the "impediments to agreement" and the purposes of "philosophical argumentation and discussion." Philosophers who believed in the possibility of unanimity were urged to consider "what methods for the systematization of philosophical inquiry, or for organized cooperation in philosophizing," would help achieve that end.[6]

The Twelfth Annual Meeting in New York produced rather less agreement on the question of "Agreement in Philosophy" than the organizers of the debate had hoped. No one wanted to suppress individual opinion, and nearly all desired "agreement upon the old questions, at least, if for no other purpose than that they might go on and disagree about new ones." Still, there was considerable disagreement over the form such agreement should, or could, take and on the possibilities of achieving any agreement at all. Toward the end of the extended debate, Ralph Barton Perry and Lovejoy, among others, suggested that "greater agreement of the desirable kind might be attained if the members of the Association would give up the philosopher's traditional lonely individualism, and make an effort to cooperate with each other, and especially try to understand each other and to be understood." As one might expect, there was further disagreement on how best to reach this goal. The meeting ended, however, on a hopeful note regarding the possibility of cooperation, if not agreement.[7]

Following the New York meeting, the problem of agreement receded from the forefront of philosophical discussion. Lovejoy, however, retained his commitment to the ideas of cooperation and agreement. During his presidency of the APA in 1916, he appointed a committee, with himself as chairman, to organize a discussion of mental and physical entities. Like most previous attempts at organized discussion, that in 1916 was disappointing. Because of the late announcement of the topic and the inability to have papers or abstracts published beforehand, the discussion lacked unity and focus.[8] Although cooperation and organized discussion had again failed, the philosophers in attendance heard Lovejoy, in his presidential address, argue for the necessity of cooperation and progress in philosophical inquiry.

"On Some Conditions of Progress in Philosophical Inquiry" addressed the questions of the function of philosophy and the role of the philosopher. Believing that philosophers should contribute to the settlement of vital issues concerning human thought, Lovejoy proposed that they cooperate so that they might rationally and conclusively settle philosophic controversies. This address thus united two concerns, one personal and the other professional. On the one hand, Lovejoy required the rational resolution of philosophic problems to make the universe intelligible. On the other hand, the philosophic discipline had become worried that, unlike the sciences, it was increasingly unable to settle any of the problems facing contemporary thinkers. Lovejoy proposed a solution that would meet both his need for rational intelligibility and, as he saw it, the discipline's apparent need for more scientific truth.

Lovejoy set out to determine "What's the Matter with Philosophy" and to suggest ways of alleviating the problems. The splintering of the philosophic discipline after the seeming certainties of the 1890s prompted his inquiry. When he studied under Howison, the great philosophic issues seemed settled; idealism reigned triumphant. Following that, the "collective mind of philosophy" had become *"divers et ondoyant"*—diverse and undulating. Although there were, no doubt, "eternal verities" among the new theories, not all of these often contradictory theses could be true. In Lovejoy's mind, this riot of diversity was a "standing scandal to philosophy."[9]

Lovejoy was not totally opposed to the diversification occurring in modern thought. He believed that the high value placed on diversity was one of the "notable gifts of Romanticism to modern thought." However, he remained totally opposed to the notion that diversity in philosophy was inherent and inevitable. Philosophy was more than the interaction of diverse temperaments upon a "many-aspected universe." It was neither the "communication of mere personal impressions about the universe," nor "the impartation of some sort of cosmic emotion from one bosom to another, by whatever method of spreading the contagion prove most effective." Lovejoy felt that argument was the "customary employment" of the philosopher. In argument, "every man steps aside out of a world of his own into a world in which is presupposed not only the existence of truths verifiable by the common reason, but also the possibility of cogency—that is, of intellectual coercion—and so the possibility of unanimity." Thus, unless philosophy gave up all scientific pretensions, it must be prepared to limit itself to verifiable truths and the consequent possibility of agreement.[10]

Philosophy, according to Lovejoy, had long had "two seemingly identical, but practically incongruous, functions." Man demanded both edification and logical certainty from his philosophers. Though Lovejoy did not want to denigrate the value of edification, he clearly felt that the scientific function needed to be carefully distinguished from the edifying. Beyond this, if philosophy was to fulfill properly its scientific function of rigorous inquiry, philosophers would have to acquire a scientific "temper." This meant that the philosopher would have to abandon his complacent assumption that his own particular method was scientific and admit the possibility that he had erred in his inquiry. The question was, How does anyone know that he has erred? Lovejoy thought that the "only objective way whereby a philosopher can judge the probable correctness of his opinions is, not by considering the cogency (to his mind) of the arguments which support them, but by viewing himself, so to say, in his statistical aspect." If he thinks, to use Lovejoy's example, that seven out of ten philosophers are wrong, then, by all rights, he, too, has a 70 percent chance of being wrong. Lovejoy was convinced that most error was accidental, and once philosophers accepted this, and its prevalence, they could take the necessary steps to remedy the situation.[11]

Lovejoy presented his fellow philosophers with a six-point program to ensure that philosophy would become increasingly scientific. The basic requirements were that philosophers become more "methodologically self-conscious," that philosophy become "more systematic in its procedure," and, finally, that the discipline devote "relatively more attention to its technique and, for a time, relatively less to the formulation of substantive conclusions." Lovejoy would not be satisfied "until no trained philosopher can ever sit down at his desk to write without an explicit, vivid and persistent consciousness of the specific causes from which error is likely to arise in the type of inquiry in which he proposes to engage."[12]

His first two proposals for introducing greater rigor into the philosophic discipline focused on ways of avoiding the omission of important "considerations" in philosophizing. He defined "consideration" very broadly as "almost any sort of logical datum that may be mentioned, according to the character and scope of the problem." Carelessness was a chief source of error; in his haste to reach conclusions the philosopher overlooked or ignored important and relevant considerations. The first step to eliminating this problem was the development of a habit of caution Reversing Danton's motto from the French revolution, Lovejoy argued that the motto of philosophy should be "not boldness, but circumspection, and again circumspection, and always circumspection." Once philosophers were aware of the need for cautious inquiry, they should undertake "a deliberate and systematic attempt at exhaustiveness in the enumeration of the elements of a problem, of the 'considerations' pertinent to it."[13]

The third and fourth elements of Lovejoy's program followed from the first two. They were a response to the question, How was this circumspection and exhaustiveness to be accomplished? Lovejoy believed that philosophy, perhaps more than any other science, was a "coöperative enterprise." Cooperation, he thought, would have to become even more important under the new scientific regime. A single mind was bound to err in evaluating all the considerations pertinent to a problem, but, through cooperation, philosophy as a whole might avoid the pitfalls of logical oversight. "Under such conditions a good many ingenious and plausible errors might conceivably never survive their trial heats."[14]

As his fourth point, Lovejoy admitted that "genuinely useful and constructive philosophical discussion" was "one of the most difficult things in the world to secure." If nothing else, the frustrations of the preceding annual meetings would have taught him that. Yet, in spite of this experience, his proposals for organized discussion were simply extensions of past experience. He first suggested "the adoption, at least for purposes of a particular discussion, of a common and unambiguous terminology, and—if so much be within human power—of a common set of initial postulates." Part of the problem with this proposal, which Lovejoy seems not to have fully realized, was that some of the most important differences among philosophers were on basic definitions and initial postulates. As Royce had pointed out, such a proposal was fraught with dangers of exclusivity. Lovejoy, nonetheless, remained optimistic about the ability of philosophic good will to overcome these difficulties. Assuming agreement on initial postulates, the discipline should then "organize discussion upon a sufficiently large scale and . . . provide for its prosecution over a sufficiently long time and with the requisite orderliness and sequentiality." If these things were carried out, then Lovejoy anticipated a "more precise joining of issue . . . [and] a richer accumulation and convergence of pertinent 'considerations,' a more tenacious following of the argument, a better understanding, at the worst, of the precise nature and grounds of our differences, than would be attainable by any other means."[15]

Lovejoy's argument centered on his fifth point. Here he took up Norman Kemp Smith's question, Is it "possible to treat individual philosophical problems in isolation, to deal with the general field of our inquiries piecemeal?" Kemp Smith and others had argued that it was not possible; philosophy dealt with wholes, not with parts. Lovejoy admitted that the isolation of philosophical elements was more difficult than in the other sciences, but he argued that there was no necessary reason why separation was impossible. He thought that "hypothetical reasoning" provided a sound logical method for isolating problems: "Philosophical discussion may be, and, conducted in an ideal manner, always would be, expressly hypothetical in form: Its postulates would be explicit, they would be assumed for the occasion and not asserted, and the question at issue would concern the conclusions properly to be drawn within the limits of the system thereby determined." Having thus established certion sound conclusions, the philosopher would move on to other questions in the same fashion: "it is precisely through such a linked sequence of provisionally limited and hypothetical discussions that the way to an increasing agreement among philosophers lies."[16]

Hypothetical discussion by itself would not have produced agreement. The possibility of agreement rested upon Lovejoy's assumption of the basic rationality of man: "We must, after all, assume that, if the question is a real one, an identical logical reaction to it will be obtainable from all rational minds capable of understanding it; and a failure to obtain such reaction from minds in which such capacity is presumed can be regarded only as a difference in specific logical sensitivity."[17] This assumption was not only the key element in his argument for progress in philosophy; it was, in many ways, the most important assumption underlying his whole philosophy. If an "identical logical reaction" could be obtained from all "rational minds," then Lovejoy had a basis for intelligibility in the multifaceted world of change. Reason and logic could establish certain limited and sound conclusions upon which one could order the alogical universe of experience. Since the principles of reason were unchanging, rational conclusions would persist unchanged by the flux of experience.

Lovejoy concluded his proposal with the suggestion that the cooperative task of philosophy be eased through the preparation of "a comprehensive *catalogue raisonné* of 'considerations,' arranged according to the problems or the theses to which they are, or have by any considerable body of thinkers been supposed to be, pertinent." This "modern *Summa Metaphysica*" would bring together those considerations which Lovejoy regarded as the "ultimate units of our inquiry." As he had earlier in his religious articles, and would later in *The Great Chain of Being*, Lovejoy argued that the "number of really distinct 'considerations' discoverable in the history of philosophy is vastly less than the unsophisticated reader of that kaleidoscopic record usually supposes." The collection, discrimination, and clarification of these various considerations would allow the philosopher to avoid the errors of the past and to build his own philosophy on sound and logical grounds.[18]

At the end, Lovejoy appealed not so much to the philosophers' reason, but to their desire to make philosophy a science commensurate with the hard sciences. He argued that his program was an absolute necessity unless philosophers were willing to abandon their "customary pretension to be dealing with objective, verifiable and clearly communicable truths, and are content to acknowledge that all our brave parade of philosophizing is nothing more than an exploiting of our temperamental idiosyncrasies, disingenuously masquerading in the garb of impersonal reason." If philosophy could minimize the chances of error, its practitioners might "give to the next generation of philosophers a fairer prospect of a common understanding; and . . . give to philosophy itself some hope of attaining the assured and steady march which should characterize a science."[19]

As might be expected, philosophers could not agree on the merits or demerits of Lovejoy's program. In one sense there was agreement; most seem to have thought that it was somehow flawed. The discussants contacted by the editors of *Philosophical Review* clearly exhibited the diverse reactions to the address. Ernest Albee questioned the notion that philosophy could become a science; Charles M. Bakewell doubted that problems could be so neatly organized or that philosophy could surmount its individual characters; and Edmund H. Hollands doubted whether philosophic issues could ever be definitely settled. These men and their colleagues, whose cooperation would have been essential to its success, all dissented in one fashion or another from Lovejoy's program. The APA soon abandoned totally any effort to organize discussion and to turn philosophy into a cooperative science.[20]

The failure of the APA to adopt Lovejoy's plan is not very surprising. The address, however, was important for Lovejoy. Aside from enunciating the rational basis of his philosophy it laid out a methodology he would attempt to follow, with only limited success, in the writing of *Essays in Critical Realism* in philosophy and with the *Documentary History of Primitivism* in the history of ideas.

Lovejoy's one venture into cooperative philosophizing pointed up many of the difficulties inherent in his proposal. *Essays in Critical Realism* was written to provide a platform for the critical realists and to challenge the cooperative volumes published by the new realists in 1912 and the pragmatists in 1917. Whereas the new realists had argued for a direct realism in which the objects of experience were directly perceived, the critical realists, for the most part, adopted a dualistic and representative epistemology. Objects were in some sense real, but our perception of them was mediated by ideas.[21] The aim of the critical realists was to present a consistent and unified defense of their position demonstrating its validity as an epistemological theory. However, even considerable reservoirs of good will were insufficient to overcome philosophical differences. When published, the volume hardly presented a unified position. Lovejoy's contribution, "Pragmatism *Versus* the Pragmatist," has already been discussed, but the nature of the cooperative enterprise bears closer scrutiny in the light of Lovejoy's call to make philosophy a cooperative science.

In January 1917, Durant Drake, professor of philosophy at Vassar College, began to solicit contributors to the proposed volume. He initially contacted James B. Pratt, A. K. Rogers, C. A. Strong, and Dickinson Miller. Within six weeks the project began to take shape. Miller had withdrawn and George Santayana and Roy Wood Sellars had joined. Already, however, differences were beginning to appear. Epistemological dualism, which several of the group held firmly, was less ardently held by others, especially Strong. There was also some confusion as to what critical realism stood for exactly, and how much would have to be modified to achieve the cooperation of all those interested. At this point, they could not even agree on what they were going to call themselves; "dualistic realist" and "representative realist" were among the suggestions. Lovejoy thought that the program of the volume should be equally against pragmatism, subjectivism, and epistemologically monistic realism. He was willing to allow some disagreement on the first two issues, but felt that the last, the opposition to epistemological monism, was the most fundamental point on which agreement was necessary.[22]

Epistemology was both the fundamental basis of the critical-realist position and the source of the greatest disagreements. Lovejoy, of course, was an avowed dualist, but the others, especially Strong, were less adamant. The contributors attempted to resolve the problem at a conference in the summer of 1917. They agreed, according to notes kept by Drake, that there was always a duality in knowledge between the object perceived and the "perception-datum." At the same time, to accommodate Strong, who was not at the meeting, they agreed that there was a monistic side to the problem: "One and the same *object* is revealed to us all by different sense-data." They also agreed that dualism did not necessarily imply either "the contention that we perceive the *datum*," or a knower or self or any similar entity. In the end, they thought the best course was to avoid the term *dualism*.[23]

This conference did not settle the issue. Strong continued to object forcefully to the concept of dualism and representative knowledge. Lovejoy, in a long letter to his collaborators, discussed the meaning of the word *exist* and the dualistic implications of his theory. For him, an existent was a "character" or a "complex of characters" that had a locus in time, in space, or in both. The existent as a physical object could never be the same as the existent as perception because of the time difference inherent in all forms of perception. This conclusion implied a dualistic epistemology. The split in the critical-realist camp became even more evident when all the papers had been written. As

Drake wrote Lovejoy, "it does seem to me that to have two or three of us disclaiming 'dualism,' & two or three espousing 'dualism' will make people think that we disagree more than we *do*."[24]

Lovejoy had argued in his presidential address that the essential elements of cooperation were "good will and determination." The collaboration on *Essays in Critical Realism* demonstrated that good will and determination might suffice for cooperation, but that they could not make philosophy a science. At times, even the good will existing among men who supposedly agreed was strained. Both Strong and Drake, for example, were concerned about the dogmatism of some of the collaborators. Drake pleaded that "we must try to understand one another better" and urged Lovejoy to try to reduce Pratt's hostility to Strong and Santayana. Strong wrote Lovejoy that they should continue the discussions until the critical realists achieved a "single front." As he put it, "if we cannot convince each other in this matter, can we convince the enemy of our main point?" In a clear reference both to Lovejoy's presidential address and his insistence on dualism, Strong noted that "the prize for which we are playing is nothing less than a scientific consensus about some things in philosophy."[25] Ultimately, that "scientific consensus" was unattainable in the *Essays in Critical Realism*.

The nature of the cooperation in this venture indicates the limits of Lovejoy's program for a scientific philosophy. In the first place, it was impossible for the critical realists to reach any consensus on the definition of key terms. One or two might agree, with qualifications, but beyond that agreement was hopeless. Faced with the decision to agree on broader, but vaguer, issues or to splinter on the problem of definitions, the critical realists decided to settle for agreement on the broader issues. Even here such agreement was impossible, as the important split over epistemological theory reveals. What, then, remained of their cooperative venture? They agreed that they opposed the theories of the new realists and, to some extent, the pragmatists. They agreed that there were certain similarities in their approaches to the problem of knowledge, but this similarity was a far cry from Lovejoy's desire for logical unanimity. Finally, they could agree that by sharing ideas in the formulative stage, they were better able to understand their collaborators' positions.[26] In the sense that Lovejoy's program would bring philosophers into closer and perhaps more fruitful discussion of the issues, his proposals had some merit. However, the failure to achieve anything near a scientific consensus in a venture in which Lovejoy himself participated suggests that "good will and determination" were not sufficient bases for a rational and scientific philosophy.

Lovejoy's emphasis on "good will and determination" is curious in a philosopher noted for his reliance on reason. There was, however, as both Philip Wiener and Lewis Feuer have noted, a nonrational, indeed a psychological, character to much of Lovejoy's philosophical criticism. Feuer has argued that Lovejoy's method of inquiry consisted of "asking whether the philosopher does, as a matter of fact, hold to the philosophy which he professes." In comparing the formal and informal beliefs of a philosopher, Lovejoy often found that thinkers denied in their writings what they instinctively believed in their "normal moments." A philosopher who rejected a demonstration of the irrationality of his position was, in Lovejoy's view, blinded by certain genetic or psychological considerations, since rational discourse should produce unanimity.[27] Lovejoy was keenly aware of these nonrational impediments to a rational, scientific philosophy, as both his presidential address and his contribution to *Essays in Critical Realism* demonstrate.

Although he recognized the genetic and psychological sources of error in philosophy, Lovejoy seems not to have recognized that his program, as well, rested on less than wholly rational grounds. In his presidential address he argued that logical observation was restricted by "the inevitable limitations of the logical sensitivity of any individual mind." He was fully aware that "unconscious emotional bias" and "inexplicit yet controlling presuppositions" created logical error and he proposed cooperation as the remedy; the collective rationality would screen out the individual irrationality of the separate thinkers. A collective program required, of course, ' good will and determination."[28] Good will and determination, however, are not rational qualities and the often frail philosophical temperaments were frequently unable to muster much good will toward a critic—even a friendly one, as his own collaborative experience demonstrated.

If Lovejoy himself did not always escape the dangers of the nonrational, he often employed genetic and psychological analysis to good effect in criticizing other philosophers. As Lewis Feuer has pointed out, Lovejoy engaged in this type of analysis of John Dewey's philosophy in "Pragmatism *Versus* the Pragmatist." However, Lovejoy's psychological analysis in this essay was more thoroughgoing than Feuer has suggested. Lovejoy repeatedly trapped Dewey in contradiction of positions he had taken elsewhere. He argued that because Dewey had certain "prejudices" against presentative theories and knowledge of the past, the Columbia philosopher contradicted the only possible rational position open to him, epistemological dualism. Lovejoy was not optimistic that Dewey would recognize the error and irrationality of his ways. Still, he felt constrained to point out Dewey's defects in reasoning and to present what seemed to him to be the only consistent and rational position for a pragmatist.[29]

Lovejoy's collaboration with the critical realists had seen his analytical skills arrayed on behalf of epistemological dualism. "Pragmatism *Versus* the Pragmatist," however, developed his ideas only indirectly in comparison with those of Dewey. By the end of the essay it was clear that Lovejoy was an epistemological dualist, but the characteristics of his own dualism were not nearly so evident. In the next decade Lovejoy tried to develop a consistent epistemological, and psychophysical, dualism, especially in "The Anomaly of Knowledge" and in his Carus Lectures, *The Revolt Against Dualism.*

When he delivered "The Anomaly of Knowledge" before the Philosophical Union of the University of California in the fall of 1922, Lovejoy gave a fuller and more direct exposition of his epistemological theories than ever before. Though he still used a critical approach, attacking Josiah Royce, behaviorism, and Samuel Alexander in turn, he did grapple with the central problem of how something could be known that was not directly before the mind. Faced with the alternative, as he saw it, of knowing through representative ideas or not knowing at all, Lovejoy gladly chose the former.

The value of epistemological inquiry had often been questioned in the early part of the century by those who did not regard it as crucial to philosophizing. Epistemology, for Lovejoy, was not necessarily a first step in philosophizing, but it was a valid "descriptive or analytic science among others"; since knowing was "an actual phenomenon," we had sufficient reason to inquire into its characteristics. He proposed to begin his study "with a plain descriptive account of what knowing is, what goes on when it occurs." There was one potential difficulty. The investigator must be certain that it was "an account of *knowing*, and not of something which happens to be associated with it."[30]

Lovejoy's first task was to define knowledge:

> By "knowledge" here is not meant perception of data immediately and sensibly present at the moment of experience to be considered, but "knowledge about" things not in that manner present; and to make the question more specific, we may take the instance of knowledge about a no-longer-existing object or a bygone event— whether it be a remembrance of a past experience of the knower, or an inferential reconstruction of a past situation.

He recognized the anomalous character of such knowledge: "Knowledge of a past object or event manifestly consists in a species of presence, within the experience of some organism at a given moment, of an object which is not at the same moment present in nature."[31]

There was another side to the problem Lovejoy considered, knowing as a function of the organism. For him, knowing consisted "in a power which the organism has to reach beyond, to transcend, both the place and the date of its own existence as an observable object in nature." The knowing organism ranged "up and down through time, annulling in some measure the transiency of things." Knowing was, regardless of its specific content or direction, "an organic process characterized by a reference to, an evocation and apprehension of, a spatial and temporal Beyond." This was not simply theory, it was a "mere description, and a description of the obvious." He recognized the anomaly of this account of knowing and proposed, not to avoid the anomaly, but to render it intelligible and, if possible, alleviate it.[32]

As Lovejoy conceived the problem of knowledge, there were two anomalies, the lesser and the greater. The lesser anomaly appeared when knowing was considered from the standpoint of physical science: "it consists in the fact that there exists an organism, itself physical, which at some moments of its life has as items in its experience, as factors in its environment, things that are not, at those moments, any part of the sum of masses and motions and forces which for the natural sciences then constitute the physical world." The greater anomaly lay in that "peculiarity of knowing which philosophers call 'meaning' or 'transcendent reference'; that is, in the fact that when we know we appear somehow to have within the field of our experience at a given moment objects which we must at the same time conceive as existing entirely outside of that field." In the case of "retrospective and anticipatory knowledge" the entities known "must apparently be said not to coexist *at all* with the organism, or with the particular exercise of the cognitive function through which they are known." [33]

After examining and rejecting several previous attempts to deal with these anomalies, Lovejoy outlined his own approach. The earlier theories had failed, at least in part, because philosophers had tried to ignore the irreducible temporal character of our experience. Lovejoy would not be satisfied unless an explanation lay within "the limits of human experience." An eternal mind was no help in alleviating the anomalies of knowing. When he examined Samuel Alexander's attempt to deal with the greater anomaly, he described his colleague as having chosen one horn of a dilemma. Philosophers appeared to have a choice between believing that there does not need to be a content of knowing at the moment it occurs or that some such content is required. Alexander, in the case of memory, argued that there was no content immediately and directly present in consciousness, thus choosing the first horn. Lovejoy, largely because of temporal considerations, seemed driven to the other horn: "we must conceive of all the content or material of an act of knowing as temporally present along with the act." The dilemma was not as real for Lovejoy as it first appeared. He thought that the two sides were not of "equal logical force; one of the alternatives is meaningless, the other, though it undeniably offers some difficulties to our ordinary habits of thought, is nevertheless capable of intelligible formulation, and is, in fact, simply an accurate description of the common natural event called knowing." [34]

Lovejoy believed that the key to intelligibility regarding knowing was a temporal perspective. He conceded that "present experience cannot without absurdity be described in terms of past events." There was, however, another approach which was more satisfactory. He began with the premise that there was always some content "existentially synchronous with the act or event of knowing." This content, of memory, for example, was not a "simple, flat, one-dimensional thing." It contained "temporal perspectives." The present images of past events have "two dates— their date of existence in consciousness . . . and what may be called their date of reference." Furthermore, the quality of "pastness" is a "present quality of the memory-images." According to Lovejoy, "we apprehend the various elements of our present content as fitting into a framework of *conceptualized* temporal relations." This temporal framework had a dual relation to present consciousness: "As a datum for psychological observation, as an existent now given in consciousness, the framework is *included in* the present moment's content; but at the same time, as a conceived scheme of relations, it logically includes the present moment and its content as a single unit in the larger system represented." This dual or "self-representative" character of thought allowed Lovejoy to explain the anomaly of the "presentness of the absent." A given thought, for example a memory, exists as a "transient bit of reality now, and at no other time; but that which *does* exist now is a representation of a more comprehensive whole in which the now is an element consciously distinguished from the not-now." Through the present content of a conceptualized temporal framework Lovejoy thought that "rational cognition" could be "conversant with a Beyond" without transcending the present.[35]

This conception of the possibility of knowing not-now-existing entities brought together several strands of Lovejoy's thought. The temporal foundation of this theory is clear. Equally important, however, was the rational component, which suggests a reason for the vehemence of his attacks on antiintellectual temporalism. Only man's rational faculty could conceptualize a temporal framework. The temporal flux was vital, but without rational conceptualization the flux remained unintelligible and useless in explaining the epistemological anomalies. Combine time and reason, however, and the anomaly of knowledge becomes explicable.

If Lovejoy's account of the temporal framework of knowing was correct, then he could explain how the "content of a cognitive experience" was "present-as-absent." The content, of a memory-image, for example, was present at the moment of knowing. However, it was, at the same time, "presented 'as absent' in the sense that, in the conceptual scheme of temporal relations which is also now presented, the memory content is assigned a position external and prior to that occupied in the same scheme by the present moment." The implication of this account was that "all knowing of things remote in time or place is indirect and substitutional." The experience of pastness was not the same as the experience of a bygone event. The past existence of the event and the present memory of its occurrence remain totally separate. We can, however, recall to the present the image of the past event and through this indirect means be said to know it.[36]

This account of knowing solved the problem of the greater anomaly. If Lovejoy was correct, he could explain how we "have within the field of our experience at a given moment objects which we must at the same time conceive as existing entirely outside of that field." The problem was that this threw one back to an acceptance of the lesser anomaly; how can we know things that do not exist as part of the physical world? Unlike "some minds" that appeared "to have an unconquerable repugnance" to the conception of indirect knowledge, Lovejoy argued that such knowledge was required by the limitations imposed upon man by his temporal existence. Man can live only in the fleeting present, but, inescapably, he has knowledge, vicarious though it may be, of other presents or of other experiences not then his own. Knowledge may well be indirect, but it is still "a presentation, within the limits of the passing moment and the individual consciousness of things apprehended as transcending those limits." The solution to the greater anomaly seemed to require him "cheerfully to accept the lesser." This solution, though, required the assumption of the existence of "representative ideas." Only with the existence of mental entities which could, in some sense, represent the not-then-existent object in present consciousness could man escape from the greater anomaly by accepting the lesser. The existence of ideas had been frequently questioned in the early twentieth century, but Lovejoy concluded: "I am still much inclined to believe that I have ideas, and that without them I and other men would know even less than we do—would, to be precise, know nothing at all."[37]

By the conclusion of "The Anomaly of Knowledge" Lovejoy had suggested the outlines of his epistemology. Postulating the conceptualization of a temporal framework, Lovejoy argued that man could know entities which were not then directly present to consciousness. Man experienced the difference between the present representation of a not-now-existing entity and the existent entity. We could hold in present consciousness both the representation of the nonexistent entity and the temporal relationship between the present moment and the entity's moment of existence. Through this indirect process of representation, man could know objects which were not immediately present in consciousness. Thus, through the use of representative ideas, Lovejoy was able to avoid the greater anomaly of knowledge by making the lesser intelligible.

Even though "The Anomaly of Knowledge" dealt more fully than before with the problems of indirect knowledge, Lovejoy had yet to take up the question of how a dualistic epistemology was possible and why it seemed to him to be the only intelligible theory of knowledge. When he began his Carus Lectures in 1928, Lovejoy again turned to these epistemological questions. After discussing the natural basis of a dualistic, indirect epistemology, Lovejoy analyzed the antidualistic epistemologies of several contemporary philosophers. In each case, he concluded that the particular revolt against a dualistic conception of knowledge had failed. He ended the book with a lecture on "The Nature of Knowing as a Natural Event," in which he attempted to demonstrate the necessity, indeed the inevitability, of a dualistic epistemology.

As he had throughout his philosophical writing, Lovejoy defended his thesis by attacking his opponents. The bulk of the argument in *The Revolt Against Dualism* was directed against the New Realists and the Objective Relativists and against Alfred North Whitehead and Bertrand Russell. Although it was important for Lovejoy to demonstrate, conclusively he thought, the failure of these various revolts against epistemological dualism, it is more important for an understanding of Lovejoy's own philosophy to examine his positive arguments for a dualistic epistemology.[38]

Lovejoy relied extensively on genetic analysis in undertaking to determine a sound basis for both epistemological and psychophysical dualism. Although the two theories—the one concerned with the possibility of knowledge, the other with the character of the universe—were not logically connected, Lovejoy thought they were intimately related and, in the end, defended the validity of both. His method in this inquiry was to review "the natural genesis of both epistemological and psychophysical dualism, the situations in experience out of which those ways of thinking (whether ultimately tenable or not) intelligibly and normally and, indeed, inevitably arise as 'moments' in the progress of man's reflection."[39] If the dualistic approach could be shown to be the natural way of conceiving the problems of knowledge, and if the attempts to overthrow dualism were all logical failures, then both forms of dualism could be said to be definitely established.

"Man," Lovejoy wrote, "is by nature an epistemological animal." He thought that men naturally accept epistemological dualism "because they have formed certain preconceptions as to what an object of knowledge ought to be, and then, comparing the characteristics of the thing directly presented in their experience with these preconceptions, have found that the two do not match." Natural man made several assumptions: the world was real, there were objects which existed apart from his own "transient being," and he could somehow know these external objects, that is, he could bring them within his experience without destroying their transcendence.[40]

Man made five natural assumptions about what Lovejoy called "*cognoscenda*—the things-to-be-known-if-possible." First, man assumed that many *cognoscenda*, especially those known visually, were at "places in space external to the body of the percipient." Second, man demanded that "he shall have a real traffic with things that are not, because they are by-gone or have not yet come into being." Third, man desired to know things "as they literally are in themselves." He was not satisfied with essences or ghostly ideas but wanted to know directly the object itself. Fourth, man wanted to have knowledge of the experiences of other humans. This, Lovejoy thought, formed the basis of man's social behavior and was one of his most characteristic features. Finally, the objects to be known must be capable of being known publicly; there was "a world of objects for common knowledge."[41]

Reflection on these five assumptions naturally produced a form of dualism, the belief that "the thing known may be other in time and place and nature than the *event or act by means of which* the thing is known." Lovejoy, however, believed in the necessity of a more philosophically precise dualism. For him, "epistemological dualism" stood for the duality of "the content or datum at a given moment immediately and indubitably presented, and the reality said to be known thereby." This theory held that "all knowing is mediated through the presence 'before the mind' . . . of entities which must be distinguished from an ulterior reality which is the true objective of knowledge."[42] That is, not only are objects external to the knower, but we are conversant with these objects only through the mediation of ideas, which are themselves distinct from the object.

Acceptance of the natural assumptions of man concerning the reality of external objects led Lovejoy to the conclusion that there were "at least five familiar aspects of experience" in which the object of knowledge must in some sense be different from the perceptual content at the occurrence of apprehension. "Intertemporal cognition" was the first instance Lovejoy cited in support of the mediate character of knowledge. In memory, for example, there must be both the past existent and the present memory-image that is in consciousness. Because of the temporal consideration, the past object or event and the memory-image could never be present together in consciousness; "the past, in being known, still inexorably keeps its distance."[43] Here, then, there was always a duality between the object known and the datum by which it was apprehended.

The second and third arguments for the duality of object and datum derived from the nature of the physical universe. The second followed from the physicist's discovery of the finite speed of light and the physiologist's detection of a lag "in the transmission of the neural impulse to the cortical center." Both these discoveries, Lovejoy argued, debarred the possibility of direct perception of an object: "Never in short, if both the physiologists and the physicists are right, can the datum or character-complex presented in the perception of a given moment be regarded as anything but the report of a messenger, more or less tardy and more or less open to suspicion, from the original object which we are said to know by virtue of that perception." The third argument for duality was a more general statement regarding the relativity of the perceived world to the actual. Experience dictated that what was perceived was "determined by events or conditions intervening in space and time between that object and my so-called perception of it." How we can know anything when our perception was so extensively determined by intervening conditions presented serious epistemological problems. Lovejoy, however, rejected any notion of escaping into direct perception, for that seemed contrary to natural experience.[44]

The fourth instance concerned the supposed knowledge of different knowers. Lovejoy argued that the "conditionedness of the data manifestly implies that the contents of the experience of percipients having different spatial and physical relations to a postulated external object cannot be wholly identical." Since we all perceived what was supposed to be the same object slightly differently, there rose the notion that what we perceived directly was not the object itself, but some representation of it. The idea of perspective distortion, Lovejoy believed, made men epistemological dualists.[45]

The final consideration that led to an acceptance of epistemological dualism was the problem of error and illusion. Lovejoy wrote that "in so far as *cognoscendum* and content are identified, error is excluded; in so far as the possibility of error is admitted, *cognoscendum* and content are set apart from one another." This duality was necessary whenever error was *conceivable*, not merely when it occurred. Since in actual error the content of perception cannot be identical with the object, error must consist of attributing some content to "*another* locus in reality" where it is not present. True judgments, then, would be the attribution of some content to another locus where it is present. The "baldly dualistic epistemology known as the correspondence-theory of truth" was "one of the most deeply ingrained and persistent of human habits."[46]

These five considerations formed the "roots of epistemological dualism in human nature, common experience, and natural reflection." This was not the product of some latter-day philosophizing: "it is simply the account which man, grown capable of holding a number of facts together in a single view and drawing what seem plain inferences from them, will normally give of the situation in which he finds himself when he is engaged in what he calls 'knowing.'" Lovejoy summarized his conditions regarding the natural and genetic bases of epistemological dualism with a hypothetical proposition:

> *if* you postulate the externality of the entities to be known, in *any one* of the five ways in which it is asserted in the natural realistic creed—*i.e.*, spatial externality to the knower's body, temporal externality to the date of the event of perceiving or remembering, causal independence of that event, the identity of the objects known by many observers, and the actual "otherness" of your neighbor's experience—then in that specific case your knowledge cannot be direct; the presented content upon which the knowledge depends must be numerically other than the thing which the knowledge is about, for one or more of the reasons given. And if you postulate externality in all five cases, then all your knowledge is indirect; the existents which convey it are not the existents which it means.

Lovejoy invited the insurgents to demonstrate either that the dualistic conclusion does not follow from realistic premises or that a realistic and monistic epistemology was not absurd.[47]

Having thus challenged those who would deny epistemological dualism, Lovejoy considered the question of psychophysical dualism. He thought that the two dualisms were independent of each other. There was nothing in the argument for epistemological dualism which required that sense data be "mental" or excluded from the physical order. On the other side, to hold that the world was composed of only one kind of "stuff" did not mean that the content of perception or memory was identical with the object known. But if percepts and memories had no place in the physical world unless they were identical with the object known, then epistemological dualism implied psychophysical dualism.[48]

As he had with epistemological dualism, Lovejoy began by inquiring into the "natural grounds and normal genesis" of psychophysical dualism. Man has a preconceived notion of "the properties which an existent ought to possess if it is to be conceived to be a true part of the physical world." When "experience and reflection" demonstrate that part of the "actual content of perception" differs from the preconception, "that content is thereupon relegated to another realm of being." The initial preconception assumed a naturally realistic order composed of five characteristics: first, it was temporal and spatial; second, some or all parts of it continued to exist even when not perceived by a single percipient and no part existed solely because of being perceived; third, the objects in this order interacted causally according to determinable laws; fourth, these causal sequences continued when not perceived by any percipient; and, fifth, this order was "a common factor in or behind the experience of all percipients." Thus, our preconceptions concerning an existent were based on this physical world—this order—which filled for thought "the temporal gaps between actual perceptions."[49]

Having explained the basis of the physical order on man's natural realism, Lovejoy theorized that man conceived the realm of ideas when he realized that not all experiences fit into the physical order completely. Dreams and hallucinations could not be made to fit the requirements of the physical world. They did not appear to act causally in the same fashion as physical objects. They also seemed not to persist in regular sequences when not perceived, and their existence could be verified by only one knower. Lovejoy argued that the "discovery—or the invention—of a second world" to which man could assign all entities incompatible with the physical world was a necessary step in the development of science: "The world of 'mental' entities served as an isolation-camp for all the 'wild data,' the refractory and anomalous facts" that could not be accommodated in the order of the physical world.[50]

He admitted that it seemed paradoxical to assign "the content of normal and veridical perception and memory" to the same realm which included the "wild data." However, this extension of the mental realm to include such normal perceptual content became intelligible when it was joined with epistemological dualism. In that theory of knowledge the datum of perception was not identical with the specific physical object, nor, apparently, with any other physical object. Since the datum had no place in the physical order, it "fell into that 'inner' world of 'appearances' which had long since been discovered by man through his experiences of illusion and phantasy and dream and error; but by virtue of the cognitive function ascribed to it, it assumed in the latter world a place of special dignity, as a (more or less) 'true' appearance, a 'representative idea.' "[51]

Lovejoy thought that his account of the natural genesis of both epistemological and psychophysical dualism provided convincing grounds for accepting the validity of both theories. If these were the ways in which men normally conceived the world, then any critic of the theories who accepted the real existence of a physical world would have to demonstrate that the theories were not an accurate account of man as knower or that the natural reasons for holding these views were invalid.[52]

In the bulk of the text Lovejoy examined several contemporary accounts which tried to escape from one or both of the dualisms. In each case Lovejoy concluded that the monistic theory was contradictory and thus absurd, or that the philosopher, Whitehead, for example, had smuggled in dualistic notions and had failed for that reason to escape. Overall, then, he concluded that the experiment to escape from the necessity and inevitability of epistemological and psychophysical dualism had failed. His inquiries into the various alternative theories only demonstrated that the "logical elements" of these theories were contradictory, "at variance with empirical facts," or could not be inferred from undeniable empirical facts.[53]

The failure of the revolt left Lovejoy's dualistic theories in possession of the battlefield. He could confidently believe that the "content of our actual experience" did not consist of entities which were wholly physical, and it was "unprovable and improbable" that they were even in part members of the physical realm. The content of experience consisted of entities that arose "through the functioning of percipient organisms," were present only within the 'private fields of awareness" of these organisms, and lacked both certain relations and properties normally ascribed to the physical world. They were, Lovejoy wrote, "essentially of the nature of 'ideas' as Descartes and Locke (for the most part) used that term." Since it was only through these entities—these ideas —that we know anything, Lovejoy was willingly driven back to Locke's conclusion: " 'it is evident that the mind knows not things immediately, but by the intervention of the ideas it has of them.' "[54]

This conclusion, based on the assumption of a real physical

world, left two questions to be answered. The first was whether epistemological dualism was a necessary belief, not only for the realist, but for everyone, idealist, pragmatist, and phenomenalist alike, who claimed to have knowledge. The second was whether epistemological dualism itself was tenable: "is mediate knowledge possible—and if so, how?"[55]

In taking up the first question Lovejoy argued that epistemological inquiry ought to begin with retrospection and remembrance rather than with perception. The idealist, by denying the separate existence of a physical world, avoids the problem of dualism in the case of perception. Remembrance, however, was another matter. Lovejoy wrote that in retrospection there was "a conscious and intrinsic reference to a reality other than the content given." As he put it, "merely to remember *is* to be aware of a contrast between the image presented and the event recalled." This fact was, or should be, as clear to the idealist as to the realist. It mattered little whether the actual existents were physical objects or ideas; what was past could not be recalled directly to consciousness, but had to be mediated by some representation of the past existent. While this instance of indirect knowledge concerned the idealist, Lovejoy also argued, as he had in "Pragmatism *Versus* the Pragmatist," that the same principle applied to "foreknowledge or expectation," especially as advanced by pragmatists. Here again was a clear case where the representation of the object or event could not be temporally identical with the object and, thus, if it occurred at all, knowing had to be indirect.[56]

The second question—"is mediate knowledge possible—and if so, how?"—was perhaps more basic than the first, but it only became compelling if one believed that we know only mediately. In arguing for the possibility of mediate knowledge, Lovejoy returned to the theory he had advanced in "The Anomaly of Knowledge." Knowing does not consist simply of isolated and random "bits of content." Whenever we have a content before us it is "permeated with relational categories." In the case of retrospection this relational category was "a pattern of dated events." We have this pattern or framework before us now and within this pattern, but not temporally identical with it, the date of the past existent is located. Only the representative images are "literally and indubitably present." The remembered events are, however, "presented." The representative image has, within the conceptual framework, "a date of givenness and a date of reference, which are clearly distinguished." The function of knowledge, then, is to bring "past and future within the scope of present consciousness." The "uncertainty and fallibility" of knowledge results from the fact that it brings only representatives of the *actual* past or future before present consciousness. This framework of relatedness enabled man to hold both the present idea of a nonexistent entity and the conception of its distinguishable date of actual existence before the mind without contradiction. If mediate knowledge was thus intelligible in the case of intertemporal cognition, Lovejoy argued that it was no more paradoxical to suppose that a similar theory applied in the case of knowledge of the physical universe.[57]

Knowing, then, was essentially "a phenomenon by which the simple location of things is circumvented without being annulled." Every existent, whether mental or physical, has its own existence, of whatever character, and the bounds of its existence are mutually exclusive. These existents are related, but this does not destroy their reciprocal exclusiveness, "for it is only where there are distinct terms that there can be said to be real relations." Though things exist in their own places, they can be "reported" elsewhere while continuing to exist in their own place. Any theory of knowledge, Lovejoy argued, must successfully maintain the separate existence of entities while providing a means by which they can be reported where they do not actually exist. If a theory did not recognize both elements of this requirement, it failed to account either for "actual knowledge or for possible error."[58]

Lovejoy, of course, thought only epistemological dualism accurately described the knowing experience and accounted for possible error. Only under this theory was there "partial or symbolic reproduction" of an entity in a consciousness that was also capable of conceiving a framework which maintained the separateness of entities and to which the representation could be referred. Lovejoy recognized that under this scheme "no judgment concerning a particular existent" could "conceivably attain experiental verification in any literal sense," for all knowledge was indirect and mediate. Since knowing was "characteristically concerned with beyonds, we know by faith." It was not, however, an unfounded faith; experience and reason helped shape what we know: "not all beyonds of which we can frame ideas are the objects of faiths for which we have motives equally persuasive, urgent, or irrepressible, equally deeply rooted in our cognitive constitution, and equally reconcilable with one another and with what—through our primary faiths in the reality of remembrance and in the existence of other knowers—we believe to have been the constant and common cause of experience."[59]

With this affirmation that man, aided by reason and experience, can, and does, know all things indirectly through the mediation of representative ideas, Lovejoy brought his study to a close. Not only had he demonstrated, to his satisfaction at least, the failure of the revolt against dualism, he had also enunciated the bases of his own belief in epistemological and psychophysical dualism. He combined his unshakeable beliefs in the temporal nature of reality, the real existence of physical objects, and the rational capacity of man with a genetic account of a natural theory of knowing to demonstrate the necessity and inevitability of both dualisms. Having presented seemingly convincing arguments for his own position and having destroyed all rival claimants, Lovejoy was confident that he had ensured the eventual triumph of a dualistic account of both the universe and the process by which we know the world.

When he completed *The Revolt Against Dualism*, Lovejoy's philosophizing had come full circle from the first essays he had written for Josiah Royce. In 1896 he had inquired as to the nature of the real world and how we could have knowledge of it. He began, even then, by criticizing other conceptions of the problem, but throughout his philosophical investigations he built up his own philosophy.

Lovejoy began with three fundamental ideas: there was a real universe of some sort, time was a real characteristic of that world, and man had ideas. Somehow, he had to use those ideas to establish an intelligible account of the world in which he lived. The idealisms of Bradley, Royce, and Howison soon lost their appeal, because they appeared incapable of maintaining both the diverse character of the world and the eternal character of the absolute. Various pragmatic and temporalistic theories recognized the multifaceted aspects of the real world, but they often went too far toward an antirationalism. Where the idealistic philosophies of Bradley and Royce had subordinated diversity to rational intelligibility pragmatists and temporalists like James and Bergson subordinated rational intelligibility to diversity and temporal flux. Lovejoy sought a middle ground, a philosophy that would maintain the real diversity and temporal flux of the actual world and yet render that world rationally intelligible. He believed he had found such a philosophy in the epistemological and psychophysical dualism he outlined in *The Revolt Against Dualism*. Here was a philosophy that maintained the separate and independent existence of the physical world and of our ideas and yet used those ideas to explain how we could have real, if indirect, knowledge of that actual world. Lovejoy recognized that this account was anomalous, but that was inevitable given our human limitations. For all its anomalies this account explained the relation between the physical world and our ideas, explained how we could know anything at all, and thus provided a rational and intelligible account of the universe.

CHAPTER V

"THE BELLING OF CATS,"

1910–1920

Arthur Lovejoy had always combined activism with scholarship, but there was a new urgency to his academic and political activism in the second decade of the twentieth century. By the first decade it was clear that the intelligibility he sought rested on the free exercise of reason and on the existence of ideas and their free expression. At the same time, reason and the freedom of ideas were challenged from two directions. Attacks on the independence and academic freedom of professors in the colleges and universities increased. An even greater challenge, as Lovejoy saw it, came from Germany. For him, as for so many others, the possibility of a German victory in World War I threatened both the freedom of ideas and the opportunity to establish a rational order. Ironically, his response to the German challenge endangered the very concept of academic freedom he had done so much to foster.

Lovejoy's initial experience with the problems of academic freedom had occurred with the dismissal of E. A. Ross from Stanford University in 1900. After some deliberation, Lovejoy decided that by remaining on the faculty he would be condoning the "abridgement of liberties which it is the right and duty of university teachers to demand." The crucial element in his decision to resign was his belief that professors should have freedom, not only in their teaching, but also in applying their expertise to the problems of society. Restrictions on professorial rights threatened "the leadership and social usefulness of universities in our democratic society." Unless professors could pursue their scholarly studies freely and advocate changes openly, they would be unable to apply their knowledge to the solution of social problems.[1] Lovejoy based his defense of academic freedom on this conviction that scholars must remain free, independent, and uncommitted to any ideology or organization.

Lovejoy's concern for the academic rights of professors lay dormant for the next several years. While at Washington University he was involved in several local issues, but he only returned to matters of national interest during the controversy over the Carnegie Foundation pension. The foundation had established, in 1906, a system of service pensions for college professors, which they could claim after twenty-five years of service. In the years following, numerous colleges and scholars joined the plan. Four years after its inception, however, the Carnegie Foundation unilaterally abolished its service pension, retaining only elements of a disability pension. Lovejoy believed that the action was a "dishonorable breach of faith," and he hoped to convince the foundation to reconsider.[2]

Although Lovejoy's efforts, and those of others, were in vain, his participation was significant. For the first time since the Ross Affair, matters of professional and national interest attracted him. It became clear during the course of the controversy that professors individually were powerless to prevent other organizations from treating them summarily. This realization increased his awareness of the need for a professorial organization.

Throughout this period the academic profession was undergoing a number of changes that lowered the barriers to organization while increasing the need for it. Walter Metzger cited the "collective effort inspired by the ideals of science" and the "constant tension between administrators and faculties" as "slowworking" factors in the rise of professional self-awareness among professors. Progressivism and ideas of reform were also influential in creating dissatisfaction with college administrators and in suggesting the need to regularize academic practice.[3] Lovejoy, of course, shared the collective ideal of science. So, too, his experiences with the college administrations of Stanford and Washington Universities had exposed him to the realities of faculty-administration tension.

The need for a national organization of university professors was heightened when the Presbyterian-controlled Lafayette College forced the resignation of John M. Mecklin, a liberal philosopher, in 1913. Mecklin filed a complaint with the American Philosophical Association and the American Psychological Association. The two groups appointed an investigating committee chaired by Lovejoy. The committee's inquiries into the facts of the case were rebuffed by Lafayette's president, E. D. Warfield. As a result, the committee was unable to draw any definite conclusion, although they suggested that Mecklin had been unjustly dismissed. The report concluded with a reaffirmation of the public's and the profession's right "to understand unequivocally what measure of freedom of teaching is guaranteed in any college." "No college," they wrote, "does well to live unto itself to such a degree that it fails to recognize that in all such issues the university teaching profession at large has a legitimate concern."[4]

Regardless of the stirring words of reaffirmation, the failure of the committee to conduct a thorough inquiry or to exert effective influence demonstrated the impotence of a divided and unorganized profession. Even the two learned societies acting together had been unable to apply any pressure in this instance. The Mecklin case and the investigation did, however, provide additional impetus to the movement toward a national organization of professors. The machinery of pressure was already present in the technique of investigation and publicity. If a national association of professors could be organized, it might be powerful enough to assert and to protect the rights of its members.[5]

The initial steps toward forming an organization occurred at The Johns Hopkins University. By 1913, Lovejoy was convinced, as he later recalled, that it was "desirable and important for the university teachers of the country to form a national organization which could deal with such cases of dismissals for improper reasons." His position at Johns Hopkins gave him both the stature and the time he needed, and he was able to persuade his senior colleagues at the university to join the effort. In the spring of that year they invited the faculties of nine other schools to send representatives to an organizational meeting. The Johns Hopkins letter recognized that professors had two interests which could be "furthered by cooperation and the interchange of views, and therefore, by organization." Cooperation in the advancement of learning was already effectively organized by the various technical societies. Lovejoy and his colleagues argued, however, that professors had legitimate concerns in the area of educational policy, and in the maintenance of professional standards and rights as university teachers. The purposes of the proposed organization were: "to promote a more general and methodical discussion of the educational problems of the university; to create means for the authoritative expression of the public opinion of the profession; and to make possible collective action, on occasions when such action seems called for."[6]

Seven universities—Clark, Columbia, Cornell, Harvard, Princeton, Wisconsin, and Yale—responded by sending delegates to a meeting in Baltimore on 17 November 1913. The delegates included John Dewey and J. McKeen Cattell from Columbia, C. S. Minot from Harvard, and Joseph Ames, Maurice Bloomfield, and Lovejoy from Johns Hopkins. The professors decided that an association should be organized, and Bloomfield, as chairman, was authorized to appoint a committee to work out the details.[7]

During the following year a committee of twenty-five, representing most fields of learning and most major universities, struggled with the organizational problems. Late in 1914 the committee issued invitations to a meeting to be held in New York on 1 and 2 January 1915. The response was overwhelmingly favorable, with many professors offering suggestions. Josiah Royce even proposed a name for the organization, "the society of the united mice, organized for the belling of cats." Over two hundred and fifty professors attended the three sessions. They discussed the proposed constitution, but voted only on general principles, leaving final details to be worked out before the next meeting. The delegates considered a program for the coming year and recommended that the questions of standardization in education, methods of appointment and promotion, and recruitment of professors be investigated. They also voted to instruct the newly elected council to join with the economic, political science, and sociology associations in formulating a position regarding academic freedom. As its final action, the meeting chose officers for the newly formed American Association of University Professors (AAUP) and elected John Dewey as president and Lovejoy as secretary. Lovejoy later recalled that it had taken him several hours to persuade Dewey to accept the presidency.[8]

Lovejoy and Dewey played key roles in the formation of the AAUP. Lovejoy performed much of the organizational work, beginning with the initial meetings at Johns Hopkins in 1913.

Throughout that year and the following, he and Dewey frequently corresponded as they tried to resolve questions of membership, problems with several academic-freedom cases, and the other details necessary in the establishment of the association.[9]

Throughout the long period of organization, the founders, especially Lovejoy, wanted to establish more than simply an association to investigate abuses. The new organization was an expression of the rising professional self-consciousness of the academic scholars. University teachers, Lovejoy thought, had "special responsibilities as the 'natural'—though not exclusive—custodians of the higher educational and scientific interests of the community." Just as doctors and lawyers had their national associations, so the university professors needed a national organization to deal with broader concerns in a rapidly changing educational environment. As John Dewey wrote, the "best way to put educational principles where they belong—in the atmosphere of scientific discussion—is to disentangle them from the local circumstances with which they so easily get bound up in a given institution." In a very real sense, this desire for the status of a profession, with all the prerogatives attendant upon it, lay behind the foundation of the AAUP. The academic freedom issue was important because it was an ever-present threat to the integrity of what Lovejoy described as the "self-governing republic of scholars." As long as politicians and university administrations established policy and controlled the machinery of admission to and dismissal from the ranks of scholarship, the status of the profession of the professoriate would remain in doubt.[10]

During the association's first year of existence these other concerns were submerged within a consideration of the problem of academic freedom. This focus is understandable, for infringements upon professorial rights posed the gravest danger to the standing of individual scholars and the viability of the association. One of the organization's first acts was to appoint a committee to meet with the previously established committees of the economic, political science, and sociological associations. Edwin R. A. Seligman chaired the committee, whose members included Richard T. Ely, Roscoe Pound, and Lovejoy. In the estimation of Seligman, Lovejoy spent some 75 percent of his time on the work of this committee. He acknowledged that Lovejoy's "share in the general report [on academic freedom] is much greater than might be supposed." After a year of work, the committee submitted a declaration of principles and several concrete proposals to the AAUP membership, which approved them on 1 January 1916.[11]

The report reflected the professors' general concern about their status as a profession and their self-conception as stewards of knowledge and expertise. Echoing sentiments long expressed by Lovejoy and others, they argued that "if education is the corner stone of the structure of society and if progress in scientific knowledge is essential to civilization, few things can be more important than to enhance the dignity of the scholar's profession." The function of the profession was to "deal at first hand, after prolonged and specialized technical training, with the sources of knowledge; and to impart the results of their own and of their fellow-specialists' investigations and reflection, both to students and to the general public, without fear or favor." This function required that the scholars be totally free from any restrictions on their investigative or instructive tasks.[12]

Academic freedom was also vitally important to the successful fulfillment of the purposes of the modern university. The university should "promote inquiry and advance the sum of human knowledge," "provide general instruction to the students," and "develop experts for various branches of the public service." Each of these functions required that the "scholar must be absolutely free not only to pursue his investigations but to declare the results of his researches, no matter where they may lead him or to what extent they may come into conflict with accepted opinion." Unless the society and the university accepted and enforced to "the fullest extent" the principle of academic freedom, the efficiency and morale of the scholars, and thus the interests of the community, would be impaired.[13]

The committee thought that the freedom of the social sciences was the most threatened. These disciplines were the most likely to suggest "extensive social innovations, or call in question the moral legitimacy or social expediency of economic conditions or commercial practices in which large vested interests are involved." In a prophetic voice, the report also described the serious danger from the possibility of the "tyranny of public opinion." They saw the university as an "inviolable refuge" from such tyranny, a place where "new ideas may germinate and where their fruit, though still distasteful to the community as a whole, may be allowed to ripen until finally, perchance, it may become a part of the accepted intellectual food of the nation or of the world." The university could guide public opinion into a more rational course only if scholars could pursue their studies unimpeded by external or internal pressures and if their advice was the "disinterested expression of the scientific temper and of unbiased inquiry."[14]

Turning to the responsibilities of individual scholars, the committee argued that academic freedom could be claimed only by those who carried on their work "in the temper of the scientific inquirer." There was no need for the professor to hide his own opinions, but his inquiry and presentation within the university must be fair and judicious. In teaching, he had a special responsibility to present all sides of the question, to entertain divergent opinions, to avoid propagandizing, and to inculcate habits of critical thought. However, the professor's right to freedom of inquiry and expression also extended beyond the university walls. Here, too, he had an obligation to avoid "hasty or unverified or exaggerated statements and to refrain from intemperate or sensational modes of expression." Beyond these constraints, scholars' freedom to speak should not be limited, nor should "they be prohibited from lending their active support to organized movements which they believe to be in the public interest."[15]

The committee, then, did not advocate total license for professors. Only activities that were scholarly, that were carried out with a disinterested, unbiased, and scientific temper, and presented in rational, temperate language fell under the protection of academic freedom. Any necessary restraints on these activities must be "self-imposed, or enforced by the public opinion of the profession." Trustees and administrative officers could rightfully act in cases of neglect of duties and "grave moral delinquency," but in all other matters the scholarly profession should have the sole power to act. Interference from outside the profession in matters of opinion would convert the university "from a place dedicated to openness of mind . . . into a place barred against the access of new light." It was not "the absolute freedom of utterance of the individual scholar" that they sought, but "the absolute freedom of thought, of inquiry, of discussion, and of teaching."[16]

The committee concluded its report with a set of practical proposals. Four measures were necessary to maintain academic freedom and the integrity of the scholarly profession. First, action on reappointment should be taken only with the advice and consent of a faculty board. Second, the conditions pertaining to the tenure of any position should be clearly and unequivocally stated and upheld. Third, the legitimate grounds for dismissal at an institution should be clearly formulated. Fourth, all university teachers were entitled to a judicial hearing before dismissal.[17] The goal of these proposals was not to make it impossible to dismiss a teacher, but to regularize the process and to ensure that dismissals were restricted to legitimate professional reasons.

Although he was only one member of a committee of fifteen, the report on academic freedom clearly reveals Lovejoy's influence, for the positions adopted were similar in most respects to ideas that he had long held. The concept of stewardship was widely prevalent during the Progressive era and Lovejoy had outlined similar views even before he began teaching. So, too, the fear of academic anarchy and the desire to regularize and order the professional aspects of scholarship were sentiments he shared fully. On only one point is there evidence that he disagreed with the report. Unlike the committee, which saw no reason to bar participation in partisan politics, he thought scholars should avoid partisan, political office, except for minor, local posts.[18]

The legitimization and protection of social service and social activism was one of the most important aspects of the committee's report. This was especially true for Lovejoy, and the committee's emphasis on the social role of scholarship may well reflect his influence. As had been the case since Lovejoy's undergraduate days at Berkeley, the social responsibilities of a professor were more than theory or principle. Beginning then and continuing well into the teens, Lovejoy was actively engaged in social service. When he went to Baltimore in 1910 his involvement slackened as academic questions required greater attention. Nonetheless, he was associated with a group of boys clubs in East Baltimore acting in "a sort of grandfatherly capacity" and worked to establish a neighborhood association in the same area. Lovejoy did not restrict his activities to Baltimore, for he retained his ties with the National Child Labor Committee.[19] These efforts on behalf of social change and social betterment, however, became even less important with Lovejoy's increased political activity before and during American participation in World War I.

Lovejoy was in Switzerland when war broke out in August 1914. His initial reaction was detached interest in the "monstrous" situation in which "a species of so-called rational animals" was involved, but he soon changed his views toward Germany and her allies. German disregard for "the principles of law" and "international good faith" in the invasion of Belgium cast that nation as the aggressor and as a potential threat to America. The German actions not only physically threatened the Western democracies of England and France, a German victory would also legitimate the ascendancy of force over the rule of law and reason. The result would be chaos. Thus, Lovejoy reasoned, England and France deserved support, because they upheld the rule of law and the rights of man while Germany endangered them.[20]

Lovejoy's attitudes toward Germany were not unique. Carol Gruber's study of American academics during World War I reveals that, in spite of some pro-German sentiment, "the preponderance of opinion on the American campus was hostile to Germany and in favor of the allies." This pro-ally sentiment included "an identification of American interests—political, economic, cultural, and strategic—with those of Great Britain and a view of Germany as the aggressor nation, whose political system and world political ambitions represented a threat to those interests and to world peace."[21] Clearly sharing these views, Lovejoy attempted to alert Americans to the German threat through his articles and letters that appeared in the *New York Times*, the *New Republic*, and the *Nation*.

His early writing on the war focused on the threat Germany posed to the liberal democracies and the dangers to scholarship under wartime conditions. As already suggested, he favored measures that would help the Allied cause. Writing on proposals to embargo arms sales, Lovejoy argued that in a neutral nation private sales should not be restricted. The fact that British control of the seas effectively restricted sales to the Allies did not disturb him. He did not consider this a violation of American neutrality, but a consequence of the fortunes of war. In any case, his sympathies were clearly with the Allies, and he supported arms sales to them regardless of the seeming violations of neutrality.[22]

Lovejoy was deeply concerned about the status of scholarship during the war. This problem rose with the publication in Germany of a propaganda tract entitled "Truth About Germany: Facts About the War." The pamphlet was published under the sponsorship, if not the authorship, of ninety-three prominent German scholars. These academics defended Germany and denied German responsibility for the war. Lovejoy was shocked that scholars of such repute would allow patriotic sentiments to pervert their judgment. By participating in the publication of this false and misleading propaganda, these German scholars had "signally failed" to perform their proper function of "detached criticism" and "cool consideration" of all the relevant facts.[23] In thus condemning the subservience of German scholarship to the interests of the state, Lovejoy warned his American colleagues of the dangers inherent during war. Ironically, Lovejoy's own activities after the United States entered the war came perilously close to the apparent German actions he so soundly denounced in 1914.

Lovejoy did not restrict his activities during the period of American neutrality to the publication of articles alerting Americans to the German danger. From 1915 to 1917 he participated in the AAUP investigations of four cases of academic freedom. These cases, at the Universities of Utah, Pennsylvania, Colorado, and Montana, were not directly related to the war in Europe.[24] They were, however, a constant reminder that the principle of academic freedom was by no means firmly established in the United States. As the war dragged on, Lovejoy grew impatient with American neutrality. Late in 1916 he apparently wrote Norman Kemp Smith in London to inquire about the possibility of a job during the summer of 1917 to help England's war effort. Smith was discouraging and was only able to suggest driving an ambulance.[25] Lovejoy's desire to go to England soon dissipated, for with the American entry into the war in April 1917, he threw himself into the campaign to sell the war to his fellow citizens and to bolster their morale and will to fight.

The American declaration of war on 6 April 1917 unleashed scholarly support of the war. The academic community responded quickly and vigorously. Colleges adjusted curricula, turned buildings over to the government, conducted special research, and granted leaves of absence. Individual scholars left their libraries, laboratories, and offices to join the crusade against the newly declared enemy. Political considerations were a major factor in the decision of many academics to support the war. Gruber has also suggested that professional concerns, indeed, professional insecurities, about the role of scholars and universities lay behind much of the impulse to serve the country during the war. These academics wanted to demonstrate that their talents were useful in meeting this crisis.[26] Lovejoy, of course, had long been concerned with the social role of professors, and he scarcely hesitated to aid in the war against Germany.

Lovejoy's activities after the declaration of war were diverse, but they were all directed toward one end, the defeat of Germany. He concentrated on educating his fellow citizens about the German threat and the need to subordinate all their other energies to the crucial task of winning the war. Lovejoy worked both for governmental organizations, like the Morale Section of the War Department and the Maryland Council of Defense, and for independent patriotic organizations, including the National Security League (NSL) and the YMCA.

The NSL was founded in 1915 by S. Stanwood Menken, a New York lawyer, to educate Americans in the need for military preparedness. Supported both by wealthy contributors and thousands of "patriotic citizens" who sent their dollars, the NSL pushed for American entry into the war. Once war was declared, "preparedness campaigns gave way to loyalty crusades, Americanization programs for immigrant groups, and civic education in schools." The NSL was one of the more effective patriotic organizations in mobilizing public support for the war, especially through the efforts of its Committee on Patriotism Through Education.[27]

Throughout much of 1917, Lovejoy channeled his educational efforts into the Committee on Patriotism Through Education. Ostensibly, the activities of this organization provided a valid opportunity for a scholar like Lovejoy to use his talents to instruct and lead the nation. Lovejoy and many other academics certainly viewed their participation in this fashion. In the introduction to the *Handbook of the War for Public Speakers*, which Lovejoy edited for the NSL with the historian Albert Bushnell Hart, the editors described the task of the scholar as "that of informing the understanding, of awakening the moral vision and the moral passion, of the entire people, concerning the cause for which they fight." Hart and Lovejoy wrote that all must be brought "to feel that America has never entered upon a more just or more necessary war." America's traditional isolationism was the chief obstacle to overcome. The war in Europe was vital to the "collective interests of the human race," and Americans should not delude themselves into thinking they had no stake in the outcome of that conflict.[28]

The two editors of the *Handbook* compiled facts and "illustrative extracts" from Allied and German documents to convict Germany of causing the war and to justify American entry. According to the editors, the material provided "pertinent evidence, in which German writers furnish material for self-conviction, upon certain of the main questions about the war" and made "easily accessible some of the best and most thought-arousing passages . . . concerning the meaning of America's war, the tasks confronting the Government, and the duty of the citizen." The extracts portrayed German culture as inherently warlike and German aggressiveness and disregard for international law as the sole causes of the conflict. The Western democracies of England, France, and especially the United States, were described as upholders of law, honor, decency, and peace, and in no fashion implicated in the events leading to war.[29]

In addition to editing the tract, Lovejoy contributed a brief discussion on "Democratic Government and Success in War." "Success in war," he wrote, "requires quickness in decision, continuity of policy, secrecy in counsel, and concentration of control." These things were, of course, foreign to democratic government, but war was an "abnormal condition." Since democracies were ill-suited to waging war, and since there were times when war was necessary to defend security or principles, "a wise democracy" will, in such a situation, "promptly and unflinchingly modify its ordinary and normal processes of government, and the customary procedure of its political life, in such ways—though only in such ways—as may be needful to ensure success in the unwelcome business at hand." In time of war, a democracy was justified in making four departures from its usual practice:

> it must: (a) concentrate power and responsibility in the
> hands of its executive; (b) subordinate thoroughness of
> discussion to celerity of action; (c) accept loyally innu-

merable restrictions of individual liberty which in time of
peace it would deem intolerable; (d) clearly understand
and firmly resolve that these departures from its usual
modes of action are to be regarded solely as exceptional
and transitory means of meeting the peril with which
democracy itself, with all the normal life of mankind, is
threatened.[30]

In spite of the scholarly pretensions of notes and bibliography,
the *Handbook* was little more than a propaganda tract. There
was no "detached criticism" or "cool consideration" of the issues. The extracts demonstrated the enormity and finality of German guilt, extolled the idealism and righteousness of the Allied
cause, and exhorted Americans to "subordinate thoroughness of
discussion to celerity of action." Hart later admitted that he
believed "oral propaganda required argument uncluttered with
academic alternatives."[31] He and Lovejoy undoubtedly guided
public opinion, but with little attention to the qualities of scientific scholarship.

During 1917 and early 1918, Lovejoy became affiliated with
the government's war effort. He worked with the Military Morale Section of the War Department for several months.[32] He left
that position to become field director of the Maryland Council
of Defense in February 1918. Here Lovejoy directed the propaganda and educational work of the Council in the state. While
in this position, he wrote a pamphlet, "What Are We Fighting
About," which went through five editions and 60,000 copies.[33]
Throughout this period Lovejoy continued to use the letters col-
umns of the *New York Times* and the *New Republic* to warn of
the hazards of war. His topics ranged from the need to grow
more wheat to the potential traps of the German peace drives,
the dangers of benevolent neutrality, and the possibilities of a
peace of conciliation.[34]

After March 1918, Lovejoy restricted himself to nongovern-
mental organizations. In the spring of that year he joined eighteen
other representatives of American labor, business, agricultural,
and industrial organizations on a mission to Great Britain and
France. Although the group had the approval of the government,
it was a private effort designed to demonstrate to England and

Lovejoy visiting the front in World War I
(Special Collections: The Johns Hopkins University)

France "the loyal devotion of the people of the United States to the common cause of all the free nations." The party visited the two countries in April and May dividing their time between viewing the war efforts of those nations and speaking to gatherings about American activities. Lovejoy, as the representative of American education, was particularly concerned about the effect of the war on educational ties between Europe and America. In an interview in the *Paris Herald* he expressed his doubts that Americans would quickly restore their close prewar contacts with German universities: "We have lost confidence in the intellectual integrity of a body of scholars capable of becoming the apologists of the conduct of the German Government in this war."[35]

When he returned from Europe, Lovejoy entered into additional war work, this time with the YMCA. He took a position as director of lectures and war aims instruction in the Educational Bureau of the organization, with responsibilities for the educational activities of the YMCA in various training camps. In the fall of 1918, for example, he sent educational directors suggestions for lectures in connection with the fourth Liberty Loan. Since it coincided with 12 October, President Wilson had declared Columbus Day to be "Liberty Day," and Lovejoy suggested talks on such subjects as "What America Means to the Rest of the World" and "Christopher Columbus and the War." He later collaborated with Ernest H. Wilkins, director of the YMCA National War Work Council, on a lecture entitled "Some Facts About the British." The two men argued that Britain's efforts early in the war had protected American interests, that England's defense of democracy, civilization, and fair play benefited America, and, as a consequence, Americans should be grateful to the British. Lovejoy remained with the YMCA until February 1919.[36]

The efforts of Lovejoy and his fellow scholars to educate Americans to the necessity of war and to bolster morale after its declaration were directed, for the most part, toward a receptive audience. Playing on the themes of idealism, of the German violation of American and human rights, of the need to make the world safe for democracy, these propagandists were largely convincing in their appeal for support of the war. Not all Americans, however, shared Lovejoy's conviction that the crusade against Germany was necessary or that the war justified restrictions on the freedom of Americans. Convinced that the defeat of Germany was necessary at almost any cost if order and reason were to be preserved for humanity, Lovejoy only grudgingly tolerated dissent and willingly sanctioned restrictions on academic freedom.

He revealed his attitude toward those who withheld their support from the crusade in his reply to a letter by Norman Thomas and others announcing their conscientious objection to the war. Using a mixture of ethical and historical argument, Lovejoy concluded that conscientious objection was fundamentally wrong. He thought it strange ethics and strange history to hold that there has never been, and never will be, anything worth fighting for. Conscientious objectors' sacrifice of everything to the one good of refusing to fight rendered them "unpleasantly parasitic" in the "history of human progress." They benefited from the freedoms won at the cost of other men's lives. Lovejoy believed that conscientious objection might be a good rule if all men abided by it. However, since men did not, and there was no prospect that they would soon begin to, he felt that man had no choice but to recognize the fact that he would occasionally have to fight. Although he had total contempt for the position, he conceded that the "ulterior question of toleration" remained. Since their number was small and unlikely to affect the course of the war, "the country may well be generously considerate." Nonetheless, while he was willing to tolerate conscientious objection, he made it clear that this was toleration "not simply of an erroneous opinion, but also of an anti-social attitude and mode of conduct."[37]

The question of dissent in time of war raised the problem of academic freedom under such conditions. Even before the war the AAUP had not sanctioned total academic license. Once war was declared, the organization faced the problem of deciding what, if any, additional conditions and restrictions were legitimate during the crisis. In October 1917 Lovejoy suggested to Allyn A. Young, chairman of the Committee on Academic Freedom and Academic Tenure, that the committee take up the question of dismissal for disloyalty, including the cases of J. McKeen Cattell at Columbia and William Schaper at Minnesota. He urged the preparation of "a supplementary statement of principles, in which we shall recognize plainly the fact that, in the abnormal conditions of wartime, the same degree of freedom of utterance is not practicable as can be, and should be, maintained in time of peace." Such a statement of principles would allow the committee to evaluate individual cases under these abnormal conditions. Lovejoy recommended that a small subcommittee be established to draw up a report. The membership of this subcommittee should consist "exclusively of men whose loyalty has never been challenged, and who have been rather conspicuous in their activity in support of the war."[38]

Young agreed with Lovejoy's recommendations, although he worried about weakening the AAUP's previous stand on academic freedom. His work with the War Trade Board left him with no free time and he urged Lovejoy to take the chairmanship of the three-member subcommittee. As he wrote Lovejoy, "first, you have in some ways a better right to speak for the rest of us on these matters than has anyone else, and second, you have been consistently anti-German and your patriotic attitude is thoroughly well known." Lovejoy acquiesced and as chairman prepared the initial draft of the report on academic freedom in wartime. Lovejoy, Young, and Edward Capps of Princeton presented their report to the AAUP in December 1917, where it was approved.[39]

The committee prefaced their report with praise for the loyal service that the academic profession had already performed. Scholars had contributed mightily to America's awareness of her vital role in the world, and had sent their students to fight for the "cause of humanity and justice and human freedom." So, too, the ability of the United States to wage war successfully was aided by the scientific investigations of its scientists. This loyal service to the nation was, however, only one aspect of the scholar's task in time of war. The profession must also take care to ensure that the "adjustments necessitated by the crisis" did not injure "the permanent interests of society" or the principles for which the war was being fought. Therefore, they considered it one of the wartime duties of the scholar, "as of all men who have been granted special opportunity for thought and knowledge," to ensure that the American democracy was able "to carry on the war with a maximum of efficiency and success—and with a minimum of hysteria and of spiritual retrogression."[40]

The Committee on Academic Freedom did not doubt that "some restrictions of normal liberty" were required. However, these limitations must not be "multiplied, as they tend to be, beyond real necessity." Recognizing that "freedom of thought and of discussion, and in particular the intellectual independence of the scholar" were extremely valuable, the committee faced the problem of maintaining these freedoms to the fullest extent compatible with the special requirements of wartime. The first question was whether "*any* special restrictions upon the expression of opinion ought to be laid upon members of the academic profession as such." The committee considered it a sound presumption that the national government had the ultimate responsibility and competence to judge what restraints were necessary and whether any acts violated necessary restrictions. If the activities or utterances of a professor were not clearly dangerous to the country or obstructive of the war effort, "the ordinary presumption of academic freedom" should prevail. There were, however, four legitimate grounds for dismissal relating to attitudes or conduct concerning the war; three of these required no prior action by the government.[41]

Any teacher convicted of "disobedience to any statute or lawful executive order relating to the war" could "legitimately suffer deprivation of academic office." Indictment was sufficient grounds for suspension. The reasons for this, the committee assumed, were "too evident to require explanation." The case of conscientious objectors, however, raised certain problems, especially if they were convicted of resisting the draft. The committee had no sympathy for conscientious objectors: they regarded the position as both "ethically indefensible, and, if it is widely prevalent, gravely dangerous to the public safety in time of war; and in such a time the public safety is the supreme law." Even though they regarded such behavior as "conscientious treachery," the committee felt there was no absolute requirement that objectors convicted of resisting the draft be dismissed. Each case should be decided on its merits and, if there was no evidence that the professor was inciting others to follow his example or otherwise obstructing the war effort, the university should not add its penalty to that imposed by the state.[42]

The second ground for dismissal was participation in "propaganda designed, or unmistakably tending, to cause others to resist or evade the compulsory service law or the regulations of the military authorities." Dismissal in such cases could, and should, come before the government took any action. The committee believed that individuals had the right to express an opinion on the terms of peace or on the "wisdom or efficacy of proposed measures or instrumentalities for the conduct of the war." No person, however, had the right "to obstruct or impede the execution of any measure lawfully determined upon as requisite for the safety of the country and the successful prosecution of the war." The university would be justified in acting before the government in order to avoid any suggestion of "complicity" in such activities.[43]

Although the first two grounds for dismissal involved at least potentially illegal actions, the third had no such basis. The committee assumed that a successful prosecution of the war necessitated extensive voluntary acts and sacrifices not specifically required by law. They admitted that the failure to perform such acts was not illegal and that individuals who shirked their patriotic duty could be "subject to no penalty except the censure of public opinion." The same was not the case for those who sought "to dissuade others from rendering voluntary assistance to the efforts of the government." Lovejoy and his colleagues argued that "participation in a propaganda of this kind" was "plainly an endeavor to obstruct the carrying out of the purposes of the majority" and was "not less dangerous to the public security, nor less reconcilable with good citizenship," than the illegal offenses that were grounds for dismissal. Accordingly, if there was conclusive evidence, the professor could be legitimately dismissed.[44]

The problems presented by the large number of professors of German or Austro-Hungarian birth or parentage, whose sympathies often lay with their homeland, was the final question considered by the committee. The three men thought it probable that a number of these pro-German professors had been "so blinded to the moral aspects of the present conflict by their affection for the land of their origin" that they desired a German victory. These men were required to refrain from any overt or covert acts to support Germany or hamper the Allies, "to refrain from public discussion of the war," and "to avoid all hostile or offensive expressions concerning the United States or its government" in their "private intercourse." The committee felt that so long as these restrictions were "scrupulously observed," there was no reason for persons of German birth and sympathy to be dismissed, indeed, "their dismissal would be neither generous nor expedient."[45]

Lest the public and the university community think that the

committee sought "to suppress all public discussion concerning the objects of the war, the terms of peace, and the military policy of the government; to silence all criticism of the methods of administrative or military officials; and to attempt to carry out this program of repression by extra-legal methods of intimidation or coercion," the members stressed their belief that there were only four legitimate grounds for dismissal. To go beyond that and enforce total unanimity would be to sacrifice the very freedoms America was fighting to preserve. Some restrictions were necessary, but no emergency yet existed which made it "either necessary or desirable" that policy be determined without "general consideration and discussion" or that "minorities should be deprived of all right" to present their views and to attempt to influence policy.[46]

At the conclusion of the report, Lovejoy, Capps, and Young included a reminder that when charges were brought against any professor "the proceedings should, as a matter of course, be strictly judicial in character, and should be in accord with the principle of faculty responsibility." They wrote that "the importance of maintaining these procedural safeguards against hasty or unjust action is, if possible, even greater at a time of popular excitement and heightened passions than under normal conditions."[47]

Although they concluded their report by urging Americans not to succumb to wartime hysteria or to overthrow judicial processes, Lovejoy and his colleagues had already capitulated to the passions of war and had weakened the judicial safeguards of academic freedom. There can be little doubt that even a democratic government has a right to restrict clearly treasonous activities during a declared war. However, the committee's report went far beyond this by sanctioning dismissal of professors who opposed the war but had not yet done anything illegal. By expecting all academics to support the war effort wholeheartedly, Lovejoy, Capps, and Young both succumbed to the passions they warned against and discarded the idea of the scholar as a dispassionate, scientific investigator. Nowhere in this report, neither in its tone nor in its specific proposals, was there a willingness to tolerate diversity of opinion or the rational discussion of differences of belief. They assumed the righteousness of the Allied cause and charged that anyone who believed otherwise was blinded by faulty ethics or by the prejudices of ethnic consciousness. Despite their injunctions regarding the continued necessity for judicial proceedings, it is impossible to conclude other than that this report endangered the principles of academic freedom and scientific inquiry at the very moment they needed the greatest protection.

Contemporaries were not unaware of the significance of this report. The *Nation* published a blistering attack on the AAUP, accusing them of returning control over thought and inquiry to the government and university administrators—the very groups that had necessitated the founding of the AAUP. Lovejoy defended the report and the AAUP. He claimed that the organization had never sanctioned unrestricted freedom or "academic anarchism" and argued that the universities had no obligation "to furnish a livelihood, and a platform, and the prestige of academic office" to men who were actively engaged in opposing the American war effort. Freedom, Lovejoy wrote, was not "an absolute and all-sufficient end in itself, to be pursued at the sacrifice of all other human interests." In times of peace, freedom was an essential means to truth, to the development of diverse personalities, and to the solution of social injustices. However, a war such as the one in which they were engaged "alters many things and suspends some of the rules of less critical and perilous times." Men and institutions must choose whether they would aid in the defeat of the United States, either directly or through complicity, and thus "do immeasurable injury to the cause of freedom throughout the world," or whether they would devote all their energies toward the American war effort and the preservation of freedom.[48]

Lovejoy's actions during World War I are explicable if they are not excusable. His prime concern was the preservation of the freedoms of thought, scientific inquiry, and rational expression. He firmly believed that Germany presented the gravest danger to these freedoms, graver even than the temporary restrictions on freedom the war conditions seemed to require. Still, his actions during the war went beyond the bounds of his own principles and the bounds of necessity. Lovejoy participated in propaganda that differed only slightly from what he had condemned when done by German scholars. He repeatedly argued that "celerity of action" took precedence over scientific and rational consideration and discussion of the issues. Finally, in the report on academic freedom, Lovejoy and his colleagues severely weakened that principle by sanctioning greater restrictions on scholars than even the government required and by giving the government the sole right to determine the limits of scholarly freedom in times of crisis. By abdicating the right of academics to follow their scholarly investigations during the war, and by allowing an external power to determine necessary restrictions on professors, Lovejoy breached the walls of academic freedom even before they had been sufficiently raised to withstand external attacks. More disturbing, perhaps, was his willingness to put aside scientific and rational investigation and discourse in favor of speed of action at the very time that the nation most needed calm and reasoned inquiry. If any one could have been expected to uphold the standards of scholarship in times of crisis it was Arthur O. Lovejoy, yet he, too, succumbed to the powerful nonrational forces abroad in the world between 1914 and 1918.

After the war's end, Lovejoy returned to his normal scholarly and academic pursuits. Like most of his colleagues, he seems to have regarded his war work as an aberration—a necessary aberration, to be sure—and to have desired nothing more than to return to the ever-present problems of academics in a world of peace.[43] For Lovejoy, this meant leading the AAUP into the postwar world and attempting to recover those freedoms given up in the heat of crisis. Related to this was the question of whether the AAUP was a professional society or a trade union and, if it was the latter, whether it should affiliate with a labor organization. In responding to these problems, Lovejoy attempted to reassert the need for independent scholarship on social questions, something that was possible only if the profession was unaffiliated with any social group and possessed the freedom for disinterested inquiry.

Lovejoy outlined his concerns for the postwar AAUP in his presidential message to the organization in December 1919. The college professors faced three major problems: the economic condition of the profession, the perennial problem of academic freedom, and the question of trade-union affiliation.

Lovejoy considered the economic problems facing professors to be ' foremost in urgency and gravity." The price rise during the war had not been accompanied by a corresponding rise in

salaries, so that professors in 1919 found themselves at an economic disadvantage. The poor economic situation of the universities, coupled with attractive nonacademic positions, tended to
pull bright young men away from teaching. The result was "a
grave menace to the future efficiency of the American universities." The scholar and teacher had a vital role to play in the modern world, for, in the future, "the well-being of men must increasingly depend, not only upon the work of the analyst of physical
processes, but also upon the work of the disinterested analyst and
interpreter of human experience and of human nature." Lovejoy
argued that maintaining high levels of "energy and competency
in the men and institutions especially dedicated to these fundamental tasks" was a matter of "deepest concern to any civilized
community." These high levels, however, could only be maintained if the economic rewards of scholarship were great enough
to attract and keep the brightest men, and Lovejoy urged his colleagues to push for the improvement of university salaries.[50]

When he turned his attention to the problems of academic
freedom, Lovejoy had to confront not only the recent aberrations
of war, but also the postwar world of strikes, labor and political
unrest, and the Red Scare. The world faced a renewed interest in
the so-called "social question—which is in the main the question
of the distribution of the collective income of society." It would
have been better, he thought, if these social problems could have
been deferred until "the distracted minds of men had in some
measure recovered from the war-psychoses." Since such a post-
ponement was unlikely, the AAUP had to consider seriously the
role of the academic profession in a time of social strife.[51]

Returning to the ideas advanced before the war, Lovejoy argued that a period of "social controversy and class conflict" required the advice and leadership of experts "habituated to seeing
social problems steadily and to seeing them whole, and competent to apply the adequately analyzed lessons of experience to
the rational shaping of the future." Scholarly influence ensured
"reasonableness, balance, patience, [and] the control of social
evolution by disinterested and informed intelligence, rather than
by empty catchwords or by blundering and lawless cupidities."
Professors, however, could only exert effective influence if their
"opinions and utterances" were the "disinterested and unham-

pered expression of their own inquiry and reflection."[52] In other words, academic freedom was an absolute necessity.

Lovejoy rejected the arguments of those who thought academic freedom had received too much attention. Since it was obvious that those who ran the universities had not yet accepted the principles of academic freedom, the AAUP needed both "to reiterate the theory of academic freedom and to insist upon the practice of it." The individual members of the association should especially push for the establishment of "permanent procedural safeguards against illegitimate removals from office" on their various campuses. If this could be done, and if the general awareness of the need for academic freedom could be increased, then there was reason to hope that those principles might be more securely established. Unconscious of the irony of his words, Lovejoy warned his colleagues that "freedom of teaching, like most of the other forms of desirable freedom, is unlikely to be won, or kept, unless those who are its natural guardians possess a certain measure of civil courage."[53]

Finally, the AAUP faced the question of trade unionism. This problem united both the economic and freedom issues, as well as calling into question the nature of the association. Unionism was especially attractive to the younger faculty, who were hardest pressed by economic difficulties. As president of the AAUP, Lovejoy had received numerous inquiries about affiliation with the American Federation of Teachers or the American Federation of Labor. Although Lovejoy thought unions were appropriate and necessary for wage earners, he argued that the AAUP should remain an "independent professional body."[54]

He opposed unionization of professors on grounds of representativeness, the function of scholarship, and the need for academic independence. Many university teachers, he thought, would not "in the near future become members of a teachers' trade union affiliated with the American Federation of Labor." Since an organization possessed influence according to its representativeness, he argued that any association of teachers should be as broadly representative as possible. Until most professors were willing to join a union, it would be better to have the greater representativeness and, thus, the influence that a professional organization offered. Furthermore, while a trade union was primarily economic in its purposes and goals, an organization of university teachers should exist for other than purely economic reasons. Lovejoy recognized the economic requirements of teachers, but argued that the "first concern and controlling purpose" of an association of university professors should be to enable its members "to discharge their distinctive function in the economy of modern society with the highest possible degree of competency and serviceableness." The requirements of scholarly independence made unionization unfeasible; the "professional investigator of social problems ought to avoid entangling permanent alliances with any of the purely economic groups" struggling for the benefit of its members. An affiliation with a trade union would compromise scholarly independence and call into question the academic's rational solutions to social problems. He also worried that affiliation with the American Federation of Labor would weaken public support of education, since most Americans opposed unionization and the AFL.[55] Lovejoy argued that the AAUP, by giving greater attention to the economic problems, and by ensuring the independence of scholarship, could more effectively perform the duties of a trade union without the disadvantages of affiliation.

As the nation returned to normalcy, Lovejoy returned to philosophy and history. He retained, however, his interest in the problems of the profession and the nation even as his participation in the search for solutions declined. He continued to discuss the advantages and disadvantages of the unionization of teachers, but his position changed little from that outlined in his presidential message to the AAUP.[56] The practical problems of ensuring academic freedom recurred all too often during the decade of the twenties, and he investigated abuses at Washburn College and Clark University.[57] After 1920 Lovejoy broke no new ground with his social and political activism, but rather followed old patterns of thought and behavior when an occasional problem required his attention. Study and writing dominated the third decade of the century as social and political problems receded into the background.

CHAPTER VI

THE MORAL OF

THE GREAT CHAIN OF BEING

During the second decade of the century, Lovejoy had continued to write in both philosophy and the history of ideas, but his efforts to establish and maintain the AAUP, to draw attention to the German threat, and to contribute to the war after April 1917 took precedence over scholarship.[1] Not until his term as president of the AAUP ended in 1920 was he again free to devote his energies completely to philosophy and history. The next sixteen years saw Lovejoy pull together the diverse strands of his thought, the masterly treatments of epistemology in *The Revolt Against Dualism* and the history of an idea in *The Great Chain of Being*. In *The Great Chain of Being* he brought together over thirty years of study and traced the ideas of plenitude, continuity, and gradation from their Platonic and Aristotelian genesis through the Romantic Revolution at the beginning of the nineteenth century. To view *The Great Chain of Being* only as a consummate example of scholarship in the history of ideas is to miss much of the significance of the book. *The Great Chain of Being* is not merely the history of an idea (although it is that too), it is also the history of Lovejoy's ideas. In this history he uncovered and examined the intellectual antecedents of the philosophical problem he faced throughout his career—the problem of making a pluralistic and temporal universe intelligible to man's reason.

Lovejoy's work in the history of ideas, like his philosophy, was part of his effort to create a rational and intelligible account of the world. From his earliest essays in the history of ideas, written just after the turn of the century, Lovejoy hoped to uncover the logical process by which man moved from belief in an absolute and a static universe to pluralism and evolution. If he could discover the logical grounds for this change in Western thought, he could be more certain that his pluralistic and evolutionary philosophy was not only possible but also necessary.

In addition to unearthing the history of man's search for intelligibility, the history of ideas lent support to two of Lovejoy's most fundamental philosophical assumptions: ideas do exist, and man, as a rational animal, uses these entities to order his world. Regardless of what contemporary philosophers argued, Lovejoy believed it was impossible to deny that since well before Plato man had had ideas and that they had made a difference. Ideas were, and, as history revealed, always had been a necessary element in man's continuing attempt to make sense of the universe.

Lovejoy's belief in historical inquiry was longstanding. He had decided to undertake graduate study in philosophy because it would commit him to nothing more than a "desire for reasonableness and an interest in the history of thought." In the summer of 1895 he was sure of only one thing: "I should want to make my study run largely along historical lines."[2] Thus, when he was faced with the problem of a pluralistic universe a few years later, it seemed as necessary to examine the historical antecedents of the problem as to investigate the contemporary philosophical implications.

Lovejoy began his investigations into the history of ideas contemporaneously with his initial efforts in philosophy. Several of his initial historical essays treated religious subjects, a legacy of the religious disputes with his father and his early interest in comparative religion. Even so, he very soon addressed the question of how mankind had lived under an absolute conception of the universe for so long and then had rapidly transformed it into something very different. Before 1905 Lovejoy had delineated the Platonic conception of the universe in a philosophical context, had suggested the moral of the tale, and had clearly anticipated his arguments in *The Great Chain of Being*.

In one of his earliest essays, "Religion and the Time-Process," published in 1902, Lovejoy began to outline the historical problem that dominated his work in the history of ideas, and that he would most fully elaborate in *The Great Chain of Being*. Concerned with the relationship of the temporal and the eternal, he examined the philosophic and religious roots of the "otherworldliness" so prevalent in Western thought. He described otherworldliness as "a disposition to define both ultimate Being and genuine Worth in terms of their 'otherness' to the characteristics of the common experience of the life in time and place." He then traced this conception to Plato: "it was in Platonism that those formal preconceptions which were to determine for many centuries all the more philosophical views about divine nature and the nature of the good, got their earliest and most influential manifestation."[3]

He had not yet discriminated the component ideas of the framework of Western thought with the clarity he achieved in *The Great Chain of Being*. He was, however, dealing with the same complex of ideas. The Good must, according to Plato, be perfectly self-sufficient: as Lovejoy described it, "the perfect must be one, simple, ontologically independent of external relations to other entities, and, above all, free from all mutability, from all activity or outreaching of volition." In such a belief, "mere diversity, richness of content as such, especially in the form of change and temporal process, absolutely is not . . . valuable or interesting in itself, but only as rationalized into a formal unity."[4] Here was one side of the Platonic conception of the universe that Lovejoy later traced in his William James Lectures.

When he turned to the fate of Platonic otherworldliness in the course of human thought, Lovejoy discovered that the idea of the absolute underwent certain changes with the passage of centuries; new ideas about change and development appeared in Western philosophy. In 1902 he believed that the ideas of history and of becoming had been introduced into Western thinking through the Judeo-Christian tradition. He had not yet discerned the principles of plenitude, continuity, and gradation within Platonic thought, which, as he demonstrated in *The Great Chain of Being*, were capable of overthrowing the tradition of which they were a part. Although in "Religion and the Time-Process" the notions of time and diversity were Judeo-Christian in basis, the process of temporalizing the self-sufficient good paralleled the temporalizing of the chain of being. Lovejoy believed that the deists began the weakening of otherworldliness by attempting to establish a "religion of this world." However, because their conception of the good was itself "a condition of perfected and stationary equilibrium," the deists had been unable to assign any "rational meaning or ultimate value to the time-process." The rise of evolutionary thought in the eighteenth century further contributed to the breakdown of the Platonic universe. Beginning with Gotthold Lessing, the notion that the world, man, and ideas were not static, but instead developing, changing, and becoming, swept through Western consciousness. In the principles of evolution man had a means whereby a world of becoming could be made intelligible. The final step was the development of a new theory of worth in the nineteenth century. This theory held that the good lay "not in perfection, not in the arrest of forthreaching process, but has its very essence in movement and process itself." As he later argued in *The Great Chain of Being*, Lovejoy then asserted that "with this radical transformation of the conception of value, the entire Platonic and Aristotelian scheme of the universe—which, as we have seen, has in its broad outlines formed the logical framework of European moral and religious thought, even where men have been least aware of it—gets now completely inverted."[5] This revolution in thought lay behind Lovejoy's own developing philosophy. Just as the nineteenth century had rejected a static absolute conception of the world, so, too, he had rejected the absolute idealism of his philosophical mentors in favor of a philosophy based on diversity and change.

Two years later, in "The Dialectic of Bruno and Spinoza," Lovejoy returned to the Platonic influences on Western thought, this time in a more philosophical context. Spinoza scholarship had long foundered on the problem of explaining how this seventeenth-century philosopher could find in the absolute the logical ground for "the existence of an infinity of attributes." Rather than another analysis of Spinoza's language, Lovejoy proposed to exhibit Spinoza's "dialectical procedure through an examination of its historical sources and affinities." He argued that "the more general and fundamental principles of Spinoza's metaphysics are in no respect original": Spinoza was a "consistent Neo-Platonist of the Renaissance type," whose approach to these problems had been "foreshadowed by Plotinus, fully worked out by mediaeval theologians and much used by Bruno." Spinoza's philosophy, Lovejoy felt, could be "understood only in the light of its relation to these earlier applications of a similar dialectic to a similar problem."[6]

Lovejoy believed that "without going back to Alexandrian Neo-Platonism little in subsequent European metaphysics can be understood in its proper historical setting" and that this background was indispensable to a study of Bruno and Spinoza. Now, he saw more clearly than before the Platonic, Aristotelian, and Neo-Platonic bases of Western thought. From Plato, of course, came the conception of the one true Being that was "perfect, simple, immutable, having no relations to anything outside itself." If the true Being was perfection, what then were its relations with the imperfect world in which man lived? Although both Plato and Aristotle suggested connections, Lovejoy argued that it was the Neo-Platonists who "would find in the abstract Platonic Deity the necessary source of all being, and also the substance of all" and, as a result, would structure much of Western thought. He still thought Judeo-Christian beliefs had influenced the alteration of Platonic thought, but now he conceded that contradictions in "Platonic and Aristotelian theology" were sufficient to explain the transformation of the tradition. The Neo-Platonists had realized that "only a Nature that included all positive being within itself could meet the requirements of the dialectic that lay behind the theology of Plato and Aristotle." The Neo-Platonists argued that all particular and relative things were "taken up within the being of the Absolute One." This idea brought the Absolute into a relationship with the relative, but it still left philosophers with a serious paradox: how could a perfect, transcendent, immutable Being "embrace within itself all the diversity of the universe?"[7]

In Plotinus, Lovejoy discovered a deduction from Platonic principles that sought to make the "concept of perfection and self-sufficiency . . . the ground and the necessity" for the existence of all "particular beings and the subjects of concrete predicates." Plotinus had argued that the perfect Being could not remain limited within itself but must give rise to all things. In what Lovejoy would later call the principle of plenitude, the Absolute was now conceived as the "maximum potentiality" involving "the necessity of the actual existence of all possible things with all possible qualities and modes of being." The Neo-Platonic dialectic, as worked out by Plotinus, had four elements: first, the Absolute Being was transcendent, immutable, and free of all limitation and relation; second, "the same Being is conceived as necessarily inclusive of all the reality that in any sense exists, and thus holding within itself the whole universe of concrete, manifold and temporal existences"; third, the Absolute must necessarily transcend itself and become "the dynamic ground necessitating the coming into existence of all possible realities in all possible modes and scales of being"; and finally, although holding all these principles was contradictory, to deny any seemed to involve an even "more radical and offensive self-contradiction." This same dialectic, Lovejoy asserted, could also be shown "at work in the doctrines of the Platonizing Christian theologians of the Middle Ages."[8] The dialectic of Bruno and Spinoza, of course, was only a legacy of this well-established tradition. By 1904, then, Lovejoy had more fully outlined his reconstruction of the framework of Occidental thought, but the complete history would have to wait for another thirty years.

"The Dialectic of Bruno and Spinoza" was primarily a historical inquiry into the intellectual antecedents of the two philosophers, but Lovejoy also hoped to uncover "some general considerations capable of pertinent application to certain contemporary tendencies in metaphysics." The problem of Bruno and Spinoza—indeed, in Lovejoy's view, the problem of all philosophers since Plato—was to render intelligible the relationship of the Absolute Being to the imperfect world. When he wrote this essay, Lovejoy was in the midst of his own struggle to find an intelligible account of the universe. By 1904 he had largely rejected the notion of an absolute as the ground of temporal existence, but the "moral" of the history he recounted in this essay lent support to his own developing theories: "The moral . . . is the hopelessness of the effort—not yet wholly given over— to make a metaphysic by framing a conception of a really 'absolute' Absolute which is at the same time to be thought as 'inclusive' of all reality, a 'comprehensive whole of experience,' the 'possessor of an infinite wealth of organized individual elements of content.' "[9] If human experience was truly pluralistic and temporal, then this real world could not be contained in any absolute without self-contradiction. His historical inquiries, by revealing the contradictions inherent in an absolute, helped Lovejoy reject the absolute philosophies of his day. The moral of this history was thus central to Lovejoy's intellectual enterprise, and he returned to it at the end of *The Great Chain of Being*.

The philosophical framework and central problem established by Plato and described by Lovejoy in these early essays formed the background against which he constructed his own philosophy. In these early essays, in the numerous studies in the history of ideas, and most fully in *The Great Chain of Being*, Lovejoy outlined the intellectual antecedents of the philosophical problem he confronted and the temporalistic realism of his solution. The history of ideas provided ample evidence that the concept of the self-sufficient absolute, and its corollary, the chain of being, had failed to make the universe intelligible, that time, evolution, and diversity were ideas more in accord with the world as man experienced it, and that ideas exist and are important. Lovejoy's temporalistic realism and his epistemological and psychophysical dualism were his answers to Plato's questions about the existence of a world of becoming and the kinds of being that made up the experienced world. His essays in the history of ideas described man's attempts to answer those questions and "to show that the scheme of things is an intelligible and rational one."[10] The absolute and the chain of being proved a failure, but out of that failure rose the ideas of evolution and the value of diversity that enabled Lovejoy to make his world rationally comprehensible.

One needs only to look at Lovejoy's essays in the history of ideas to realize the extent to which his studies illuminated episodes in man's attempt to work out the implications of the Platonic universe. The bulk of his historical essays focused on eighteenth-century thought, evolutionism, or romanticism (in Germany, 1790–1830). His essays on the Enlightenment pointed up the contradictions in the thought of the period, although Lovejoy admired Enlightenment thinkers for their devotion to reason and their rejection of historical and mystical religion. His studies on evolutionism traced the modern discovery of time and change, while his investigations into romanticism eventually uncovered the transformation of the chain of being into a becoming. All these studies, of course, demonstrated, if only indirectly, the importance and value of ideas to rational man.

The thinkers of the Enlightenment took the legacy of Plato to its highest development in their reliance on reason and the chain of being. At the same time, however, the contradictions inherent in their beliefs were becoming increasingly obvious. Lovejoy began his studies of the eighteenth century because the deists had been among the first modern thinkers to argue against historical Christianity and for a rational, universal religion. In their arguments, Lovejoy had found support in his dissent from the evangelical religion of his father. But the Enlightenment thinkers were more than allies in the attack on historical religion. Of all modern philosophers, they had valued reason most highly, and it was, of course, upon rational foundations that Lovejoy worked to build his own philosophy. The problem, as Lovejoy quickly discovered, was that the Enlightenment was too rational. As he suggested in "The Dialectic of Bruno and Spinoza" and demonstrated at length in *The Great Chain of Being*, the contradictions inherent in the full elaboration of the ideas of plenitude, continuity, and gradation soon undermined the "hypothesis of the absolute rationality of the cosmos."[11] Reason was a key to intelligibility, but other elements of man's experience, especially time, were equally important.

At the same time that he began to write on the Platonic legacy, Lovejoy discovered the beginning of modern, scientific evolutionism in the eighteenth century. Evolutionism was important in the history of thought, Lovejoy believed, because through these ideas thinkers gained a theory whereby they "could assign rationality and spiritual significance to the temporal order of phenomena." Just as Lovejoy's own reflections on the temporal process led him to reject the absolute doctrines of his teachers, so the nascent evolutionary thought of the eighteenth century did much to undermine the absolute imbedded in the chain of being. Beginning with "Some Eighteenth Century Evolutionists" in 1904, Lovejoy described several episodes in the development of evolutionary thought before Darwin.[12] Although Lovejoy's essays on evolution were characteristically precise and discriminating, he was well aware of both the religious and philosophical implications of evolutionary theory. The theory had helped make possible a "religion of evolution" and ultimately temporalized the chain of being. Not solely responsible for the major shift in Western thought, "the evolutionist tendency" had, nevertheless, worked "to increase the pressure towards the transformation" of the principles of plenitude, continuity, and gradation into their "temporalized form."[13] And when that had happened, especially after Leibniz, it was only a small step to the universe of becoming celebrated by the Romantics.

The study of romanticisms and the thinkers of the early nineteenth century formed a major part of Lovejoy's work in the history of ideas. As with the Enlightenment and pre-Darwinian evolutionary thought, the ideas associated with romanticism were important in the transformation of the absolute and static world to one of diversity and becoming. Although Lovejoy did not begin his studies of the period until the 1910s, he recognized as early as 1902 that ideas characteristic of romanticism, in at least some of its guises, were antithetical to what had come before. The new value placed on the belief in the good as "movement and process" meant that the "entire Platonic and Aristotelian scheme of the universe" was "completely inverted."[14]

The essays on romanticism, products of Lovejoy's search for intelligibility, were valuable historical studies of the period. In his articles, "Schiller and the Genesis of German Romanticism" and "On the Discrimination of Romanticisms," Lovejoy did much to clarify the murky intellectual history of the period. Only in *The Great Chain of Being* did Lovejoy explicitly connect the Romantic thinkers to the overthrow of the chain of being and the absolute, uniformitarian concept of the universe of which it was a part. In the writings of Friedrich Schelling, Lovejoy discovered that the "complete and immutable Chain of Being" had "been converted into a Becoming." The ideas of plenitude, continuity, and gradation were still imbedded in Western thought, but the fullness of the universe was no longer "the permanent character but the flying goal of the whole of things."[15] The way was now open for a pluralistic, temporalistic universe ordered by the principles of reason.

The existence of ideas, indeed their necessity, was an integral part of Lovejoy's philosophy, and the history of ideas, if only indirectly, lent support to Lovejoy's philosophical arguments. Ideas were, of course, central to any rational philosophy and indispensable in Lovejoy's representative theory of knowledge. As he put it at the conclusion of "The Anomaly of Knowledge": "I am still much inclined to believe that I have ideas, and that without them I and other men would know less than we do—would, to be precise, know nothing at all." Lovejoy's working assumption in the history of ideas drew upon this philosophical position: "Whatever other definitions of man be true or false, it is generally admitted that he is distinguished among the creatures by the habit of entertaining general ideas." Not only did man have general ideas, "his thoughts have at all times had a good deal to do with his behavior, his institutions, his material achievements in technology and the arts, and his fortunes." Given the rational nature of man, the history of ideas "has its own reason for being":

> To know, so far as may be known, the thoughts that have
> been widely held among men on matters of common hu-
> man concernment, to determine how these thoughts have
> arisen, combined, interacted with, or counteracted, one
> another, and how they have severally been related to
> the imagination and emotions and behavior of those
> who have held them—this, though not, indeed, the whole
> of that branch of knowledge which we call history, is a
> distinct and essential part of it, and its central and most
> vital part.[16]

Although the existence of general ideas justified the history of ideas, the historian must not falsely assume that man is, or was, totally rational. Lovejoy cautioned against the belief that the terms *idea* and *intellectual* implied "any assumption of the solely or chiefly logical determination of opinions and behavior and of the historical movement of thought." If man was not wholly rational, neither was he the prisoner of his subconscious, irrational desires, passions, and interests, and the historian of ideas had the responsibility to discriminate between the rational and nonrational elements of the history of thought. Despite his recognition of man's nonrational side, Lovejoy believed strongly that the historian of ideas should concentrate on the rational side: "It must still be admitted that philosophers (and even plain men) *do* reason, that the temporal sequence of their reasonings, as one thinker follows another, is usually in some considerable degree a logically motivated and logically instructive sequence." And, in the sequential record of Western thought, Lovejoy tried to trace man's attempt "to make the world he lives in appear to his intellect a rational one."[17]

Most of his essays in the history of ideas examined some facet of this unfolding world order, but only in *The Great Chain of Being* did Lovejoy bring together all the "general conceptions" in a masterful study of an influential complex of ideas in Western thought. More importantly for the development of his own ideas, he described, more fully than before, the intellectual antecedents of the philosophical problems he had confronted throughout his career. He concluded that the history of the chain of being was the history of its failure, but a failure with a moral: no static, absolute, and completely rational conception of the universe could render the actual world intelligible. Out of the ruins of the Age of Reason, however, arose a newly dominant view of the cosmos, a scheme of things that made the temporal and pluralistic character of the experienced world comprehensible. From the time he began to write philosophy under the guidance of Josiah Royce, Lovejoy faced "a world demanding to be made intelligible." Not alone in his desire to make sense of the universe, he discovered that the ideas implicit in the chain of being had long provided a basis for showing that the order of the world is "an intelligible and rational one." When he came to write *The Great Chain of Being*, Lovejoy discerned two questions at the heart of much of Western philosophy: Why was there a "World of Becoming" in addition to the "eternal World of Ideas," and what principle determined the character of the experienced world? These questions remained as important for Lovejoy as they had for Plato, Plotinus, Spinoza, or the other philosophers of Occidental civilization: "For to acknowledge that such questions are necessarily insoluble or meaningless is to imply that, so far as we can judge, the world is in final analysis nonrational." If no "intelligible reason" could be given for the character of the world as experienced, then "the constitution of the world is but a whim or an accident." And that was a conclusion Lovejoy could not accept.[18]

Plato and most subsequent philosophers had assumed that these questions about the nature of the universe could and should be asked. Lovejoy shared that assumption, although he recognized that there was no assurance of success in the quest for complete intelligibility. Using an image he took from William James, he wrote: "No doubt man's quest of intelligibility in nature and in himself, and of the kinds of emotional satisfaction which are conditioned by a sense of intelligibility, often, like the caged rat's quest of food, has found no end, in wandering mazes lost."[19] If not all philosophers were successful, their failures were instructive nonetheless, and the history of the chain of being was part of the history of man's attempt to make his universe comprehensible.

As he had in the essays at the turn of the century, Lovejoy began *The Great Chain of Being* by turning to Plato to find the beginnings of Western thought. He discerned in Plato the sharp cleavage between otherworldliness and this-worldliness that influenced the course of most subsequent philosophical and religious thought. Otherworldliness, of course, held that the "genuinely 'real' and the truly good" were radically antithetic to "man's natural life." This-worldliness embodied "the chief value of existence" in struggle and development in time and in "antipathy to satisfaction and finality." Lovejoy argued that Plato's otherworldliness was clearly evident in the Greek philosopher's Idea of the Good, which was the direct opposite of all change, distinct from all particular existence, and "the most indubitable of all realities."[20]

Having conceived of "an Idea of Ideas which is a pure perfection alien to all the categories of ordinary thought and in need of nothing external to itself," Plato, according to Lovejoy, grounded the "necessity and worth of all conceivable kinds of finite, temporal, imperfect, and corporeal beings" in the "Self-Sufficing Being." These considerations gave rise to the two questions already mentioned: "*Why* is there any World of Becoming, in addition to the eternal World of Ideas" and what principle determines how many kinds of being make up "the sensible and temporal world"? Lovejoy believed that Plato assumed that finite and imperfect entities were "inherently desirable" and thus transformed the "Self-Sufficing Perfection" into a "Self-Transcending Fecundity." As for the number of possible beings, Plato answered: "*all* possible kinds." These two answers Lovejoy saw coming together in the "principle of plenitude"—in the notion that all conceptual possibilities must be realized in actuality.[21] Plenitude, continuity, and gradation were the three closely associated "unit-ideas" that were components of the chain of being in Lovejoy's analysis.

The second principle, that of continuity, Lovejoy found emerging in the philosophy of Aristotle, though it could also be "directly deduced" from the Platonic notion of plenitude. The idea of continuity required that if there was a theoretically intermediate type between two natural species, that type must be realized, otherwise there would be gaps in the universe implying a lack of fullness and an inadmissible inadequacy in the good or absolute.[22]

The principle of gradation, the third element in the complex of ideas Lovejoy studied, was also rooted in Aristotelian thought. Aristotle had suggested arranging all animals in a single *scala naturae* according to their "degree of perfection," an idea later extended to all things. This hierarchical approach gave rise to the "principal of unilinear gradation," which became attached to the principles of plenitude and continuity.[23]

The union of these three principles produced "the conception of the plan and structure of the world which, through the Middle Ages and down to the late eighteenth century, many philosophers, most men of science, and, indeed, most educated men, were to accept without question—the conception of the universe as a 'Great Chain of Being.'" This complex of ideas was first "fully organized into a coherent general scheme of things" in Neoplatonism. Plotinus, more clearly than Plato, deduced "the necessity of the existence of this world, with all its manifoldness and imperfection" from the self-sufficient Absolute.[24]

Although Neoplatonism established an otherworldly conception of the universe, Lovejoy noted that elements of a this-worldly conception remained alive, even during the Middle Ages. Some philosophers assumed that there was "a true and intrinsic multiplicity in the divine nature," that the good consisted of "the maximum actualization of variety" and that "the temporal and sensible experience" was therefore good.[25] These ideas, when freed from the dominance of otherworldly philosophy, would provide the basis for a new conception of the universe that celebrated the temporal, diverse world of becoming —the very conception Lovejoy attempted to make intelligible through his philosophy.

When Lovejoy wrote "The Dialectic of Bruno and Spinoza" in 1904, those two philosophers represented for him the culmination of the Neoplatonic dialectic. In *The Great Chain of Being*, he argued that Leibniz and Spinoza most clearly expressed the chain of being as the ruling conception of thought. The philosophy of Leibniz revealed the chain of being at its "most conspicuous, most determinative, and most persuasive." However, at the very time that this world received its grandest exposition, it revealed the paradox inherent in it. Spinoza, according to Lovejoy, had argued that the " 'fullness' " of the temporal world was necessarily grounded in "the timeless immutability" of the absolute. Drawing on his own arguments against the absolutes of the late nineteenth century, Lovejoy attacked Spinoza. "Being and change," he asserted, "simply do not fit into an eternal rational order"—the imperfect world could not be logically deduced from an eternal absolute.[26] In this criticism of Spinoza, Lovejoy recapitulated his earlier attacks on the eternal and foreshadowed the moral of his history of *The Great Chain of Being*.

Following his discussion of Spinoza, Lovejoy devoted three chapters of his book to the influence of the chain of being in eighteenth-century thought, for it was then that the conception and the three principles of plenitude, continuity, and gradation "attained their widest diffusion and acceptance." Citing examples from philosophy, theology, journalism, poetry (especially Pope's *Essay on Man*), literature, and science he traced the impact of these ideas on man's view of his place in the world, on the belief in optimism, and on the development of eighteenth-century science. The chain of being had the effect, Lovejoy argued, of making man aware of "his littleness in the scheme of things"—of putting him in his place. If this promoted a salutary modesty, it also discouraged attempts at reform. Reform might encourage the human species and individual man to rise above his assigned station in the chain. Eighteenth-century optimism, according to Lovejoy, was not simply blind cheerfulness in the face of obvious evil. The principle of plenitude required that goodness lie not in the paucity of evils but in their multiplicity. A completely good universe, by this reasoning, would not be completely and fully realized. Finally, the chain of being influenced eighteenth-century science by stimulating a search for missing links—for example, Monboddo's ape between the lower primates and humans. Ironically, the frustrations and problems encountered in this search would soon help to overthrow the idea of the chain.[27]

As a philosopher and historian, Lovejoy clearly liked the climate of the eighteenth century and he devoted much time studying the age. His admiration for the Age of Reason was tempered by the eighteenth-century reliance on "an absolutely rigid and static scheme of things," the opposite of Lovejoy's own temporalistic and pluralistic universe. Eighteenth-century faith in reason elicited Lovejoy's admiration, but so did "the temporalizing of the Chain of Being" which, to him, was "one of the principal happenings in eighteenth-century thought." Toward the end of the century, the necessary existence of all beings implied by the chain of being came to be seen "not as the inventory but as the program of nature, which is being carried out gradually and exceedingly slowly in the cosmic history." Difficulties and contradictions in the conceptions of plenitude, continuity, and gradation caused the "static and permanently complete Chain of Being" to break down "largely of its own weight."[28]

Lovejoy believed that one "fatal defect" of the principle of plenitude and of optimism was that "it left no room for hope, at least for the world in general or for mankind as a whole." The argument so often employed in the eighteenth century—though satirized by writers like Voltaire—held that all the evil in the world was a consequence of the universal good. To increasing numbers of thinkers in the eighteenth century and to Lovejoy, "this optimistic paradox was a grotesque mockery." They felt, as did Lovejoy concerning his own efforts at social and political reform, that "it was better to admit the world to be not at present entirely rational, and retain some hope of its amendment, than to conceive of it as perfectly rational—and utterly hopeless." The growing revolt against this absolute rationality did not result in the total disavowal of the chain of being. Instead, the chain was "reinterpreted so as to admit of progress in general, and of a progress of the individual not counterbalanced by deterioration elsewhere." This reinterpretation, in turn, stimulated the revival of the belief that man's destiny was a gradual ascent through all the stages toward, but never reaching, the Perfect Being. Lovejoy believed that this idea of "unending progress" had emerged "as a consequence of reflection upon the principles of plenitude and continuity." The ideas of plenitude and continuity thus contained within themselves "hidden implications" that would destroy the rational world they had supported for so long.[29]

The tendency of these "hidden implications" of a principle to destroy the "*Zeitgeist* to which [the principle] was meant to minister" was, to Lovejoy, "one of the instructive ironies of the history of ideas." The ideas embodied in the chain of being had been used "to justify the belief in the rationality, the perfection, the static completeness, the orderliness and coherency of reality."[30] This static conception did provide one means of making the universe intelligible, but the denial of the reality of time proved as unacceptable to many thinkers at the end of the eighteenth century as it would to Lovejoy at the beginning of the twentieth century. The temporalizing of the chain of being, which began in the late eighteenth century, pointed toward a new conception of the world that would recognize the reality of time.

Lovejoy went on to argue that the early nineteenth-century Romantics had added a belief in the value of diversity to this recognition of temporal reality. The "substitution of what may be called diversitarianism for uniformitarianism," he wrote, "more than any other *one* thing has distinguished, both for better and worse, the prevailing assumptions of the mind" of the nineteenth and twentieth centuries.[31] Here, then, lay the foundations of his own philosophical pluralism.

Lovejoy valued the revolt against uniformitarianism, but it was not an unalloyed good. He feared that "the revolt against the standardization of life" could easily become "a revolt against the whole conception of standards." Man, however, possessed "a reason which demands selection, preference, and negation, in conduct and in art." The task of man was not simply to succumb to Romantic diversity but to balance between rational standards and the real diversity of the world: "The delicate and difficult art of life is to find, in each new turn of experience, the *via media* between two extremes: to be catholic *without* being characterless; to have and apply standards, and yet to be on guard against their desensitizing and stupefying influence, their tendency to blind us to the diversities of concrete situations and to previously unrecognized values; to know when to tolerate, when to embrace, and when to fight." Though diversity undermined the legitimate value of standards, it remained, nonetheless, "one of the great discoveries of the human mind." And, insofar as the discovery of the value of diversity was the result of the principle of plenitude, Lovejoy thought it "among the most important and potentially the most benign of the manifold consequences" of the chain of being.[32]

Lovejoy uncovered the culmination of the revolt against the chain of being in the writings of Friedrich Schelling. Here "the Platonistic scheme of the universe" was "turned upside down." Lovejoy argued that Schelling had converted the "originally complete and immutable Chain of Being . . . into a Becoming." Now, even God was identified with the Becoming. In Lovejoy's view, however, this "inversion of the Platonistic scheme of things" did "not alter its essential character." Schelling and much of the subsequent thought of the nineteenth century retained the Platonistic attributes of "insatiable generativeness, the tendency to produce diversity, [and] the necessity of the realization of the greatest possible 'fulness' of being." But things had, nevertheless, changed radically: "the generativeness is now that of an insufficiency striving unconsciously for richer and more various being; and the fullness is not the permanent character but the flying goal of the whole of things."[33]

With his discussion of Schelling and the discovery of this new and more intelligible account of the universe, Lovejoy brought his history of the chain of being to a close. There remained to be told only the moral of this history of man's quest for intelligibility—the last chapter, after all, was entitled "The Outcome of the History and Its Moral."

Why should Lovejoy, renowned for his rational and discriminating scholarship, conclude his major work in the history of ideas with a moral? That he did so suggests that the moral held great significance for him, that his history of the chain of being was more than an abstract exercise in scholarship. The moral of *The Great Chain of Being* was the same as that which he had outlined at the conclusion of "The Dialectic of Bruno and Spinoza" some thirty years earlier: As long as one assumed "the existence of this world of temporal and imperfect creatures" to be a "genuine good," then "the otherworldly Idea of a Good," the idea embodied in the chain of being, must be "the idea of a spurious good." Furthermore, "an Absolute which is self-sufficient and forever perfect and complete cannot be identified with a God related to and manifested in a world of temporal becoming and alteration." As Lovejoy had argued in "The Obsolescence of the Eternal" (1909), the eternal was no longer necessary. —

The history of the chain of being, then, "in so far as that idea presupposed such a complete rational intelligibility of the world" was "the history of a failure," but one with "an instructive negative outcome." It revealed "the hypothesis of the absolute rationality of the cosmos to be unbelievable" because it conflicted with "one immense fact," "the fact that existence as we experience it is temporal." Finally, this history revealed "that rationality, when conceived as complete, as excluding all arbitrariness, becomes itself a kind of irrationality." The thinkers of the Enlightenment were too rational, for the "complete realization of all the possibles" excluded "any limiting and selective principle."[34]

In the history of the chain of being, Lovejoy traced the historical antecedents of, and discovered a historical justification for, his own religious and philosophical beliefs. Underlying his philosophical enterprise was his assumption that "an actual world given as diverse is a world full of differences requiring to be united and harmonized; it is a world demanding to be made intelligible." In the years after 1900, Lovejoy found a large measure of the intelligibility he sought in the conception of a pluralistic and temporalistic universe, epistemological and psychophysical dualism, and the principles of reason. The actual world was "a contingent world" but that characteristic allowed men to choose rationally "among the infinity of possibles."[35] Without the legacy of the chain of being, Lovejoy would not have confronted the seeming chaos of a diverse, nonrational world, but neither would he have found his way toward intelligibility.

CHAPTER VII

EVOLUTION AND THE

NATURE OF MAN

The study of the chain of being occupied Lovejoy for over thirty years, from the turn of the century to the mid-thirties. The chain of being had been, especially in its seventeenth- and eighteenth-century conceptions, an attempt to structure the universe and to determine man's place in it. Early in this century Lovejoy discovered that the rigid forms of the chain had been temporalized by a current of evolutionary thought which converted the chain of being into a becoming. Lovejoy dealt only tangentially with evolutionary thought in *The Great Chain of Being*; he did, however, inquire into the promise and problems of evolution in a series of essays beginning in 1904 and continuing until just before his death in 1962.

Lovejoy conceived of the world in evolutionary terms. As with the problems of plenitude, gradation, and continuity, his study of evolution ran "largely along historical lines."[1] Early research into eighteenth-century thought uncovered not only the chain of being, but also the beginnings of evolutionary thinking in men such as Buffon, Kant, and Herder. Lovejoy traced the argument for organic evolution in the nineteenth century up to the publication of *The Origin of Species*. His studies had implications beyond their historical interest. By the twentieth century, evolutionism had largely triumphed as the reigning conception of the universe. That is not to imply, however, that all the problems with this view were solved. Lovejoy, in a series of articles closely related to his historical studies, inquired into the nature of evolution. How did evolution proceed; through mere rearrangement

Arthur O. Lovejoy

of a finite number of units, or were there discontinuities in the
process whereby something totally new was added to the make-
up of the world? His arguments that evolution was discontinuous
and that there had been wholly new additions to the world, had
clear philosophical implications, especially in the construction of
a theory of human nature and an ethics.

The cornerstone of Lovejoy's reflections on human nature, and
the ethical theory he derived from them, was the human capacity
for self-consciousness. Men had desires and passions, they could
think and reason. More importantly, men realized that they
shared this capacity for self-awareness with other humans and
that passions, desires, and thoughts motivated human action.
The development of self-consciousness was, in all probability,
one of the discontinuities of evolution. At some point in our evolutionary past, the emergence of self-consciousness had added a
whole new dimension to the character of the world. Lovejoy
drew upon the characteristics of the self-conscious animal and
upon the ethical ideas of David Hume and Adam Smith in developing his own ethical views. Focusing on the notion that self-
conscious man desires to perform praiseworthy actions and to
avoid the pain of disapproval, Lovejoy's ethical theories received
their fullest expression in *Reflections on Human Nature*.

Lovejoy began his historical investigation of evolutionary
thought contemporaneously with his examinations of the dialectic of Bruno and Spinoza and of the influence of the time process
on religion. The same inquiry that uncovered the manifestations
of the chain of being also revealed the early evolutionary writings
of men like Maupertuis, Diderot, Herder, and Monboddo. Their
evolutionism was neither as thoroughgoing nor as scientific as
nineteenth-century versions, but they were key figures in the revolution in the world order that accompanied the temporalizing
of the chain of being.

Lovejoy published the first of his essays on evolution, "Some
Eighteenth Century Evolutionists," in 1904, the same year he
published his study of Bruno and Spinoza. He claimed that "a
satisfactory history of the theory of descent is a chapter in the
records of human opinion that is still to be written." Darwin was
not the first to assert the evolution of species; the thesis had orig-
inated "as a respectably fathered and militant hypothesis, in
France in the middle of the eighteenth century." Developments

in both embryology and comparative anatomy fostered this rise of evolutionism.[2]

In 1909, fifty years after the publication of *The Origin of Species*, Lovejoy turned his attention to the early nineteenth-century precursors of Darwin. This essay, "The Argument for Organic Evolution Before 'The Origin of Species,' " took up two questions: "at what date can the evidence in favor of the theory of organic evolution . . . be said to have been fairly complete" and "by what English writer was a logically cogent argument for the theory first brought together and put before the public?"[3] The answer to the first question was the mid-1840s, specifically 1844, and the answer to the second was Robert Chambers in his anonymously published *Vestiges of the Natural History of Creation.* These answers, however, raised another question. If the evidence for organic evolution was available and even collated by the mid-1840s, why was that evidence not widely accepted by noted scientists such as Darwin, Thomas Huxley, Charles Lyell, and Asa Gray until after the publication of Darwin's book? Lovejoy's explanation for this fifteen-year lag in the general scientific acceptance of the theory anticipated Thomas Kuhn's idea of a paradigm shift.

Lovejoy contended that Chambers, who was not a scientist, was "sound in his main thesis" and that "his thesis was based upon sound and sensible arguments." Chambers had based his arguments for organic evolution on the increasing evidence against special creationism, on the growing biological evidence concerning rudimentary organs, on the unity of organization, and on the theory of recapitulation developed in comparative embryology. In these crucial respects, Chambers anticipated Darwin by fifteen years, yet his theories were sharply attacked by almost all the noted scientists studying evolutionary problems. Why? Lovejoy concentrated on Thomas Huxley's reaction to Chambers's work, but implied that the negative reaction of the other scientists was similar. He suggested that "certain wholly non-logical influences" kept Huxley and the others from accepting Chambers's arguments and the evidence for organic evolution in the 1840s. In Huxley's case, these nonlogical influences derived, not from "religious tradition or temperamental conservatism," but from a too punctilious regard for the proper form of scientific inquiry and discourse. Huxley was unable to see the essential validity of

Chambers's theory behind the author's "exuberant and rhetorical style," the "pious and edifying tone" of the volume, and his "blunders in matters of biological and geological detail." More conservative and religious scientists balked at the "religious heterodoxy" of *Vestiges*. The one scientist, apparently, who saw the essential truth of Chambers's arguments was Alfred Russel Wallace, for whom the new problem became that of solving the mystery of the origin of species.[4]

Lovejoy's emphasis on the nonlogical components of resistance to Chambers's book and the reluctance of scientists to accept organic evolution before 1859 suggests the process Thomas Kuhn outlined in *The Structure of Scientific Revolutions*. The Chambers episode in the history of thought provided Lovejoy with an "object-lesson in the logic of scientific reasoning." It revealed "how far, even in the minds of acute and professedly unprejudiced men of science, the emotion of conviction may lag behind the presentation of proof."[5] Similarly, Kuhn argued that "the emergence of new theories is generally preceded by a period of pronounced professional insecurity."[6] He, like Lovejoy, suggested that in the crisis preceding a paradigm shift, professional insecurity or other nonlogical factors may keep the scientist from changing his allegiance to the new paradigm. The phenomena that Lovejoy described as "an interesting, if not an encouraging, fact in the history of the human intellect," Kuhn later developed into a central feature of the structure of scientific revolutions.[7]

Lovejoy's interest in the nature of the scientific enterprise did not result in a full-scale theory of scientific development. He did, however, examine the possible bases for a unified science and, finding serious problems with any proposed unification, pointed the way toward his theory of emergent evolution. Lovejoy felt that the largest barrier to the unification of the sciences was the evidence that evolution had produced "discontinuous mutations and genuine, not-wholly-predictable innovations."[8] The most radical evolutionism would hold that not only do living creatures, or chemical and physical processes, evolve in a discontinuous fashion, so also do the laws and uniformities that describe these processes. His speculation on the possible discontinuities of evolution and their implications shifted the focus of Lovejoy's study of evolution from history to philosophy.

Lovejoy first addressed the question of the unity of science and the nature of the evolutionary process in an essay, "The Unity of Science," originally given as part of a series of nontechnical lectures at the University of Missouri in 1909–10. As the opening speaker in the series, Lovejoy had been enlisted to take up the broad questions of the possibility of scientific unity and the characteristics of any possible unity. He was determined to demonstrate the "broad outlines" and connections between the parts of science, to suggest the "unity and total sweep" of contemporary science, and to remind his readers of the hopes and tasks of science—"tasks at once baffling and alluring to that highest expression of man's play-spirit which is the desire to know, to that wholesomest manifestation of his fighting spirit which is the inability [sic] to take a dare from an unsolved problem."[9]

He reviewed the developments in science in the preceding centuries but concentrated on the notable and fundamental discoveries of the previous twenty years. Einstein's theory of relativity was only one of the developments he cited. Many of the contemporary discoveries had taken place at the boundaries between the special sciences and had encouraged the hope of an "eventual reduction of all sciences to one, the interpretation of all phenomena in terms of a single general type of phenomenon and the description of all of them in terms of relatively few, fundamental, all-comprehensive laws." In discussing the unity of science, he planned to consider whether the special sciences constituted a "single system," whether they were "separate and independent bodies of knowledge," and the characteristics of "the logical relations between them."[10]

Clearly, if the sciences were to be unified as a single system described by relatively few fundamental laws, the laws of science would have to be logically related to each other; there could be no gaps in the interconnected laws. Lovejoy discerned, however, two discontinuities that, if upheld, would debar the possibility of unification. In so far as "two or more comparatively specific laws" were "incapable of being deduced from any common, more general law," then those laws were "discontinuous with one another." Laws could also be discontinuous when "they refer to phenomena so different in kind that there is no possibility that the laws should conflict." In this case, Lovejoy used the example of a bit of matter becoming a part of a living organism and thus moving according to laws not applicable to the motion of inorganic matter. In summary, he wrote that "two laws may be discontinuous in the sense that one does not follow from, though it conforms to, the other; or in the sense that (the two relating to a single general kind of phenomenon) the one *neither* follows from nor conforms to the other."[11]

In tracing the history of science since the Renaissance, Lovejoy uncovered three broad periods in which concern for and the possibilities of unification varied widely. Modern science, he believed, began by emphasizing the unity of scientific law, though that emphasis was a hypothesis rather than the product of empirical study. There followed, in the eighteenth and nineteenth centuries, the development of specialization in the sciences and the emphasis on empirical research. The early twentieth century saw a return to the hope of a unified science. This new expectation, however, resulted from "the actual, detailed progress of the special sciences" and the limited unity achieved through the formulation of new laws. At the same time Lovejoy recognized the emergence of vigorous voices denying the possibility of the unity of science and proclaiming the primacy of scientific pluralism, that the world is so characterized by discontinuities any comprehensive unification is impossible. Without resolving the issue between unification and pluralism, he noted that if unification did take place, it was "necessarily a unification downward." That is, "thorough unification of science . . . would mean the 'reduction' of each of these sciences [biology, chemistry, etc.] to the one next below it in the series, until all were finally 'reduced' to mechanics." To reduce all phenomena to mechanics would, of course, eliminate the possibility of human consciousness and rational thought, and here Lovejoy objected.[12]

Such a reduction, if true, posed a fundamental challenge to Lovejoy's pluralism and faith in the existence of ideas and in the efficacy of human consciousness and rational thought. He stated, for example, that "the law that a rational being who fully understands the premises of a syllogism will always feel constrained to admit the conclusion, does not seem to bear any resemblance to any known or imaginable law of mechanics or chemistry, or to be capable of any conceivable deduction from such laws." To deny the possibility that all characteristically human activity could be reduced to the "laws of the motion of matter" was to deny the possibility of the ultimate unification of science. Such a denial introduced "a real discontinuity into the fabric of science."[15]

The efficacy of thought introduced a discontinuity into science at a relatively high level; Lovejoy also suggested that other discontinuities could be found lower in the scale of phenomena. Here he returned to the problems of evolution. He argued that just as the world evolved from the barren interaction of inorganic matter, through chemical reactions to biological processes, so the sciences could be arranged in an evolutionary order. For example, a "seraphic biologist" would have been unemployed until the development of biological phenomena because, until then, there could have been "no exemplifications of specifically biological laws." The evolutionary sequence suggested that "at certain points . . . matter begins to behave in essentially new ways, develops novel properties and methods of action which were in no true sense contained in or implied by its earlier characteristics and performances." If all scientific laws were reducible to some fundamental set of laws, then "the first morning of creation wrote what the last dawn of reckoning shall read." Though he did not explicitly oppose in this essay the reduction of science, Lovejoy's pluralistic and rationalist sympathies clearly implied support for an "especially radical form of evolution" —that "the very 'laws' or uniformities of action of the physical world themselves evolve, exhibit in the course of time discontinuous mutations and genuine, not-wholly-predictable innovations." Two years later, in correspondence with the Johns Hopkins biologist H. S. Jennings, he returned to these themes with a stronger presumption in favor of the discontinuities.[14] The problems of academic freedom and World War I soon intervened, and Lovejoy did not again take up his studies of evolution until the 1920s, when he attempted to provide a solid philosophical foundation for the idea of emergent evolution suggested by the discontinuities of science.

When Lovejoy addressed anew the philosophical implications of evolution he did so as an advocate of the discontinuities of evolution. The occasion was the second annual Howison Lecture at the University of California, which Lovejoy delivered in March 1924. He recalled that his former professor, George Holmes Howison, had insisted upon the evolutionary character of the world and had struggled with the problems of the continuity of the evolutionary sequence. Where Howison found a difficulty that could be resolved only in a form of idealism, his former student suggested that events in the preceding thirty years had done much to confirm the theory that the "evolutional process . . . is not, properly speaking, continuous, that it does indeed, in certain respects, show breaks or 'chasms,' that it exhibits the 'emergence' from time to time of absolute novelties, discontinuous variations in no way deducible from, or explicable by, any characters of the prior members of the series." [15]

Lovejoy characterized contemporary thinking on the problem as creative or emergent evolution and considered it "a revolt of the temporalistic, and usually realistic, philosophers against the same features of the older evolutionism." The emergent evolutionist declared that it was impossible to unite the conception of evolution with the idea that a complex reality could be deduced from a "very small number of relatively simple laws of the redistribution of a quantitatively invariable sum of matter and energy." Such a view coincided well with Lovejoy's own temporalistic realism, and he asserted that "the doctrine of emergent evolution is manifestly important if true; and there are, I think, good reasons for believing it true." [16]

He proceeded to his analysis of the problem in typical fashion, by discriminating among the possible meanings implicit in the concept "new." Emergence implied the appearance of something new, but "new" was an equivocal term. If the concept was to avoid the banality of every novelty being labeled emergent, the concept required more careful distinction. He thought that three types of novelty would provide a solid foundation for a theory of emergent evolution. "They would consist in the appearance at certain points in the history of some system of (a) *qualities* not previously found anywhere in that system; or (b) *types of objects or events* not previously existent therein, not mere combinations of anything previously existent, and characterized by new qualities; or (c) *laws*, i.e., modes of uniform action, not previously exemplified by any entities in the system." He pointed out that these types of emergence were not logically dependent on each other, and one might accept one instance and not the others. In this address Lovejoy returned to the problems he had considered in "The Unity of Science" and concentrated on "the hypothesis that laws of nature have themselves been evolved in the course of time, that they too, or some of them, are 'emergents.' " More specifically, he focused on those laws that concerned the motion of material things, including living things, for they raised "a peculiarly momentous and critical problem for any realistic philosophy." Particularly, what effect, if any, did the emergence of such new processes as "feeling, perception [and] thought" have upon already existing entities? Was "sentiency and rational thought" anything more than a "transitory surface-iridescence upon an underlying and abiding world?"[17]

Lovejoy set his first task as clarifying the issues involved in the emergence of new laws. He pointed out that laws are a product of human thought and thus do not emerge until there are humans to generalize about phenomena. He then defined more precisely what he meant in speaking of the emergence of novel laws "I mean the appearance of some correlation of events or method of action which cannot be correctly described by the generalizations that would have correctly described all the correlations of previous events or methods of action." He distinguished his ideas from C. S. Peirce's tychism, which held that at one phase in evolution phenomena conformed to no laws at all. Lovejoy assumed that motion had always occurred "in accordance with some sort of ascertainable laws." He believed, however, that the evolutionary process had seen certain "junctures" at which entities "begin to move in accordance with new laws that are logically discontinuous with those which their motions previously exemplified."[18]

Two or more laws were discontinuous when "neither can be deduced either from the other or from any more general law from which the other can also be deduced." Lovejoy distinguished four types of discontinuities between laws. First, "the instances of a given type of event . . . might all conform to laws expressible in terms of the same variables, but the *same* law might not hold good for all values of those variables." He suggested that if Newton's law of gravitation was found to be inapplicable when bodies were separated by more than a given distance, such an occurrence would be an example of the first discontinuity. Second, a discontinuity would be present if "different instances of the same generic type of event required for the correct formulation of the laws of their occurrence the introduction of different variables." Third, a discontinuity arises "whenever science finds itself obliged to invoke different 'forces' —in the traditional language of physics—in order to bring under the notion of law even a single event." Fourth, "the laws of two classes of events may be said to be discontinuous if the events are so different in nature that they cannot be described in the same generic terms." Here Lovejoy noted that the impact of light upon the retina exemplified the discontinuity; the laws that explained the physical properties of light are incapable of explaining what happens after the retina is stimulated.[19]

Just as there were four types of discontinuity, so Lovejoy postulated four types of "juncture" at which a discontinuity might conceivably occur: "(1) the mere completion of a period of time or of a number of repetitions of a process; (2) the attainment of a certain distance between the units of matter concerned; (3) the entrance of any such unit into some particular region of space (relative to a given set of coordinates)"; and (4) the creation of new entities that exhibited uniformities not deducible from the laws which had governed the behavior of the separate parts. Lovejoy considered the fourth juncture the most interesting, for "most (not all) of the phenomena which tend to indicate a discontinuity of the laws of the movement of matter are such as to suggest that these discontinuities hold between persisting integrations of matter differing in the number or configuration of their components." The classic example was the question of "whether there exist any material systems which are organic rather than atomic or mechanistic . . . in their mode of action."[20] This old philosophical problem had developed new relevance in the early twentieth century in the debates over vitalism in biology and behaviorism in psychology.

These discontinuities and junctures came together in the theory of emergent evolution. Lovejoy characterized emergent evolution as simply a form of scientific pluralism, the belief that the world is heterogenous and complex and continuously experiencing new differences and multiplicities. Emergent evolution held that some of these diversities and complexities had emerged in "a serial order in the history of certain material systems." The pluralism of the universe was not eternally established by some creative act, but was continually augmented by the appearance of new entities, new discontinuities in the long course of the evolutionary process. This lengthwise pluralism was more significant than crosswise pluralism, for an emergent theory asserted "a genuine progressiveness in the cosmical processes . . . as the pre-supposition of the otherwise incomprehensible diversification of her products and the ascending scale of *their* powers."[21] Here, some nine years before he delivered his lectures on the chain of being at Harvard, Lovejoy suggested the moral of that history. An evolutionary theory, a theory of becoming, could more accurately account for the gaps, discontinuities, and junctures of natural history than could an absolute and static chain of being.

Although Lovejoy believed that scientific pluralism and emergent evolutionism were the most accurate descriptions of the world, he recognized that these theories collided with the natural scientific bias toward simplicity. The scientist desired simplification through "the correlation of things already verified in experience [to] enable him to foretell things not previously verified in experience." The ultimate goal, of course, would be the reduction of all science to one science and to one fundamental law. Lovejoy doubted the possibility, for there was no assurance that the world was "indefinitely accommodating to our intellectual convenience in this matter." The presumption of ultimate simplicity had deleterious implications for science itself, and Lovejoy suspected that there was "something secretly suicidal for science in an unrestrained craving for the elimination of intrinsic diversity from nature." A totally simplified world might well become "so simplified as to be not worth living in—so simplified, indeed, as to imply the uselessness and even the impossibility of science itself."[22] It should be obvious that such a complete unification of the universe was foreign to Lovejoy's temperament and his entire philosophic enterprise.

Lovejoy concluded his address by considering whether one could come to a reasoned decision on the possibility of discontinuities in evolution and science. The fact that at a given date science had not resolved all discontinuities was not conclusive evidence that they were ultimately unbridgeable. After a brief look at discontinuities in the inorganic world and at the apparent chasm between the inorganic and organic worlds, Lovejoy turned to the operation of the laws of motion in "those material systems called human bodies." The best he could do in the first two inquiries was to suggest that if unification was not impossible, it had not yet been proven possible. He felt more comfortable

Arthur O. Lovejoy

in dealing with humans and more confident that here the laws of motion would exhibit a real discontinuity.[23]

Lovejoy conceded that, as with all matter, many of the actions of component parts of the human body could be reduced to the laws of motion. But, he asked, did that not leave "a residuum of the unique and irreducible in the behavior of these aggregates?" There was, Lovejoy thought, one postulate underlying all science and all civilization that suggested a discontinuity with the laws of motion. It was "the assumption that intelligence is capable of being a factor in the control of human action and thereby of man's physical environment." The essence of all intelligent or planned action was "adjustment to future situations, the determination of some present particular arrangement of bits of matter partly through its relation to some other particular arrangement of other bits of matter which does not yet exist." If intelligence was ever successfully applied to the control of any external events, then "*some movements of certain complexes of protons and electrons are, in part, functions of other movements which are to occur afterwards.*" The determination of some present action by future actions or consequences was totally foreign to the laws of chemistry and physics.[24]

To Lovejoy, such a conclusion clearly implied a dualism of mind and body, but other considerations were more pertinent to his inquiry in this case. The key question was whether there were at least "two radically distinct kinds of causal law exemplified in physical processes, i.e., in the movements of matter." The major difference concerned the appropriate variables: "one set of laws in the formulation of which the only variables which are admissible are prior or simultaneous physical events or situations, another set in which *possible or actual physical events subsequent to the occurrence of the phenomena to which the laws relate are among the variables in concomitance with which the laws declare such phenomena to happen.*" Though he could not say with assurance how future arrangements of matter could determine present movement of humans, such occurrences must be admitted if foresight was not to become "an absolutely useless redundancy in nature and human life."[25]

Forethought, Lovejoy believed, was one of the emergents that introduced a fundamental discontinuity into the fabric of the universe. Given the existence of forethought, there were only two possibilities that could account for the behavior of human beings. Either forethought had emerged in the evolutionary sequence as a "specific psychic process" capable of modifying "subsequent physical processes in the neuro-muscular system, and indirectly the motions of external things," or "certain late-evolved integrations of matter" considered future events and modified their actions without any psychic phenomena. Lovejoy clearly preferred the first alternative, but concluded that one or the other must be accepted. If future events were not among the conditions determining "present physical events," then "the practical intelligence has no function, and in all his experimenting and all his planning man walketh in vain show and disquieteth himself in vain." To reject both alternatives in the name of the unity of science was "to proclaim the futility of science."[26]

Two years after his address in Berkeley, Lovejoy returned to the theme of emergent evolution before another audience, the philosophers gathered at Harvard for the Sixth International Congress of Philosophy. He took up the problem of the meanings of "emergence" and its modes in a talk that was both briefer and more philosophical than the earlier one.[27] Most broadly, the address was an essay into the nature of the causal relation. More specifically, he proposed to inquire whether all things must be caused by some prior entity or activity or whether, in fact, totally new entities or activities had emerged that were discontinuous with any prior entity or activity.

The brevity of his speech forced Lovejoy to compress his argument, and he concentrated on supporting the possibility, indeed the probability, of existential emergence. He began by clarifying "emergence" and "emergent evolution" through definition, discrimination, and correlation of the various considerations. The key term, obviously, was "emergence." Loosely speaking, "emergence" signified "any augmentative or transmutative event, any process in which there appear effects that . . . fail to conform to the maxim that 'there cannot be in the consequent anything more than, or different in nature from, that which was in the antecedent.' "[28] To understand fully the philosophical implications of the theory of emergence, Lovejoy broke it into two separate notions—general emergence and specific emergence.

A theory of "general emergence" would reject the assumption that all attributes of all entities must be possessed by the first cause. Though many of the theological arguments had lost their force, some contemporary thinkers still held to a first-cause theory and Lovejoy was well aware of the implications of this problem. He remained, however, unconvinced that absolute or general emergence was impossible. The argument for a primal cause, in either its theological or philosophical form, was similar in at least some respects to the arguments he had rejected as early as 1909 in "The Obsolescence of the Eternal." First-cause theories all required the inclusion of temporal reality in some concept of the eternal and, as Lovejoy commented, "no ingenuity has ever succeeded in showing this to be other than a self-contradiction."[29]

Specific emergence denied the preformationist idea that natural events were merely "combinations or rearrangements of relatively simple, preëxistent entities, of which the total number or quantity remains invariant, and of each of which the qualities and laws of action remain the same through all the combinations into which it may enter." Under the theory of preformationism there was "nothing *substantive* in the consequent which was not in the antecedent" and presumably all sciences could be reduced to one and all laws to one, or very few, fundamental laws. Specific emergence, then, asserted that empirical evidence accessible to science had demonstrated that there were events which were not "mere rearrangements of preëxistent natural entities in accordance with laws identical for all arrangements of those entities." Lovejoy noted that some who deny general emergence accepted specific emergence, though he suggested that any example of specific emergence would seem to augment the sum total of things and imply general emergence.[30]

Lovejoy attacked the problem of emergence by inquiring what "types of emergent there conceivably *may* be." Emergent evolution was possible if the present phase of history contained one of five "features" lacking in any prior phase. First, an instance of change in some type of motion between two phases in which "the manner or conditions of occurrence" in the subsequent phase "could not be described in terms of, nor predicted from" laws which would have described all instances of that type of behavior in the first phase. This idea drew upon Lovejoy's earlier discussion of the emergence of laws. Second, "new qualities and, especially, classes of qualities (e.g., the so-called secondary qualities) attachable as adjectives to entities already present, though without those accidents" in a prior phase. Third, "particular entities *not* possessing all the essential attributes characteristic of those ' in a prior phase "and having distinctive types of attributes (not merely configurational) of their own." Fourth, "some type or types of event or process irreducibly different in kind" from any found in an earlier phase. Finally, "a greater quantity, or number of instances, not explicable by transfer from outside the system, of any one or more types of prime entity common to both phases." Lovejoy described the first type of emergence as "functional" and the last four as "existential." The emergence of laws is, of course, a function of our ability, or the ability of some other being, to formulate them. The other types of emergence could exist without dependence on a law-formulating being.[31]

After disposing of some logical objections to these types of emergence, Lovejoy turned to a particular hypothesis of existential emergence which he believed true. This hypothesis held that "both the third and fourth modes of emergence—i.e., emergence of new types of entities and of new kinds of event or process—have appeared in evolution, in the form, but only in the form, of what may be called 'trans-physical' emergence." In other words, existential emergence was embodied in the appearance in "certain complex and late-evolved integrations of living matter," such as humans, of "psychical events and psychical objects." Psychical events included "an act of awareness," and presumably, reasoning and desiring. "Sensa and images" whether delusive or veridical, were both included in psychical objects. Lovejoy believed that living organisms evolved from the first emergence of such trans-physical events and objects to the apparent culmination in "the cognitive and affective functions of the human organism."[32]

Lovejoy recognized that there were contemporary philosophers who severely criticized emergent theories, behaviorists and pan-psychists among them. There was no need for Lovejoy to reiterate his own criticism of behaviorism, but he noted his agreement with C. D. Broad's description of that theory as "silly." A full critique of pan-psychism was out of the question, but he doubted that the hypothesis could withstand sharp scrutiny. Having dismissed these critics, Lovejoy was left with the belief that there was "abundant reason to believe that in the history of our planet there have occurred genuine new births of time, a sheer increase

and diversification and enrichment of the sum of things here."
Though there was good reason to believe that emergence has
occurred, there were also "no empirical reasons for asserting—
and serious reasons for doubting—that a similar process is the
general rule throughout the physical universe." Man's contemporary knowledge about evolution did not justify the widely prevalent "cosmic meliorism," which often substituted for religion,
but neither did it justify a cosmic despair, for there lay

> before our terrestial race in its own little corner of the
> world a future which, if dim with uncertainties and beset
> with perils, is not necessarily devoid of possibilities im-
> measurably transcending all that the past has brought
> forth. There perhaps yet remain to mankind, we are told,
> some thousand million years; if it be so, before this long
> day ends it is possible that, besides all that man's labor-
> ing reason may achieve, there may yet emerge out of the
> latent generative potencies of matter, as there quite cer-
> tainly have emerged before [in] our strange planetary
> history, new and richer forms of being, such as no pre-
> science of ours could foresee and no contrivance of ours
> create.[33]

The most important and distinctive fact about the history of
evolution was the emergence of psychic phenomena and particularly the evolution of the sensate and thinking animal, man. The
evolution of animate objects represented an apparent discontinuity with the inanimate world, and the reasoning animal capable of intelligent foresight seemed to be another discontinuity.
Modern scientific studies, especially with primates, might question the location of Lovejoy's discontinuous junctures, but if the
discontinuity was still observable, even at a lower level of evolution, Lovejoy's arguments would, in their main thrust, still hold.
Lovejoy himself recognized the inevitability of a degree of im-
precision in locating such junctures. More important than the
question of when or where sentient, intelligent beings had developed was the fact that they had developed. One result was individuals who could formulate scientific laws of behavior. Another consequence was that ethics and morality became possible,
indeed necessary. Since man was an apparently unique creature,

any ethical or moral theory would have to be based on an understanding of human nature. In two works written after his retirement from Johns Hopkins, "Terminal and Adjectival Values," and *Reflections on Human Nature*, Lovejoy attempted to outline an ethical theory solidly grounded in the characteristics of human nature.

Lovejoy built his ethical theory, as we have seen, on two particular characteristics of man—he had desires and could reason. The key question was to determine the relationship between reason and desire in human nature and to use that relationship as the basis for an ethical theory. As he did so often, Lovejoy approached the problem historically by examining certain seventeenth- and eighteenth-century conceptions of human nature. Having understood these earlier developments, he could go on to develop his own ideas.[34]

These earlier theorists on human nature were significant because, Lovejoy believed, they had been particularly astute in their reflections on the relationship between human nature and ethics and scarcely less "penetrating" than twentieth-century thinkers, including Freud. Lovejoy noted, in his only written mention of the Viennese psychologist, that Freud's contemporary theories were "incomplete, deficient in scientific caution, and (in some of its details) extravagant"; Freud's value came in promoting inquiry into the problems and in "some highly original and suggestive conceptions." Freud aside, Lovejoy concentrated on a particular part of the history of ideas regarding human nature that had potentially important implications for any contemporary theory. The writers of the seventeenth and eighteenth centuries, like those of the twentieth, were "much occupied with the attempt to chart the *terra incognita* of the irrational and to extract its implications." These thinkers held that man was "in the main an irrational creature," that the key to understanding and controlling man lay in these nonrational forces.[35] Because they lived in an age when reason was valued highly, these thinkers confronted the problem of the relationship of reason and desire and, thus, suggested to Lovejoy ways in which his own problems might be resolved.

One objective of Lovejoy's historical survey was to counter the widely prevalent notion that during the eighteenth century, the Age of Enlightenment, philosophers had subscribed to a theory that man was innately good and capable of being guided by reason in all things. Lovejoy argued that historians like Carl Becker who held to such a view regarding the eighteenth century had committed "a radical historical error," and Lovejoy illustrated his point with the theories that lay behind the framing of the American Constitution. The framers of the Constitution, especially James Madison, had written that document while fully cognizant of the theories that held man was dominated by passions and desires which reason was powerless to contradict. Madison's political philosophy was fully in accord with this psychological theory, for it included

> two crucial propositions: (1) that the political opinions and activities of individuals will, with perhaps the rarest exceptions, always be determined by personal motives at variance with the general or "public" interest—in short, by bad motives; but (2) that, in framing a political constitution, you can construct a good whole out of bad parts, can make these conflicting private interests subservient to the public interest, simply by bringing all of them together upon a common political battleground where they will neutralize one another.

Madison's political theory embodied the principle of counterpoise, reliance upon "an essentially external, political, and quasi-mechanical device" to offset "the irrational and mutually antagonistic motivations of individuals." Lovejoy distinguished this political theory from a related theory which explained how non-rational forces within the individual could balance and account for moral behavior.[36]

In the remainder of his historical survey, Lovejoy concentrated on the second theory, on the passions characteristic of man and on how they motivated his behavior. He traced the ideas that developed in the seventeenth and eighteenth centuries concerning three "passions":

> (a) "approbativeness," the desire for approval or admiration of oneself, one's acts, and one's achievements on the part of one's fellows, and for the expression by them of this feeling—"the love of praise"; (b) "self-esteem,"

the propensity to or desire for a "good opinion" of one-self and one's qualities, acts, and achievements; and (c) "emulation," the craving for a belief in one's own superiority to others in one or another of all of these respects, and a desire for the recognition of this superiority by those with whom one associates, and for the express admission of it by them.

For a wide range of writers, theologians, philosophers, satirists, Catholics, Protestants, and freethinkers the concept of approbativeness was the "most powerful and persistent motive of men's outwardly observable behavior." Among the writers he cited, Pascal, Malebranche, Locke, Samuel Johnson, Edward Young, and Rousseau stand out, and, like Lovejoy, they did not always distinguish so clearly the separate elements of what they usually called approbativeness. These men agreed that approbativeness, or pride as they often called it, was of paramount importance, but they did not always agree that the possession of pride was good for man. But good or bad, it was an irrefutable fact of human nature.[37]

Lovejoy fully recognized that two contradictory conceptions of the value of pride ran through the thought of those centuries. On one side was the view that " 'pride' in the sense of self-esteem, individual or racial was admittedly a sin . . . and humility the most necessary of virtues." The religiously devout could obviously not value pride as either "an emotion or as a spring of action." More importantly, many thinkers of the period argued against this negative view and held, instead, that "all men are incapable of being actuated by any other motive in their social conduct, that the craving for admiration or applause is not only universal in the human species but also that it was ingeniously implanted in man by his Creator as a substitute for the Reason and Virtue which he does not possess, and is the sole subjective prompting of good conduct, and the motive of virtually all the modes of behavior necessary for the good order of society and the progress of mankind." Lovejoy traced this second view of pride through the writings of Edward Young, Alexander Pope, Bernard de Mandeville, Voltaire, Kant, and others. David Hume and Adam Smith were, however, the two most important theorists on this subject.[38]

Hume was an especially important philosopher for Lovejoy because he went further than any other in asserting that it was "a psychological impossibility for the Reason to influence volition." Hume had two goals in his inquiry into the relationship between reason and desire: " '*first*, that reason alone can never be a motive to any action of the will; and *secondly*, that it can never oppose passion in the direction of the will.' " The best that "a reasoned knowledge of the relations of cause and effect" could show, Lovejoy argued, was how to satisfy a desire "by adopting the means without which the end cannot be attained." Reason was restricted to judging whether propositions were true or false, while desires could be neither true nor false, and thus could never be subject to reason. Desire was the only motive to action and a particular desire could be "combatted or overcome, not by reason, but only by another desire." Though Lovejoy criticized Hume for some inconsistencies, he thought that, on the whole, the Scottish philosopher's account was correct.[39]

Lovejoy described Adam Smith's *Theory of Moral Sentiments* as the "most original and systematic eighteenth-century inquiry concerning the motivations of human behavior." Smith, like most of his contemporaries, believed in the "supreme potency of approbativeness." More than any other thinker, Smith considered both aspects of the problem of motivation. Not only did he consider the "craving for the esteem of others" to be one of the key passions of human nature, he also saw the reverse, "the fear of disapprobation and contempt," as equally important.[40] Both the positive and negative elements of approbativeness were central features of Lovejoy's own theory of human nature.

Hume and Smith were not only astute observers of human nature, they also based their ethical theories on those observations. A central problem for these eighteenth-century philosophers, as for Lovejoy, was to distinguish between and to analyze two types of phenomena that applied to morals: "moral judgments, and the motivation of moral choices or acts." Lovejoy noted that moral judgments were propositions, which meant that the crucial question was whether the proposition was true or false. Since judgments of truth or falsity, however, fall within the domain of reason, not desire, the problem, was how to connect these moral judgments, an ethics, with moral motives, desires, which were the effective springs of action.[41]

Hume's solution, Lovejoy argued, was to maintain that "the moral judgment itself is, at least in part, the *expression* of an affective, or emotional, state or attitude of the person making the judgment." A moral judgment was primarily, "if not exclusively, a proposition asserting, or rather disclosing, the existence in the subject of a certain state of feeling, which can eventuate in a desire." For Hume, and Smith, moral judgments were "exclusively judgments of approbation or disapprobation of persons or their motives, feelings, or purposes"; in other words, they were concerned with adjectival values not terminal values. Hume argued that we feel pleasure or pain in thinking about the idea of a thing; we can, for example, feel pleasure in considering an act of generosity or pain in thinking about an act of cruelty. In approving or disapproving these reactions to these ideas Hume thought he had described the moral judgment. To describe certain qualities or motives as admirable or vicious was to say that "the ideas of the qualities give rise in us to pleasant or unpleasant feelings, of varying degrees of intensity."[42]

Hume's "descriptive psychology of moral experience," as outlined by Lovejoy, raised a serious problem. Hume's theory was based on what Lovejoy called adjectival values, but were adjectival values "genuine, independent, and irreducible values?" Were the "*qualities* of the *inner states* of human beings from which their actions arise" valuable in themselves, or only as a means to some ulterior end? Hume's answer, with which Lovejoy agreed, was that if one assumed the existence of "aesthetic, noninstrumental values," then there was no a priori reason that "the subjective qualities and characters of human agents" should not have similar validity. There was good evidence, Lovejoy thought, that "we admire or despise *persons* as agents, not the ends which their acts accomplish, and we admire them because of what they *are* (or are believed by us to be)." An ethics which concentrated on the nature of the good, on terminal values, and ignored the "nature of goodness," adjectival values, would miss "the most conspicuous and distinctive characteristic of the moral judgments men actually make."[43]

Lovejoy saw two problems in Hume's theory. Hume had argued that there was a "universality and uniformity of the approbations and disapprobations of all men," but Lovejoy thought that the Scottish philosopher was "obviously in error." Lovejoy agreed that all men were motivated by feelings of approval and disapproval, but asserted that "the *kinds* of conduct approved or disapproved" had "varied immensely in the course of human history." Lovejoy also thought Hume weak on a "detailed analysis of the actual process of motivation." Hume, and to a greater extent Smith, approached this problem by considering the "individual as an approver or disapprover."[44] Since Smith developed this idea more fully, Lovejoy turned his attention to the *Theory of Moral Sentiments*.

Smith, more clearly than Hume, employed what Lovejoy called "the approbational triangle." That is, there were three "persons" involved in the "phenomenon of approval or disapproval: There is John, the spectator, who is approving or disapproving; there is James, the agent whose acts or motives are to be the subjects of John's approval or disapproval; but there is also Thomas, who is . . . the third person, on whom James is acting or who is affected by his acts." As developed by Smith, the approbational triangle embodied the idea that John has a tendency to sympathize with Thomas, to share Thomas's emotional reaction to James's actions. These sympathetic attitudes of John "constitute John's disapprovals, or approvals, of James." The important characteristic of this triangle for Lovejoy was that "deriving approbation or its opposite from sympathy with a third party or parties" gave Smith grounds for "concluding that approbational judgments are essentially disinterested and impersonal" and "that they are, in their broad features, uniform." Eventually the individual spectator generalizes his reactions; "it becomes habitual with him to approve certain *kinds* of acts and disapprove others, to feel pleasure or displeasure at the 'view' of them." The next step was for John, the spectator, to pass such judgments upon his own actions, a step Lovejoy thought inevitable. And the judgments John applies to himself as agent are the same he would apply to any agent. Smith, according to Lovejoy, had argued that when we judge an act or motive of our own, "we implicitly assert a claim that any disinterested observer . . . would *feel* the same way about that act or motive." For Lovejoy, this "created a sort of social situation inside the individual; he has as it were, admitted another man within his breast, to sit in judgment upon him, and with whom he engages in a sort of internal debate."[45]

Lovejoy considered this account to be "a correct description of an aspect of ordinary moral experience." The problem was that it did not explain "how John's judgments of himself *motivate his* action." He found two different answers in Hume and Smith. Hume suggested that the "association of pleasant or unpleasant feeling with the ideas of such acts becomes *fixed* in John's mind." Consequently, "when he thinks of himself as performing similar acts, he is pleased or displeased with himself." Hume's solution meant that the desire of self-esteem was derived directly from "the propensity to pass judgments of approbation, or the contrary, upon others."[46]

Smith's solution, which Lovejoy found more compelling, was to derive the desire of self-esteem from approbativeness. In passing judgments upon others we soon learn that they are doing likewise on our actions. As a result we develop a new "passion," we want to be approved and to avoid disapproval. This new desire, in Smith's terms, was the "love of praiseworthiness." As Lovejoy put it, "the wish to be the kind of person who is *entitled* to the approval of a genuinely competent and impartial spectator."[47]

The theories of Hume and Smith provided Lovejoy with the foundation on which he built his own ethical theory. With them, he shared the view that reason alone could never motivate any action and that desire is always stronger than reason. Given that fact of human nature, the problem for Lovejoy became one of determining the place of reason in moral behavior. He was certain reason had a central place in any valid ethical theory, for if reason alone could not motivate behavior, the chaotic, undisciplined passions could not make reasonable moral choices. The solution he worked out followed Hume and Smith in its reliance on the desire for approbation as the motivating force leaving reason the decision-maker in moral judgments.

Lovejoy's ethical theories also embodied ideas developed in a lifetime of reflection on philosophical problems. Though the "facts" of human nature as he understood them lay at the heart of his thinking on ethics, Lovejoy's earlier philosophizing placed certain constraints on any possible theory. Lovejoy had long fought a priori, static, and eternal systems and they were no more palatable in ethics than elsewhere. As he had argued with William James, in an open, pluralistic world in which real choices existed, rational thought was the only consistent basis for choice. Though reason could not motivate action, it could make judgments in the moral realm. Clearly then, Lovejoy's ethical ideas would have to embody an open moral world in flux in which one made rational moral judgments. Within these constraints the key problem became that of relating these moral judgments to the passions that motivate behavior.

Lovejoy recognized that the efficacy of reason was central to his ethical system. Reason, whether in recognizing the truth of a statement or the validity of an argument, could not alone determine choice; "there must at least be associated with it some emotive state or desire." Reason was impotent before desire: "reason neither is nor can produce a desire, it can not even tell us what we *should* desire—can not evaluate desires . . . a desire can be combatted or overcome not by reason, but only by another desire." If, then, reason can never determine choice and action, the primary problem for the ethical theorist "is to identify the *particular feelings or desires* which in fact lie behind the choices commonly called moral, and to investigate the precise manner of their connection with the processes of the understanding."[48]

The next step to a workable theory involved temporal considerations. Judgments could be divided into two classes: "*appraisals of the values of ends of action*, and *approbations or disapprobations of the actions or of the qualities of agents* (including oneself)." The first, which Lovejoy called terminal values, referred to desires for "states-of-things" that will be fulfilled at some future time; they will provide satisfaction "*when realized through* the act." Adjectival values, on the other hand, are embodied in the chooser at the moment of choice as he regards himself as "having or manifesting qualities *in* the act" which he can regard with satisfaction or at least without dissatisfaction. Lovejoy believed that what ordinarily determined choice was "the relative intensity of the pleasantness or unpleasantness attaching, *at the moment preceding choice*, to the *ideas* of the two or more possible courses of action—*not necessarily the anticipated pleasantness or unpleasantness of their future results*." Though "the stuff of moral experience consists largely in the interaction of the desire for adjectival values and the desires for particular terminal values," Lovejoy thought that the adjectival values had long been neglected by theorists, and he proposed to return them to their proper role.[49]

The self-consciousness of man was essential to Lovejoy's theories. In fact, he had titled an early essay on the subject "The Desires of the Self-Conscious." The existence of adjectival values differentiated the human from all other species. As a result of self-consciousness, "man is a habitually self-judging and self-appraising animal; and he has, as no one, surely, can deny, an intense desire to think well, or at least not to think ill, of himself and his qualities and acts and performances." Beyond our own self-consciousness, there was an "inexpugnable belief" in the existence of other beings who not only experience similar sensations, feelings, and desires, but are also no less capable of "recognizing adjectival values and of manifesting—or failing to manifest—these in their voluntary choices and actions." We do not exist in an isolated ethical world, but in a world of ethical actors whose actions and motivations are subject to our adjectival judgments and who, in turn, approve or disapprove of our own actions and motives.[50] In this public realm of moral valuation reason played a crucial part. If there was to be any consistency within a particular cultural context, similar moral propositions must always be judged similarly and only reason can judge so consistently.

One learns the approbative and disapprobative judgments we apply to our own behavior from applying those judgments to the behavior of others. We are forever judging our neighbors and consequently experiencing certain feelings, whether of approval, esteem, disapproval, or contempt. We soon, however, confront a situation in which we are required to pass judgment on some action or motive of our own. And here, we are "caught in a trap —or, to better the metaphor, [our] approvals or disapprovals of others act as a boomerang." It is difficult, though not impossible, "to approve in oneself what one condemns or despises in others." We can delude ourselves, as Lovejoy realized, but, still, there seemed to be "a simple logic of consistency" that controlled our judgments about our own acts. There was, in effect, a new form of the categorical imperative: "Judge yourself by the same standards that you apply in judging others." Since most valuations, or the rationalizations expressed, take place in the public realm our friends and family tend to enforce an elemental consistency. Lovejoy concluded that there was "a kind of implicit rationality in the actual operation of the desire for adjectival values: the primary rationality which requires that an accepted general proposition shall be recognized as valid for all particular instances which fall under it."[51]

Adjectival values occupied the central place in Lovejoy's thinking, but he also realized that they were intimately related to terminal values. The relationship derived from the public interplay of approbative desires between ourselves and others. We ultimately desire that actions which affect us shall be beneficial or at least not harmful. That is, of course, a terminal value. That terminal value can only be achieved through adjectival values. We approve or disapprove of certain actions, and since other individuals desire our approval of their acts, and fear disapproval, they are constrained from acting in a way that lessens our ultimate pleasure. In this fashion "generalized terminal values may become incorporated in adjectival values." Actions approved by us are not always related to terminal values; they may simply reflect the mores of the society in which we live. Why particular approbations are applied in any society is complex; that they are applied, Lovejoy believed, could not be denied.[52]

Though our actions could only be motivated by desires, reason had a critical role in the process of choice. "A self-conscious agent" continually makes judgments about the "adjectival values" of the actions of other men and of his own behavior. Our passions are "profoundly modified by the interplay of these two modes of valuation, and in this interplay 'reason' . . . can, and usually does, creep in." Reason creeps in because one who desires an adjectival value desires to assert that a particular kind of proposition applies to "an actual or potential mode of [his] action." Unlike desires, propositions can be tested by reason, they are either true or false. Our desire to be thought of as honest, or to avoid being called cowardly, is not subject to reason. But, we commonly use propositions in judging behavior. A judgment such as, "If I did do so-and-so I could not consider myself an honest man," is a proposition, which, like all propositions, "purports to be objectively valid." Lovejoy believed that if one could show an individual that his actions did not conform to some proposition regarding his behavior, through that reasoning one might induce him to modify his desire for certain adjectival values. Since adjectival valuations are expressed in propositions, Lovejoy assumed a reasonable consistency between the truth of a judgmental proposition and the associated desire. If someone is told that his behavior is inconsistent with honesty, his desire for approval, and his self-esteem, should influence his behavior. It is not the reasoning that modifies the behavior but the desire for a favorable adjectival value. The very nature of man as a desirer of adjectival values meant that "reason becomes capable of influencing his voluntary conduct and even of modifying—though not of creating—the desires of which his conduct . . . is the expression."[53]

This approbative system in which moral behavior rests upon a favorable adjective operated on three levels, the individual, the interplay between two or more individuals, and relations between nations. For the individual, there was "self-approbativeness, or the desire for self-esteem": the desire of man to think well of himself. Though self-esteem does not always conform to social values, as, for example, in the case of a martyr, the logic of consistency suggests that one's self-esteem is enhanced by the approbation of others. The approbational triangle in which we continually make judgments of other's actions and are, in turn, judged is evident in the course of normal social interaction. Finally, there was a collective form of self-esteem, what the English writer A. Clutton-Brock called "pooled self-esteem," a collective, national sense of superiority.[54] Whereas the feeling of superiority is often repressed by an individual in his relationships with others, partly because it is behavior that receives disapproval, pooled self-esteem frequently manifests itself "in the behavior of nations toward other nations." Patriotic behavior that asserts the superiority of one's nation receives widespread approval and is thus encouraged; this, Lovejoy felt, would be no bad thing if restricted to parades and national anthems. But all too often, this feeling of national superiority contributed to "the launching of an international war"; "pooled self-esteem is the trait in human nature which has played the greatest and most disastrous part in the history of mankind in the first half of the twentieth century."[55]

Pooled self-esteem and its unfortunate consequences presented Lovejoy with a real problem. It was as much a part of human nature as approbative and disapprobative desires, yet something seemed to have run amok. The approbative and disapprobative constraints that operated to keep individual self-esteem within bounds did not work on the collective level. Here approbation increased the feelings of superiority vis-à-vis other nations. Lovejoy searched Clutton-Brock's essay for an answer, but what he found—the hope that human nature could be purged of its propensity to self-esteem—was clearly unsatisfactory. Without self-esteem it would not be human nature. The best remedy Lovejoy himself could suggest was "to find ways of correcting the worst of the psychic diseases which arise from, and are made possible but not permanently inevitable by, the same constituents of man's make-up by which his happier and distinctively human functioning is made possible."[56] Human nature could not be remade, but there was the hope that through reason and adjectival values even so destructive a part of human nature might be brought under control.

Lovejoy's advocacy of emergent evolution and approbative ethics brought together several strands of his earlier thought. Emergent evolution offered an explanation of the unique character of human nature that could combat those who, like behaviorists and pan-psychists, tried to deny that individuality. If there had been junctures in the evolutionary past that introduced real discontinuities, then, in all probability, the self-conscious animal represented such a discontinuity. Emergent evolution was also important because it introduced time and change into a scientific explanation of the universe. Unlike the chain of being, which had been static and absolute, emergent evolution embodied the sense of becoming; creation was not completed, but was, instead, a process that began on the dawn of the first day and would continue to the last minute of the last day. Though Lovejoy spoke the language of science and philosophy, his ideas harked back to the more religious conceptions of George Holmes Howison. Howison, too, had seen evolution as a creative process, but one in which we were active partners with God in the evolutionary striving toward the ideal. Lovejoy was never so explicitly religious in his later writings, but he continued to believe that there was something "out there,"[57] and his view of evolution left open the question of the impetus, if any, behind the process.

The approbative ethics he articulated near the end of his career enabled Lovejoy to unite the rational and nonrational sides of man's nature. Early in his career he had agreed with William James that the universe was open and pluralistic, while he disagreed with James's espousal of the nonrational. Lovejoy had believed that reason was the only basis for choice in a pluralistic universe, but not until his essays in ethics did he elaborate on the relationship between the rational and nonrational. He could not deny that man was largely nonrational and that only desires motivated man's actions. However, man's desire for approbation and self-esteem was articulated by and mediated through moral propositions. And moral propositions, like all propositions, were subject to rational judgment. Reason can judge whether a moral proposition is true or false, valid or invalid. That judgment has the capability of influencing and possibly modifying our desire to be well thought of, and consequently, our behavior. We can, then, make rational choices in a pluralistic universe, choices that influence the way nonrational man thinks, feels, and acts. Lovejoy may not have entered James's "Celestial City," but he seems, at least, to have found a way across "the dark Jordan" that had previously barred his entrance.[58]

CHAPTER VIII

TO THE RAMPARTS AGAIN,

1930–1962

When Lovejoy gave the William James Lectures at Harvard in 1933 he was fifty-nine and at the height of his powers as a philosopher and historian. Three years previously he had published *The Revolt Against Dualism* and Harvard would publish *The Great Chain of Being* in 1936. Although these two books were capstones of his philosophical and historical inquiries, Lovejoy gave little thought to retiring from the scholarly arena. Moreover, as the world stumbled toward war during the thirties, Lovejoy renewed his participation in politics. Especially concerned about Hitler and Germany, he moved to mobilize public opinion on the increasingly urgent need to defend anew American freedom. The end of war in 1945 could not be marked by complacency, for by then there was another threat to freedom, communism. Official retirement from Johns Hopkins came in 1938, but as long as he was able Lovejoy never retired from his studies nor from his defense of reason and the freedom of ideas.

Because Lovejoy's major influence on scholarship and academics came outside the classroom in his writing and his crusade for academic freedom, it is easy to overlook the fact that he was professor of philosophy at Johns Hopkins from 1910 until 1938. For most of this period he was the only full professor in the department (George Boas, who began teaching at Johns Hopkins in 1921, was promoted to professor of the history of philosophy in 1933) and he taught almost all the graduate courses. He refused to teach undergraduates; that task fell to Boas and a succession of part-time instructors. Lovejoy never taught more than four hours per week and during the twenties and thirties was often away on leave. His seminars were usually organized around a particular theme in philosophy or the history of ideas. Among the topics he offered were romanticism, the implications of the theory of relativity, the appeal to nature, the idea of continuity, evolutionism, and the problem of perception.[1]

Lovejoy's classes were two hours long and met in the late afternoon, usually from four until six. This schedule accommodated his habit of working through the night and then rising late in the day. His classes were small, seldom more than half a dozen students. He arrived in class carrying his notes in a manila envelope and the books he wanted to cite. Lovejoy primarily lectured, and though he invited discussion, it was clear that he expected to have his say first. He "delighted" in confounding a commonly held and, as he thought, erroneous view of some issue and then proving his point. He was not an orator and his presentation was often involuted, but one former student recalled that if you thought along with Lovejoy you discovered how "rich" his presentation was.[2]

In spite of his growing reputation in philosophy and the history of ideas, Lovejoy had very few graduate students during his tenure at Johns Hopkins. George Boas once described him as a "very reluctant teacher" and Frank Trager recalled that during his time as a student in the late twenties and early thirties Lovejoy did little, if anything, to enroll students. The smallness of the department, only two full time members, Lovejoy and Boas, discouraged students. Lovejoy's reputation, though substantial among his colleagues, had apparently not diffused to many of the undergraduates thinking of graduate school. Most of his writing had been in philosophical and literary journals; not until 1930 did he publish his first book, *The Revolt Against Dualism*. Graduate students found the diversity of schools like Chicago, Columbia, and Harvard more attractive, especially since they were known for placing their students in jobs. Moreover, for some prospective students Baltimore seemed like an intellectual and cultural backwater when compared to New York or Boston. Finally, the larger schools could offer more in the way of financial support, making their other advantages seem even more attractive. The answer, then, to the question of why Lovejoy had so few students is probably that he did not want many, and, as a result, did little to build the kind of department that would attract them.[3]

A lack of interest in academic empire building contributed to the small size of the Johns Hopkins philosophy department, but a commitment to interdisciplinary work was probably as important in keeping the department small. He believed that only by ignoring the traditional boundaries that had fragmented scholarship could one pursue a consideration in all its ramifications or explore the implications of a philosophical position. At Johns Hopkins this conviction was best expressed through the History of Ideas Club, which he took the lead in establishing in 1923. The club was established "to bring together members of the University for the occasional presentation and discussion of papers and informal communications in the field of the 'history of ideas.' " The founders hoped that "the existence of such a society may perhaps promote a useful cross-fertilization of the work of the several historical and humanistic departments." Membership was open to the "Philosophical Faculty of the University, . . . graduate students recommended for membership by professors in their departments, [and] . . . other persons invited to membership by the Club." Although the club had a formal constitution, Lovejoy later recalled that "most of the provisions of the proposed constitution were, I think, soon forgotten—and so much the better, perhaps!"[4]

The club normally met six times a year, usually in the evening, to hear a thirty-five- to forty-minute paper, followed by discussion. Most of the papers were given by faculty members at the university or the medical school, although faculty from area colleges and scholars who happened to be in the area were frequent guests. When the speaker finished, Lovejoy, from his "accustomed seat at the speaker's right," usually began the questioning. The papers ranged widely over the history of Western thought, and so did the questions, which might come from a dozen or more specialists. The discussions, while stimulating, could often wander far afield; Boas once described them as something "that could only be found in a zoo."[5] The small size of Johns Hopkins and the high quality of its faculty in literature, languages, and classics fostered the interdisciplinary exchange Lovejoy advocated and made unnecessary a larger philosophy department.

The History of Ideas Club provided a forum in which these scholars could test the results of their research against the sharp scrutiny of their colleagues.

The club was one expression of Lovejoy's conviction that interdisciplinary contact and cooperation was an essential part of the method of the history of ideas. But, as with philosophy, effective and fruitful cooperation was an elusive goal. In the late twenties Lovejoy began a project to provide a documentary history of the ideas of primitivism from classical times to the twentieth century. By employing the talents of specialists in the many fields, Lovejoy hoped to provide documents and scholarly commentary on the development of "man's reflection upon the general course of his own history and upon the value of those achievements of his which have been most distinctive of that history." The only tangible result of this effort in cooperative history was the first volume of the *Documentary History of Primitivism*, which Lovejoy edited with George Boas. *Primitivism and Related Ideas in Antiquity* was designed "to exhibit the classical background—and thereby, in many cases, the probable classical sources—of the manifold expressions of primitivism, and also of ways of thinking opposed to it, in modern literature, early modern historiography, and modern social philosophy and ethics."[6]

Cooperation in this scholarly enterprise proved difficult to sustain. For one thing, working with Lovejoy was extremely demanding. George Boas recalled that it meant "you must be prepared to push along toward perfection until every possible source of information has been explored, every possible error has been anticipated and eliminated, and furthermore to submit your conclusions to one of the sharpest critics who has ever existed." With later periods, the task of ferreting out the myriad expressions of primitivism became immense. Frank Trager, who worked as a research assistant on the project for three years at fifty cents an hour, recalled that his instructions were to read everything printed in English in the seventeenth and eighteenth centuries in search of expressions of primitivism. Beyond these difficulties, even Lovejoy found that the close work required on the project could be confining. When the primitivism study threatened to interfere with his own research, even he had second thoughts. He felt committed to the second volume only because of the work Boas and Panos P. Morphopoulos had already done and because

Arthur O. Lovejoy

the project was supported, in part, by a grant from the American Council of Learned Societies. Referring to this support, he concluded that you should "never sell your soul to a foundation or learned society for a grant."[7] Although several collateral studies were completed, only the one documentary volume appeared under Lovejoy's editorship.

Twice during the thirties Lovejoy taught at Harvard, in 1932–33 and 1937–38. Although Lovejoy was one of the most distinguished Harvard-trained philosophers of his generation, the university kept him at arm's length for most of his career. Harvard's reluctance to appoint Lovejoy, even to a visiting position, can be traced to tensions within the department and to the hostility of President A. Lawrence Lowell. In 1914, Ralph Barton Perry, who had been in graduate school with Lovejoy and who was then chairman of the department, recommended that Lovejoy be appointed to a full professorship. Hugo Münsterberg was reluctant to have Lovejoy in the department but eventually acquiesced, and the department pushed for his appointment. Lowell, however, rejected Lovejoy because he had helped establish the AAUP. After Royce's death in 1916, the department again proposed Lovejoy, and Lowell again rejected him on the grounds that he was a " 'mischiefmaker.' " Lowell was blocking Lovejoy's appointment as a visiting professor as late as 1931.[8] Not until his appointment as the second William James Lecturer in 1932 did Lovejoy return to Harvard.

In addition to the lectures on the Great Chain of Being, which he gave in the spring of 1933, Lovejoy offered a seminar on the theory of meaning during the previous fall. Lovejoy's seminar, conducted in his usual style of lectures and some discussion, was unusual at Harvard, where most graduate seminars consisted of students reading papers. Even so, it was well attended, which Lovejoy found a bit disconcerting; "My seminary is much too large to conduct as such, in the absurdly brief time available; how they manage to deal here with large subjects in about twelve weeks, allowing time for lectures by the instructor, student reports, and general discussions, I can't imagine. At any rate, the art is beyond me, so my course will probably consist only of a mixture of the first and third." Much of the course dealt with the logical positivists, and he did to them what he had done to the pragmatists in "Thirteen Pragmatisms"—dissect their writings and point out the contradictions in them. Since many of the graduate students were positivists, Lovejoy's sharp criticism of that philosophy did not sit well. His reputation among the graduate students was not helped by his low speaking voice, his digressions within digressions, and the reading of long passages. Though some students found it stimulating, the positivists referred to him as "The Old Goat" and "The German Chancellor." If discussion was inhibited in his seminar, Lovejoy encouraged it outside the classroom. During the fall semester he opened his lodgings in Adams House every Sunday evening to the graduate students, though few took advantage of the opportunity.[9]

If the young positivists were unhappy about Lovejoy's attacks on logical positivism, the philosophers as a whole seem not to have shown much interest in his lectures on the Great Chain of Being. Lovejoy himself was aware that a historical topic might not be to the department's liking and that they might have preferred a subject "dealing more directly with contemporary issues." Few of the philosophy faculty attended the lectures, and the size of the audience dwindled as the series progressed. Faculty and students from the literature departments found more of value in Lovejoy's lectures than did the philosophers. Though Lovejoy had hoped to use the lectures to further the "desirable *rapprochement*" between philosophers and the "modern-literature people," the philosophers at Harvard were not prepared to respond.[10]

Lovejoy returned to Harvard as a visiting professor in 1937–38 He offered two courses, "Philosophical Anthropology" and a seminar on the concept of romanticism. The first was primarily an examination of psychophysical dualism and alternative theories. In the second, he attempted "to exhibit and clarify the historical and logical confusions associated with the past and present use of the term 'Romanticism' in historiography and philosophy." In the four years since his previous visit, many of the graduate students had become Marxists. Like the logical positivists, the Marxists had no use for Lovejoy's kind of philosophy. However, good students not committed to a particular school and those interested in the history of philosophy were attracted to Lovejoy's courses.[11]

Harvard apparently made an effort to convince Lovejoy to accept an appointment to the faculty following his second visit, but he declined. He would be sixty-five in October 1938 and he was attached to Baltimore. He once told Boas that he refused Harvard's offer because no one in Cambridge called him Arthur— not that anyone did in Baltimore. Another consideration in declining Harvard's offer was his retirement benefits from Johns Hopkins. His year at Harvard was Lovejoy's last as a teacher. He might well have continued to teach at Johns Hopkins, but his dislike of President Isaiah Bowman and his desire to write convinced him to retire. Lovejoy disagreed with many of Bowman's administrative decisions and was repelled by the president's anti-Semitism. Boas tried to mediate an agreement that would keep Lovejoy on the faculty, but he was unsuccessful. Though Lovejoy's teaching load had always been relatively light, retirement offered him even more time to write: "I should get better results in the study than in the classroom, although I do feel strongly that a teacher loses something by having no contact with students. . . . Classes take too much time and energy, however." He thus left the classroom in May 1938.[12]

Lovejoy's retirement from the classroom was not accompanied by a lessening of his scholarly activities. Numerous essays appeared in the late thirties and early forties, especially his reflections on the practice of the history of ideas. In 1939 he gave a series of lectures at Princeton University, which, after much revision, were published as *The Reason, The Understanding and Time*. Two years later he gave another course of lectures at Swarthmore College. They were eventually published as *Reflections on Human Nature*.

Late in the decade, scholars working in the history of ideas began to consider ways of increasing the opportunities for cooperation in the discipline and for expanding the influence of the study of ideas. In 1937, George Sarton, editor of *Isis*, a journal devoted to the history of science, proposed to Lovejoy that he conduct a "department" in the journal which could serve as "a clearing house for this new discipline." Lovejoy was receptive to the idea, but he wanted to consult with other members of the Committee on the History of Ideas of the American Council of Learned Societies before making any definite commitment. His major reservation was that literary historians did not read *Isis* "as much as they should," and they were the people he most wanted to reach.[13]

Arthur O. Lovejoy in 1940
*(Ferdinand Hamburger, Jr., Archives,
The Johns Hopkins University)*

Arthur O. Lovejoy

Shortly after this exchange, Philip P. Wiener, then teaching philosophy at the City College of New York, wrote Lovejoy proposing the formation of a journal devoted to the history of philosophy. Lovejoy responded enthusiastically, but suggested that the journal should be more broadly conceived as a journal of the history of ideas. After two years of work securing funding, appointing an editorial board, hiring a staff, finding a printer, and attending to all the myriad details involved in the production of a journal, the first issue of the *Journal of the History of Ideas* appeared early in 1940. Lovejoy was editor and Wiener served as managing editor. The board of editors included Crane Brinton, Morris R. Cohen, Perry Miller, Marjorie Nicolson, John Herman Randall, Jr., and Louis B. Wright. The journal began auspiciously with articles by Lovejoy on the history of ideas, Bertrand Russell on Byron, Louis B. Wright on the English Renaissance, and Robert R. Palmer on French nationalism, among others.[14] Although the journal provided a forum for scholars working in the history of ideas, Lovejoy did not use his position as editor to become a central arbiter for the discipline. To be sure, articles submitted to him were subjected to rigorous scrutiny and often returned with several pages of criticism and commentary. He was always helpful and supportive of younger scholars whose work he respected, but he was in no sense an academic entrepreneur in directing their careers or research.[15]

These efforts to establish the *Journal of the History of Ideas* and so bring the new discipline to a wider audience were accompanied by several essays in which Lovejoy set out the intellectual and methodological premises behind the history of ideas. Lovejoy's reflections on the history of ideas came out of a lifetime of work in the field; as he noted, "the general conceptions . . . grew out of rather than preceded most of the inquiries into special topics." The history of ideas was an important development in scholarship because it helped break down the "lines of division" between the "nominally distinct disciplines." Since ideas were "the most migratory things in the world," scholarship bound by traditional divisions would tend "at best, to produce serious lacunae in the study of the history of man, and at worst, sheer errors and distortions." Although boundaries were to be breached, philosophy retained its primacy in the study of ideas, for in "the history of philosophy is to be found the common seed-plot, the *locus* of initial manifestation in writing, of the greater number of the more fundamental and pervasive ideas." These were, of course, the "unit-ideas" that underlay the history of Western thought, and Lovejoy urged scholars to undertake "the study of the (so far as possible) total life-history of individual ideas." Such a task, however, was beyond the capabilities of any one scholar: "Trustworthy historical synthesis is not a one-man job." There was an "imperative need of more definite, responsible, organized collaboration between specialists . . . than has hitherto been customary." It was to foster "more cross-fertilization among the several fields of intellectual historiography" that the *Journal of the History of Ideas* was established.[16] Although he advocated greater cooperation and collaboration as a central feature of the discipline, nowhere in these essays did Lovejoy confront the practical difficulties that had marred even his own cooperative efforts.

Lovejoy's teaching, writing, and editing might well have kept him sufficiently busy, but as the political and international situation worsened during the thirties, he again became politically active. Although concerned about the effects of the depression, Lovejoy remained relatively aloof from the national debate over the role of the federal government in ending the economic crisis. He had no confidence in Herbert Hoover and was doubtful that Franklin D. Roosevelt could provide the leadership the country needed. Since he was in Boston during the 1932 election, he decided not to return to Baltimore to vote, as that relieved him of "the difficult necessity of choice between two incommensurable evils." He could not, however, ignore repeated violation of civil liberties, especially the lynching of Blacks on Maryland's Eastern Shore, and he helped establish the Maryland Civil Liberties Union in 1931 with Elizabeth Gilman, the daughter of Daniel Coit Gilman, the first president of Johns Hopkins.[17]

Sooner than most Americans, Lovejoy came to believe that Adolf Hitler and Nazi Germany posed a potential danger to the security of Europe and the United States. In a speech to the Baltimore branch of the American Jewish Conference on 14 November 1933 he took up the question, "*Is* Hitler a menace to world-peace?" Although Hitler had denied any aggressive intent and his denials were widely believed, Lovejoy remained skeptical, for the assertions of German pacifism ran counter to the whole National Socialist program. After comparing Hitler's statements in

1933 with his earlier writings, especially *Mein Kampf*, Lovejoy concluded that Hitler could not be trusted and that, in all probability, he was planning aggressive, military moves to achieve his oft-stated objectives. He warned that "Hitler *is* a menace to the peace of the world; but I hasten to add that he need be a serious menace only if the rest of the world believes his present protestations that he isn't." He advocated effective implementation of the Kellogg-Briand Pact and the Covenant of the League of Nations, but, above all, the United States and other governments must make it clearly known that "any aggression by any European power would be ruinous to the aggressor." Only if such steps were taken could peace be maintained "upon a secure foundation."[18]

As the German threat to world peace became more apparent and imminent late in the decade, Lovejoy took the lead in organizing activities in Baltimore to alert the citizens of Maryland to the dangers. After 1939 he directed his efforts to increasing United States aid to the Allies. He chaired several committees whose major purpose was to encourage the government to counter German and Japanese aggression. They included the Maryland Committee for Concerted Peace Efforts, the Maryland Committee for Non-Participation in Japanese Aggression, and the Maryland Chapter of the Committee to Defend America by Aiding the Allies. Lovejoy was intimately involved in the formation and operation of these organizations and in the dissemination of their views. George Boas recalled that, in leading the "Hopkins war-mongers," Lovejoy revealed the same enthusiasm, capacity for hard work, and demanding standards that marked his scholarly work.[19]

A prime function of these organizations was to get their views before a wide segment of the public and before Congress; this they accomplished through press releases, letters to the editor, and testimony before Congressional committees. Lovejoy was particularly outspoken in support of these committees' positions. Hitler's actions since 1933 had only confirmed his earlier fears, and he believed that aiding the Allies was the only reasonable policy: "It is plain to every intelligent person that the Allied armies and navies *are* America's first line of defense, and that, if it holds, the last line—our own forces—need never be engaged." Aiding the Allies might prevent American entry into the war and would, in any case, give us time to prepare our military forces. These organizations pushed for the repeal of the neutrality acts that hampered American aid to the victims of Nazi aggression and for Roosevelt's lend-lease program. They also lobbied for an embargo on the shipment of militarily useful materials to Japan. Testifying before the Maryland delegation in Congress in May 1939, Lovejoy summarized the position of these organizations. He argued that "a formidable coalition of autocratic governments' was attempting to suppress "all the liberties for which western mankind had struggled for more than 3 centuries." The "traditions, the principles, and the interests of the American people" demanded that United States foreign policy give no encouragement or aid to the dictatorial governments. Since the existing neutrality laws denied "to law-abiding and peace-desiring nations the opportunity to purchase in the United States means of defending their liberties, independence, and territorial integrity," those laws should be amended to allow the victims of aggression access to American resources. He concluded his address by appealing to Congress to take action so that America would not "contribute to the triumph of international lawlessness and violence and to the defeat of those political ideals, and those hopes of a freer, more secure, and more just ordering of human life for which this Republic, despite all its shortcomings, has always stood."[20]

After war was declared in December 1941 Lovejoy, as he had in World War I, volunteered his services in the effort to build American morale. However, unlike the earlier crusade against Germany, his pamphleteering during World War II was more moderate in tone and more clearly educative in nature. This more cautious and reasoned approach, which was also characteristic of the government's propaganda efforts, may well have reflected a desire to avoid the excesses of the earlier instance, while still aiding in the defense of the country.[21]

Part of Lovejoy's educational efforts were channelled through the Historical Service Board of the American Historical Association. The Historical Service Board directed the preparation of numerous pamphlets for the educational division of the War Department designed for orientation and education officers to use in conducting their programs among off-duty troops. Lovejoy prepared two pamphlets for the G.I. Roundtable Series: *What*

Shall Be Done About Germany After the War? and *Can We Prevent Future Wars?*

Neither pamphlet was designed to present an authoritative opinion on the subject. Rather, Lovejoy wrote them to provide background material for thought and discussion. In *What Shall Be Done About Germany After the War?* he examined the background of the ongoing conflict and the reasons behind the rise of Hitler. He suggested that German aggression in the thirties was not merely the result of an unfair peace after World War I, but was also the result of certain ideas in German culture for which Hitler became an effective propagandist. He wrote that six things were necessary to achieve a stable peace: Germany must be prevented from starting another war, the victims of German aggression must be given justice, the speedy economic recovery of Europe must be assured, the responsible Germans must be punished, Germany must be assisted to become a free and democratic country, and Germany must be converted into a "peaceful, law-abiding, and cooperative member of the community of nations." Under each of these headings he raised the pertinent considerations needing discussion. In his second pamphlet, *Can We Prevent Future Wars?* Lovejoy outlined the major proposals for future international organizations. He first discussed the means to prevent war that had clearly failed, such as promises and economic sanctions. There followed an examination of the various proposals for an international organization and enforcement of peace, and of the difficulties in getting any plan accepted. He recognized that the chief problem was "to choose the right plan —one that will be really effective and the *most* effective, for safeguarding peace between nations." However, he did not presume to suggest which plan should be adopted. Instead, he asked his readers to inquire of themselves whether they were willing to pay the costs involved in the adoption of one of those plans to prevent future wars.[22]

Even more than with the Historical Service Board, for which he simply wrote pamphlets, Lovejoy was deeply involved in the organization and operation of the Universities Committee on Post-War International Problems. Established in the fall of 1942 under the chairmanship of Ralph Barton Perry, this committee had two purposes:

1. To recognize, and to develop interest in, the grave international problems with which this nation and all nations will be faced in the post-war period, and which must be examined now if they are to receive a timely and intelligent solution.

2. To provide a form of organized activity by which members of the faculties of American institutions of higher education can discuss the major international problems, and by which their reasoned opinions, and agreements and disagreements, can be brought to the attention of the public and of responsible government officials.

The committee was supported by the Rockefeller Foundation and the New York Foundation and maintained offices in Boston, where it worked closely with the World Peace Foundation. At regular intervals the committee published a "Problem Analysis," which examined the issues involved in a particular post-war problem. These pamphlets were sent to Cooperating Groups on various college campuses where discussions were held and reports of the opinions expressed were returned to Boston. Summaries of the opinions of the nearly one hundred Cooperating Groups were then sent to various members of government and to the press. Lovejoy served as vice-chairman of the group and in that capacity oversaw the preparation of the "Problem Analyses," wrote several himself, and in June 1943 chaired a special conference, "The Enforcement of Peace by Military Sanctions."[23]

Lovejoy wrote at least two of the Problem Analyses. The first, in 1943, examined the proposal to give any permanent international organization the power "to employ military sanctions to repress aggression." He outlined the problems involved in a consideration of the end desired—the prevention of aggression—and the means proposed—an armed force at the disposal of an international organization. He thought there was little disagreement over the ends desired, but, as he pointed out, previous proposals to end aggression had failed, and the new plans had numerous obvious problems. On each issue Lovejoy set forth both the arguments in its favor and those detrimental to it. Similarly, in February 1945, he took up the question of the Dumbarton Oaks proposals for the enforcement of peace. Lovejoy wrote that the failure of the League of Nations made it imperative that the tentative proposals for an international organization "be subjected to searching and detailed scrutiny and wide public discussion." He examined in detail the proposals coming from the Dumbarton Oaks Conference and, where appropriate, compared them with the League of Nations. He asked whether this plan would be more effective than the League of Nations, and if certain weaknesses were evident, what could be done to remedy the deficiencies.[24] Lovejoy later supported the United Nations. While he had no illusions about the power of the U.N. to stop all future wars, he believed "*any* association of nations having as its purpose the maintenance of peace" was "better than none" and that the organization at least provided a "permanent political mechanism for regular consultation and collaboration" among the world powers.[25]

Unlike World War I when the passion of Lovejoy's involvement in the crusade against Germany weakened his dedication to "detached criticism" and "cool consideration" of the issues, his work with both the Historical Service Board and the Universities Committee encouraged reasoned and informed discussion of the problems of the post-war world. His pamphlets, designed for members of the armed forces in the first instance and for university faculties in the second, examined specific problems from a variety of perspectives. Although he assumed that positive steps would have to be taken to ensure future peace and that these steps would necessarily include an effective international organization, he did not attempt to dictate the form of such an organization. Instead, he pointed out the strengths and weaknesses of the various plans, raised questions that needed consideration, and, thus, encouraged his readers to form their own opinions after a rational consideration and discussion of all the issues. Lovejoy's work for these two organizations, more clearly than his activities in World War I, served that scholarly function of guiding the formation of public opinion through a rational investigation of the nation's problems.

The end of the war meant the end of the German and Japanese threat to freedom, but only made more apparent a danger that had been largely suppressed by the overwhelming necessity of defeating the fascist dictatorships. Notwithstanding the wartime alliance of the United States and the Soviet Union, Lovejoy had long suspected that the ultimate goals of communism were inimical to human freedom and especially to the freedom of thought.[26] Lovejoy had been disturbed by the Marxist sympathies of students during the thirties, though he accepted Marxism as an intellectual position. The danger of communist sympathies was that they tended to destroy one's intellectual rigor. He was particularly disturbed when a younger colleague at Johns Hopkins became an open Communist-party functionary. At this point Lovejoy's attitude changed "from tolerance to divorce."[27] Lovejoy's concerns regarding communism during and after the war focused on the question of whether communists should be granted the privilege of academic freedom in America's colleges and universities. There were some qualifications, but he repeatedly concluded that members of the Communist party should be excluded from faculties.

Lovejoy first addressed the question late in 1941, long before the heated controversies of the McCarthy era. "No teacher," he wrote, "should be dismissed for holding and expressing publicly the opinion that Communism is an economic system preferable to the existing one." Nor should such a teacher be forced to refrain from expressing his views in a classroom, so long as he did not proselytize and gave a fair hearing to alternative views. The difficulty lay in other areas concerning the program of organized Communist groups and faculty participation in them. Lovejoy thought that since the "working premise" of Communist groups was that the goal of social revolution justified any means to that end, including "constant underhand intrigues to gain quasi-political power within the institution" and "lying for the sake of the cause," participation in such groups was "a proper ground for dismissal, as inconsistent with decent professional ethics." Furthermore, since a "party Communist teacher . . . is one who has surrendered his 'academic freedom' " by being bound "to accept the opinions prescribed for them by a party-committee or dictator." Lovejoy "reluctantly" concluded that it was "inconsistent with academic freedom to appoint to a teaching position in an institution of higher education any person who is pledged to alter his professed conclusions, and his teaching, on scientific or philosophical questions, at the dictates of an external, non-scientific, political organization." He supposed "it to be the fact that all regular members of the Communist Party are so pledged," thus

Arthur O. Lovejoy

invalidating any claim they might have to the protection of academic freedom.[28]

After the war, the issue reappeared with the dismissal, in January 1949, of two professors at the University of Washington who were admitted members of the Communist party. The two men, Joseph Butterworth, a professor of English, and Herbert J. Phillips, a professor of philosophy, were dismissed after a public hearing before the university's Committee on Tenure and Academic Freedom. The issue was not whether they had been dismissed improperly under the standards of the AAUP, but whether membership in the Communist party rendered one unfit to be a member of a faculty at an American university.[29]

In an essay entitled "Communism *versus* Academic Freedom" Lovejoy considered the question, "Are there sufficient reasons for holding that adherents of the Communist Party should be excluded from the teaching bodies of schools and universities?" He began with his longstanding assumption that "the distinctive function of university teachers and of the institutions in which they serve" was to furnish "the results of the investigations of disinterested experts in the several provinces of thought and knowledge." Only "open-minded inquiry" and "frank and unhampered discussion, carried on by men trained in the disciplines to which they devote themselves" could fulfill society's need for reasoned expert advice. Academic freedom was thus vital to the university's purpose and "every new threat to it should encounter the determined resistance of the entire academic profession."[30]

Central to Lovejoy's conviction that members of the Communist party should be barred from university faculties was his belief in "the indispensability of academic freedom." He put his argument in the form of five theorems. First, "freedom of inquiry, of opinions, and of teaching in universities is a prerequisite, if the academic scholar is to perform the function proper to his profession." Second, the aim of the Communist party was to establish in the United States a political and economic system similar to that existing in the Soviet Union. Third, "that system does not permit freedom of inquiry, of opinion, and of teaching, either in or outside of universities." Fourth, a Communist-party member was "therefore engaged in a movement which has already extinguished academic freedom in many countries and would—if it were successful here—result in the abolition of such freedom

in American universities." Thus, no one who desired "to maintain academic freedom in America can consistently favor that
movement, or give indirect assistance to it by accepting as fit
members of the faculties of universities, persons who have volun-
tarily adhered to an organization one of whose aims is to abolish
academic freedom."[31]

Lovejoy realized that some might object that the exclusion
of Communist-party members from universities itself restricted
"freedom of opinion and of teaching." However, he argued that
"the conception of freedom is not one which implies the legitimacy and inevitability of its own suicide." There was one freedom which was inadmissible, "the freedom to destroy freedom."
Lovejoy reiterated his belief that there was a vast difference between the exclusion of committed Communists and proscriptions
on the study and discussion of Communist economic and political doctrines within the university. Appropriate departments had
an obligation to present the writings of Marx, Engels, and other
theorists and to discuss contemporary communism under the instruction of professors competent to deal with the subject with
"the cool and critical temper of the man of science." The freedom to discuss communism was one of the freedoms Lovejoy
wanted to protect when he urged the exclusion of those "allies of
the most threatening enemy of that freedom now existing in the
world."[32]

Lovejoy's argument for the exclusion of Communists was criticized two years later by Victor Lowe, professor of philosophy at
Johns Hopkins. Lowe argued that Lovejoy had made a logical
mistake in his rational argument against Communists. According
to Lowe, the argument ran: "Professor X is a Communist; a
Communist has no respect for freedom of inquiry or for objectivity in teaching . . . ; therefore X is not fit to be a professor."
Lowe claimed that the "logical subject" of the second premise
was the perfect Communist, while the person dismissed was Professor X. He characterized this reasoning as an instance of "vicious intellectualism," which he described as "the treating of a
name as an assurance that the fact named has to perfection all
the characteristics which the name's definition includes and con-
notes." Lowe urged that a Communist professor be considered
"*as an individual* and *as a professor*" [Lowe's emphasis] rather
than being assumed to be the perfect embodiment of the defini-

tion of a Communist. The argument then would run: Professor X is a Communist; as a Communist this particular professor has shown he has no respect for freedom of inquiry; therefore X is not fit to be a professor.[33]

Lovejoy did not see the article until it was in print, and his first reaction was to tell Victor Lowe that the argument about vicious intellectualism was "irrelevant, immaterial, and contrary to fact." In his published reply Lovejoy defended his logical arguments, though in private he attributed Lowe's piece "to an excess of good nature; he doesn't like to see even a C.P. member hurt if any excuse can be found for *not* doing anything that will hurt him." Lovejoy thought he stood on sound logical ground; he replied that in his initial article he had expressly avoided passing judgment on the University of Washington case because he could not determine, from the evidence available to him, the extent to which the dismissed men fit the description of a perfect Communist. The "real argument for exclusion," he wrote, contained no definitions and so avoided the problem of vicious intellectualism. The first proposition was a principle: "Freedom of inquiry and of teaching in his own field is essential to the proper exercise of the scholar's function." The second was a statement of fact: "The political . . . program of the Communist Party is the establishment of a one-party dictatorship which does not permit freedom of inquiry, of opinion, and of teaching either in or outside of universities." The third was also a statement of fact: "Any individual member of the Communist Party is therefore, *eo ipso* contributing . . . to the triumph of a worldwide organization" that has already destroyed academic freedom where it is in power and may be expected to do so wherever it comes to power in the future. Such individuals were, of course, unfit to be professors in an American university.[34]

After his exchange with Lowe, Lovejoy continued his campaign against Communists in the universities by working with Sidney Hook, George S. Counts, and Paul R. Hays on the Academic Freedom Committee of the American Committee for Cultural Freedom, an organization composed of liberals and other politically minded individuals who were particularly concerned about the Communist threat to America. The Academic Freedom Committee operated "on an *ad hoc* basis by phone" and drew up a statement concerning Communists and academic freedom as well as inquiring into the details of several cases involving alleged Communists. Sidney Hook recalled that Lovejoy was a "very sympathetic member" of the committee and was, in fact, "much more extreme in his position on the punitive action that should be taken with respect to teachers who violated the standards of professional ethics" by membership in organizations such as the Communist party. Although his health prevented Lovejoy from attending the meetings in New York, he supported fully the actions of the Academic Freedom Committee. That support is evident in a letter to the *New York Times* regarding academic freedom and signed by Lovejoy, Hook, Counts, and Hays. The letter reiterated positions that Lovejoy had long taken, beginning with the assumption that "academic freedom is an essential part of our system of liberty." In the early fifties "academic freedom everywhere in the world is under the implacable threat of Communist aggression," even in the United States as the result of "the Communist conspiracy in our own midst." They concluded that a "Communist teacher" had no place in the American university, because he had "transgressed the canons of academic responsibility" and had "engaged his intellect to servility." However, because the number of actual Communists and fellow travelers on the campuses was "exceedingly small," the committee felt that the problem should "be left in the hands of the colleges, and their faculties." Because Communists were such "a tiny fraction" of the profession, and because government interference threatened the whole principle of academic freedom, the committee concluded that there was "no justification for a Congressional committee to concern itself with the question." The college faculties were fully capable of keeping their own houses clean.[35]

Lovejoy's position with regard to Communists was consistent with both his long defense of academic freedom and his assumptions about the rational nature of man. His ideas about the social function of the university and the indispensability of academic freedom went back as far as the Ross Affair at Stanford in 1900–1901. So, too, Lovejoy had long argued that although nonrational factors affected man's thinking, man was basically a rational animal and it was reasonable to assume a certain consistency in his adherence to his professed beliefs. Thus, he thought it reasonable to assume that a member of the Communist party was working, however indirectly, for the establishment of a system inimical to the freedom of thought. One can question, as did Victor Lowe, whether man was as rational as Lovejoy believed, or whether Lovejoy mixed logical and moral arguments.[36] These considerations could easily weaken Lovejoy's position, but it is clear that his arguments for the exclusion of Communists were the result of longstanding and deeply felt convictions and assumptions, and not merely a response to the hysteria of the McCarthy era.

In February 1951 Lovejoy became the center of a controversy when Governor Theodore McKeldin appointed him to the University of Maryland Board of Regents. Though his appointment was welcomed by the *Baltimore Sun* for bringing "something new and vital" to the Board, Lovejoy ran into considerable opposition at his nomination hearing before a Senate committee. The committee pressed him on his belief in God, his views of President H. C. Byrd, and his stand on the state's loyalty-oath law. Some members of the committee were unhappy with his response to the question, "Do you believe in God?" Lovejoy replied by trying "to explain the word God has been used in the history of human thought in a great number of different, and often inconsistent senses, some of which I tried to explain, unsuccessfully, to the committee. I said that there is a sense of the term in which I believed—that is, that there is an intelligence in the universe superior to man's. I said I regarded this as a reasonable belief." Committee members were also concerned about his opinion of President Byrd, and Lovejoy had to admit that while he recognized "the abilities and resourcefulness of Dr. Byrd, there were certain of his policies of which I completely disapprove." The committee then inquired as to whether Lovejoy was a Communist, apparently because his belief in God was unorthodox, and he recounted his long opposition to communism. He noted that since he was not a member of any organization seeking to overthrow the government by force and "had no intention of becoming one," he had no objection to signing a statement to that effect. Apparently Lovejoy's answers, especially about God and Dr. Byrd, were unsatisfactory, for the committee rejected his nomination.[37]

President Byrd's opposition was the major factor in Lovejoy's rejection by the Senate committee. Byrd opposed the appointment because he had long dominated the Board of Regents and he knew that Lovejoy would bring a measure of independence to the board. Governor McKeldin, however, ensured Lovejoy's approval by the full Senate; he let it be known that if Lovejoy was not approved, he would appoint a Black, Dr. Martin D. Jenkins, president of Morgan State College, to the vacancy. Lovejoy may have been unpalatable, but Byrd and the Senate found the alternative worse and Lovejoy was confirmed. Once on the board, he took an active part in its proceedings, becoming, as one member later recalled, "our conscience." Lovejoy was especially concerned with improving the academic quality of the university. He opposed athletic scholarships and special subsidies for athletes. The emphasis, he felt, should be on scholarship, and athletes should not receive favored treatment simply because they were athletes. He was especially proud of his successful efforts to establish a classics department at Maryland. Lovejoy resigned from the Board of Regents in September 1955 because, as he wrote Governor McKeldin, "some physical—and, perhaps, other —infirmities naturally incident to the age I have now reached make it seem not only expedient but obligatory to do so."[38]

After his retirement from the Maryland Board of Regents Lovejoy continued to work at his writing as much as his health would permit. With the assistance of Bernard Matthews, a graduate student in philosophy at Johns Hopkins, he prepared for publication both *The Reason, The Understanding and Time* and *Reflections on Human Nature*. He also revised several of the essays that appeared in *The Forerunners of Darwin*. These projects were aided in 1957 by a special $10,000 grant awarded by the American Council of Learned Societies to help support the work of senior scholars. Throughout much of the decade he continued to read and criticize manuscripts for the *Journal of the History of Ideas*. Slowly, however, the problems of age, especially his declining sight, limited his working hours.[39]

Lovejoy was at least partially resigned to the toll that age exacted. He admitted that age "has some agreeable privileges, and may have some real advantages, though they don't always offset the losses." He wrote that "thoughts come more slowly and the hours of work *per diem* are fewer—though the results, perhaps, are no worse than before." "This limitation of *pace*," he noted, "has just to be accepted."[40] Even as late as 1961 he

Arthur O. Lovejoy

Arthur O. Lovejoy in 1951
*(Photograph by Robert M. Mottar: Ferdinand Hamburger, Jr., Archives,
The Johns Hopkins University)*

continued to work on his projects. The following year, however, Lovejoy's health failed and he died at his apartment in Baltimore on 30 December 1962.

Near the end of his life Lovejoy set forth some reflections on his career. He thought that "a man's personal character is often best revealed by his admirations, his heroes, the historic figures whom he would wish to be like." He found the "most congenial personality in David Hume, and even fancies, or would fancy, that in the external circumstances of his life, in the natural disposition of his mind, and in his dominant intellectual interest, he —*si licet parvos componere magnis*! [if lesser men may be compared with the great]—he is of the same *species* of philosopher as Hume." No man in modern America could share the specific opinions of an eighteenth-century Englishman, but, Lovejoy wrote,

> the present writer has in fact, as a philosopher, spent a good deal of his time in the latter age and has liked its climate, and is a respectable bachelor scholar of the lower-middle economic class, has never engaged in trade or commerce, and not eager for more income than will enable him to philosophize in comfort, security and without mundane distractions, chiefly interested in analyzing the meaning of the more abstract general concepts, and the psychology of human volition—in particular in its relation to ethics—*nullius adictus jurare in verba magistri,* [to swear that nothing has been added to the words of the master], not concerned to edify his readers, highly unorthodox in religious matters, not innocent of ambition for reputation among his fellow-workers in his own or kindred fields of inquiry, but not eager for the applause of the *profanum vulgus.* Most of all he is sensible of the danger of accepting without searching criticism premises or methods of reasoning learned in his immature years, and, of avoiding final conclusions on any controverted philosophical problem until he has, so far as possible, methodically collated, correlated and appraised all "considerations" really pertinent to that problem which have

been presented by previous philosophers or schools of philosophy.

Lovejoy thought that all these "substantive conclusions and methodological premises" except the last had been accepted by Hume, and, thus, if he were "compelled by law to label his own philosophical beliefs with the name of some one great thinker of the past, he would, with least reluctance (though not without reluctance) let it be called Humian."[41]

Lovejoy's self-portrait was a remarkably accurate description of his long career, but his self-characterization excluded any mention of the basic theme that underlay these characteristics. The fundamental purpose of his distinguished career was his quest for an intelligible account of the universe. The eighteenth century had possessed a rational account of the world which, even though it was beginning to reveal its inconsistencies, still successfully ordered much of man's experience. The Romantic movement brought those inconsistencies to the fore and in so doing overturned the wholly rational account of the universe. In the succeeding century the principles of diversity, change, and time came to dominate man's thought. They did not bring with them, however, readily apparent principles of intelligibility, and without these there remained the real possibility, and real danger for men like Lovejoy, that chaos would triumph over order. Lovejoy confronted this potentially chaotic world when he began his career, and his search for intelligibility in this diverse world shaped his religious views, his philosophical and ethical reflections, his historical studies, and his social and political activism.

From the late 1890s when he began to realize the inadequacy of traditional Christianity and Absolute Idealism, Lovejoy sought a means of making his experienced world comprehensible. He faced the necessity of reconciling two fundamental and antithetic conceptions. On the one hand, he was convinced that the real world was a world of diversity, flux, and temporal becoming. On the other hand, the only certainties were the self-sufficient principles of reason. Lovejoy firmly believed that, paradoxical as it might seem, only by making reason the sole guiding principle and basis of choice in a pluralistic universe of change could that world be made intelligible. The major portion of his career was the attempt to work out the implications of this conception of the universe. In philosophy, he argued that only epistemological dualism was consistent with the assumed existence of ideas and the reality of the diverse world. Only in this fashion could man know anything and thus have any hope of making sense of his experiences. In the history of ideas, Lovejoy traced the antecedents of his own intellectual problems and, in uncovering the history of man's centuries-long quest for intelligibility, vindicated his belief that ideas did exist and that they did make a difference. Finally, by working to establish and defend a social and political environment in which ideas could freely exist, he hoped to ensure that man continued to be free to seek the fundamental bases for understanding his world.

Throughout his long career Lovejoy received the recognition due one of the major philosophers and historians of his generation. He served as president of both the Western Philosophy Association and the APA, as well as the AAUP. He was the second Carus Lecturer of the APA, following only John Dewey, and gave the second set of William James Lectures at Harvard, again following Dewey. From 1900 to 1950 he was a powerful critical voice in philosophy and the prime exponent of a new kind of intellectual history. *The Revolt Against Dualism* remains a powerful defense of epistemological dualism and *The Great Chain of Being* is perhaps the best example of the history of ideas. Yet, almost twenty years after his death, Lovejoy's work is little noticed by scholars. This is not to suggest that Lovejoy has had no influence on subsequent thinkers, but it does raise the question of why his work seems to be of only limited importance in current philosophical and historical debate. The answer, I think, lies in the character of his philosophical and historical writing, which was a response to the issues of his time—issues that scholars no longer find compelling.

Lovejoy's philosophy was the product of the particular problem he confronted early in his career and was tied very closely to the general philosophical questions of the first third of the century. Questions of idealism, realism, pluralism, temporalism, and dualism or monism no longer provide the wellsprings of philosophical discussion. In part, that may be the result of Lovejoy's own work. As the culmination of a long philosophical debate, *The Revolt Against Dualism* dealt with epistemological questions with a finality that made future discussion along those lines seem largely repetitious. Even as early as the 1930s, philosophical discussion began to flow in other channels in response to logical positivism and the questions a new generation of philosophers was asking. Should philosophic debate return to the questions Lovejoy considered, his work will have an immediacy it now lacks. Furthermore, most of Lovejoy's philosophical writing was critical of idealists, pragmatists, the new realists, and the epistemological monists. Such criticism is a vital part of any philosophical debate, but it has also a certain ephemeral quality. What is often remembered is not the criticism, regardless of how acute, but rather the original philosophy, whether of Josiah Royce, William James, or John Dewey. The shifting winds of philosophical debate have brought new questions and problems to the fore and reduced Lovejoy's work to a largely historical interest. Still, his legacy of reasoned and rational argument, vigorous criticism, the possibilities of philosophical debate, and faith in man's reason remain valuable regardless of the course of philosophy.

As with philosophy, intellectual history has moved beyond the concerns of the twenties and thirties when the history of ideas opened new doors to scholarly inquiry. The history of ideas lent historical support to Lovejoy's philosophical views while providing a useful methodology for investigating the role of ideas in history. The years since the publication of *The Great Chain of Being* have seen increasing interest in intellectual history and a broadening of its field of inquiry: intellectual history is no longer simply the history of philosophy or the history of ideas, but embraces semantic and linguistic studies, the examination of national myths and symbols, the social role of intellectuals, and intellectual biography. For tracing the influence and diffusion of an idea, the history of ideas remains valuable, but in confronting problems that Lovejoy never faced, the intellectual historian must often turn to other methodologies. Nonetheless, all intellectual historians must, in some measure, share Lovejoy's conviction that men have ideas, that they think and reason, and that their thoughts form an important part of human history.

Since Lovejoy believed strongly in combining scholarship with activism, it should come as no surprise to find that he is often cited today as the author of the principles of academic freedom in the United States. His statements on academic freedom for the AAUP and in the *Encyclopedia of the Social Sciences* provided the basis for most subsequent discussion of the problem.[42] Just as Lovejoy felt constrained to make certain compromises in those principles during World War I and in the 1950s, so scholars today, confronting new problems, have had to work out ways to apply the concept in novel situations. And, perhaps more clearly than Lovejoy, we can see the dangers inherent in too great a faith in government and in dubious arguments for the exclusion of certain groups or individuals from the protection of academic freedom.

That scholarship in philosophy or history has moved on to other questions should not lessen the value of Lovejoy's achievement. After all, in a world of change and diversity, a static, unchanging conception of the universe is doomed to failure, whether that conception is expressed as the great chain of being or as the principles of reason. For many twentieth-century thinkers the principles of reason upon which Lovejoy relied were simply incapable of ordering and making intelligible the increasingly complex world. New ideas about man's nonrational drives, relativity, and probability spoke more directly and convincingly to the problems man has faced in the last eighty years. Still, there can be no denying that in the concepts of reason, temporalism, and pluralism, Lovejoy found the intelligibility he sought and, in the process, left to his successors a legacy of reasoned thought, rigorous inquiry, and spirited defense of the freedom of ideas.

NOTES

Most of the manuscript citations in the notes are to the Arthur O. Lovejoy Papers, Special Collections, Eisenhower Library, The Johns Hopkins University. If there is no identification of a manuscript source, it is from the Lovejoy Papers; in several instances, to clarify the source of a manuscript the Lovejoy Papers have been specifically identified. In all citations of correspondence, Arthur O. Lovejoy is cited as AOL and his father, Wallace W. Lovejoy, as WWL. A list of manuscript sources, with the shortened form used in the notes, follows.

AAUP Archives: Archives of the American Association of University Professors, Washington, D.C.
Harvard University Archives, Cambridge, Mass.
Havens Papers: Raymond Dexter Havens Papers, Special Collections, Eisenhower Library, The Johns Hopkins University, Baltimore, Md.
Historical Library, Young Men's Christian Association, New York, N.Y.
Howison Papers: George Holmes Howison Papers, University Archives, Bancroft Library, University of California, Berkeley, Cal.
James Papers: William James Papers, Houghton Library, Harvard University, Cambridge, Mass.
Johns Hopkins Archives: The Ferdinand Hamburger, Jr., Archives, The Johns Hopkins University, Baltimore, Md.
Jordan Papers: David Starr Jordan Papers, Stanford University Archives, Stanford, Cal.
Lovejoy Papers: Arthur O. Lovejoy Papers, Special Collections, Eisenhower Library, The Johns Hopkins University, Baltimore, Md.
Philosophy Department Files, Harvard University Archives: Files of the Department of Philosophy, Harvard University, Cambridge, Mass.
Registrar, University of California, Berkeley, Cal.
Sarton Papers: George Sarton Papers, Houghton Library, Harvard University, Cambridge, Mass.
University of California, Berkeley, Archives: Bancroft Library, University of California, Berkeley, Cal.
University of Maryland, Board of Regents, Baltimore, Md.

University of Missouri Archives, Columbia, Mo.
Washington University Archives, St. Louis, Mo.

PREFACE

1. Arthur O. Lovejoy, "William James as Philosopher," pp. 88–89; Allan Janik and Stephen Toulmin, *Wittgenstein's Vienna*, pp. 13–32.
2. George Boas, "A. O. Lovejoy: Reason-in-Action," pp. 536–37.

CHAPTER I
THE MAKING OF A PHILOSOPHER, 1873–1899

1. AOL to Wallace W. and Emmeline D. Lovejoy, 21 June 1903; AOL to Emmeline D. Lovejoy, 26 June 1903.
2. Clarence Earle Lovejoy, *The Lovejoy Genealogy with Biographies and History*, pp. 51–55, 188, 254; Philip J. Greven, Jr., *Four Generations*, pp. 92–95; WWL to AOL, 17 June 1895, 11 October 1920.
3. WWL to AOL, [October 1896], 11 October 1920, 13 January 1921.
4. Wallace W. Lovejoy, "*In Memoriam Matris Suae*, Sara Agnes Oncken. Written for my son, Arthur Schauffler Lovejoy," ca. 1875–77, unpaginated.
5. W. W. Lovejoy, "*In Memoriam*"; WWL to AOL, 7 April [1912].
6. W. W. Lovejoy, "*In Memoriam*."
7. Ibid.
8. Ibid; WWL to AOL, 10 October 1892, 11 October 1920. Arthur Schauffler Lovejoy was apparently named after his father's brother Arthur and his mother's recently widowed sister, Margaret Oncken Schauffler. However, sometime before 1890, Arthur Lovejoy took as his middle name his mother's maiden name, Oncken. William Oncken to AOL, 19 December 1890.
9. W. W. Lovejoy, "*In Memoriam*"; WWL to AOL, 11 October 1920.
10. W. W. Lovejoy, "*In Memoriam*"; Sara Oncken Lovejoy to WWL, 31 December 1873, 1 January 1874.
11. W. W. Lovejoy, "*In Memoriam*"; WWL to AOL, [October 1896]. According to a medical formulary of the period, fluid extract of gelsemium was an arterial sedative that lowered the pulse and depressed the nervous system. It was normally used in early stages of acute "inflamatory affections" and for some "spasmodic diseases," such as whooping cough and spasmodic asthma. The normal dose for an adult was two to five minims, or drops. Laurence Johnson, *A Medical Formulary*, p. 190.
12. W. W. Lovejoy, "*In Memoriam*"; WWL to AOL, 11 October 1920. Johnson, *A Medical Formulary*, does not give the fatal dose, but the instructions contain this warning: "In overdoses it is a very dangerous poison." Johnson, *A Medical Formulary*, p. 190.
13. W. W. Lovejoy, "*In Memoriam*."
14. WWL to AOL, [October 1896], 10 October [1917], 11 October 1920.
15. WWL to AOL, 11 October 1920.
16. WWL to AOL, 10 October [1917], 11 October 1920.
17. WWL to AOL, 17 June 1895, 10 October [1917]; AOL to Emmeline D. Lovejoy, 17 December [n.d.].
18. AOL to Wallace W. and Emmeline D. Lovejoy, 21 June 1903; AOL to

Emmeline D. Lovejoy, 26 June 1903; WWL to Emmeline D. Lovejoy, 8 August 1884.

19. WWL to Emmeline D. Lovejoy, 8 August 1884; WWL to AOL, 10 October [1917]; AOL to Emmeline D. Lovejoy, 25 June 1907; George Boas, interview, Baltimore, Md., 13 September 1974; Lewis S. Feuer, interview, Charlottesville, Va., 7 June 1979.

20. ACL to Emmeline D. Lovejoy, 17 December [n.d.]; WWL to AOL, 10 October [1917]; George Boas, interview, 13 September 1974.

21. Arthur O. Lovejoy, Application for Admission, The University of California, 1 September 1891; Arthur O. Lovejoy, Transcript of Record, University of California, Berkeley; these items were provided by the Registrar of the University of California, Berkeley. Peter Thomas Conmy, "History of the Entrance Requirements of the Liberal Arts Colleges of the University of California," pp. 275, 285.

During the nineties Wallace Lovejoy taught Old Testament languages and literature at the Pacific Theological Seminary in Berkeley. Clarence E. Lovejoy, Lovejoy Genealogy, p. 254.

22. William Warren Ferrier, Origin and Development of the University of California, pp. 279–393.

23. Robert Sibley, ed., The Golden Book of California, unpaginated.

24. Arthur O. Lovejoy, Transcript of Record, The University of California, Berkeley.

25. Peter A. Bertocci, "George Holmes Howison," Encyclopedia of Philosophy, 4:66; John W. Buckham and George M. Stratton, George Holmes Howison, Philosopher and Teacher, pp. 1, 12–13; Elizabeth Flower and Murray G. Murphey, A History of Philosophy in America, 2:486–90.

26. Buckham and Stratton, George Holmes Howison, pp. 1, 5–6, 12–14.

27. AOL to WWL, 30 March 1897; WWL to AOL, 24 December 1896, 28 December 1896; Arthur O. Lovejoy, "A Temporalistic Realism," in Contemporary American Philosophy, 2:85–86.

28. AOL to Jesse D. Burks, 5 October 1894, University of California, Berkeley, Archives; Buckham and Stratton, George Holmes Howison, pp. 78–79.

29. Arthur O. Lovejoy, "James Burnett, Lord Monboddo," pp. 68–79. The article should be compared with Arthur O. Lovejoy "Monboddo and Rousseau," in Essays in the History of Ideas, pp. 38–61. The later article covers much the same ground, but in greater detail.

30. Arthur O. Lovejoy, "Rain at Dusk," p. 23. See also a poem dedicated to his father, 9 May 1920, in Wallace W. Lovejoy Date Book 1918; and AOL to Raymond Dexter Havens, 22 July 1950, Havens Papers.

31. AOL to WWL, 2 June [1895]; Robert A. Woods and Albert J. Kennedy, Handbook of Settlements, pp. 14–15.

32. WWL to AOL, 17 June 1895; AOL to WWL, 27 June and 1 July 1895.

33. Allen F. Davis, Spearheads for Reform, pp. 27–29; Laurence R. Vesey, The Emergence of the American University, pp. 220, 280.

34. AOL to WWL, 30 March 1897, 2 June [1895].

35. AOL to WWL, 27 June and 1 July 1895.

36. WWL to AOL, 22 May 1895, 17 June 1895.

37. WWL to AOL, 22 May 1895; AOL to WWL, 2 June [1895], 27 June and 1 July 1895; WWL to AOL, 5 July 1895.

38. George Herbert Palmer and Ralph Barton Perry, "Philosophy, 1870–1929," pp. 3–32; Rollo Walter Brown, Harvard Yard in the Golden Age,

pp. 41–85; Bruce Kuklick, *The Rise of American Philosophy*, pp. 233–58; Vesey, *American University*, pp. 227–33; and Arthur O. Lovejoy, Speech to Department of Philosophy and Psychology, Harvard University, 22 October [1932].

39. AOL to WWL, 7 January 1896, 19 May 1896, and 8 November 1896.

40. AOL to WWL, 8 November 1896.

41. Arthur O. Lovejoy, "William James as Philosopher," pp. 110–11.

42. List of courses taken by Lovejoy, supplied by Harvard University Archives; *Harvard University Catalogue, 1897–98*, pp. 347–49; AOL to [WWL], [October or November 1897].

43. AOL to [WWL], [October or November 1897]; [Arthur O. Lovejoy], "Romantic Philosophy," p. 140; Lovejoy, Speech to Department of Philosophy and Psychology, Harvard, 22 October [1932].

44. List of courses, supplied by Harvard University Archives; *Harvard University Catalogue, 1896–97*, pp. 73, 75, 99; AOL to WWL, 8 October and 10 October 1896, [October or November 1896].

45. AOL to WWL, 3 April 1896.

46. AOL to WWL, [October or November 1897], [November 1897], 8 November 1896; "Minutes of the Graduate Philosophical Society of Harvard," Lovejoy Papers; "The Graduate Club of Harvard University," Harvard University Archives.

47. AOL to WWL, 8 November 1896; *The Prospect Union, 1891–1899*, pp. 15–18; Thomas H. Fay, "The Prospect Union," Harvard University Archives.

48. *Thirty-Fifth Annual Report of the Boston Children's Aid Society, 1899*, pp. 5, 27–28; "A. O. Lovejoy H[ome] L[ibrary] Group 32," notebook; AOL to WWL, 20 October 1898.

49. Arthur O. Lovejoy, "Some Harvard Notes," pp. 114–16.

50. AOL to WWL, 10 September 1896, 28 September [1897], [November 1897], 1 February 1898.

51. WWL to AOL, 13 March 1897; AOL to WWL, 30 March 1897.

52. WWL to AOL, 6 April 1897; AOL to WWL, 30 May 1897.

53. AOL to WWL, 30 March 1897; William James, "The Ph.D. Octopus," pp. 336, 345; AOL to David Starr Jordan, 19 May [1899], Jordan Papers; George Boas, interview, 13 September 1974.

54. AOL to WWL, 17 October 1898, 1 December and 5 December 1898; Lewis S. Feuer, interview, 7 June 1979.

55. AOL to WWL, 17 October 1898, 20 October 1898, 1 December and 5 December 1898.

56. AOL to Emmeline D. Lovejoy, 26 March 1899; Josiah Royce to David Starr Jordan, 1 May 1899, in *The Letters of Josiah Royce*, p. 389; C. C. Everett to [no addressee], 23 April 1899, Lovejoy Papers; AOL to David Starr Jordan, 19 May [1899], Jordan Papers.

57. AOL to David Starr Jordan, 19 May [1899], Jordan Papers.

CHAPTER II
"TOWARD A RATIONAL THEOLOGY OF
THE FUTURE," 1895–1910

1. AOL to WWL, 16 October 1899.

2. Arthur O. Lovejoy, "Pragmatism and Theology," p. 77.

3. WWL to AOL, 22 May 1895.

4. AOL to WWL, 3 April 1896.
5. AOL to WWL, 30 March 1897, and 10 December 1897.
6. AOL to [WWL], [Summer 1896].
7. AOL to WWL, 8 and 10 October 1896, 8 November 1896.
8. ACL to WWL, 8 November 1896.
9. WWL to AOL, 21 October 1896.
10. AOL to [WWL], [Summer 1896].
11. Arthur O. Lovejoy, "The Origins of Ethical Inwardness in Jewish Thought," pp. 230–33, 247–49.
12. AOL to WWL, 30 May 1897.
13. Arthur O. Lovejoy, "The Entangling Alliance of Religion and History," pp. 259–60, 262–63, 265–67, 271, 274–76.
14. Ibid., pp. 258–59.
15. "Additions to the Faculty," *Daily Palo Alto*, 12 September 1899, p. 3; AOL to David Starr Jordan, 19 May [1899], Jordan Papers; George Holmes Howison to AOL, 22 June 1899; Ralph Barton Perry to AOL, 12 February 1900.
16. Leland Stanford, Jr., University, *Ninth Annual Register, 1899–1900*, pp. 79–148; "Philosophical Society," *Daily Palo Alto*, 22 January 1900, p. 1; AOL to WWL, 16 October 1899.
17. Orrin Leslie Elliott, *Stanford University*, pp. 326–41; Richard Hofstadter and Walter P. Metzger, *The Development of Academic Freedom in the United States*, pp. 438–45; James C. Mohr, "Academic Turmoil and Public Opinion," pp. 39–61.
18. AOL to Upton Sinclair, quoted in Upton Sinclair, *The Goose-Step*, pp. 156–57; AOL to B. W. Kunkel, 2 December 1957; AOL to David Starr Jordan, 29 April 1901; Lewis S. Feuer, interview, Charlottesville, Va., 7 June 1979; Mary O. Furner, *Advocacy and Objectivity*, p. 241.
19. AOL to David Starr Jordan, 29 April 1901; Arthur O. Lovejoy, "Some Harvard Notes," pp. 114–16; Arthur O. Lovejoy, "The Social Role of the French University," pp. 134–35; AOL to WWL, 27 June and 1 July 1895; AOL to B. W. Kunkel, 2 December 1957.
20. Laurence R. Vesey, *The Emergence of the American University*, pp. 61, 220; Hofstadter and Metzger, *Academic Freedom*, pp. 400–407; Furner, *Advocacy and Objectivity*, pp. 1–9.
21. AOL to George Holmes Howison, 22 July 1901, Howison Papers; W. S. Chaplin to AOL, 12 August 1901; Lewis S. Feuer, interview, 7 June 1979; AOL to WWL, 4 October 1901.
22. AOL to Emmeline D. Lovejoy, 21 August and 23 August 1903; AOL to WWL, 7 December 1903; Ralph Barton Perry to AOL, 19 March 1904.
23. Robert A. Woods and Albert J. Kennedy, *Handbook of Settlements*, p. 114; "Annual Report of the North Broadway Social Settlement," p. 12; AOL to Emmeline D. Lovejoy, 10 October 1905; AOL to WWL, 30 August 1907.
24. [Arthur O. Lovejoy], "The North Broadway Social Settlement," unpaginated, Washington University Archives.
25. Laurence R. Vesey, "The American Academic Revolution, 1880–1910"; Vesey, *American University*, pp. 61–66, 76–81, 233–41; [Lovejoy], "North Broadway Social Settlement."
26. Arthur O. Lovejoy, "Ecclesiastes Instructed," p. 285.
27. Lewis S. Feuer, "John Dewey and the Back to the People Movement in American Thought," pp. 567–68.

28. Arthur O. Lovejoy, "Increase in the President's Power," pp. 102–3; Arthur O. Lovejoy, "The Child and the State," speech, ca., 1905; Arthur O. Lovejoy, "Social Legislation in Missouri," pp. 326–28.

29. Arthur O. Lovejoy, "Christian Ethics and Economic Competition," pp. 328–29, 332–34, 342–44.

30. AOL to Emmeline D. Lovejoy, 30 July 1905, 17 August 1907; William James to AOL, 1 November 1902; C. S. Peirce to AOL, 27 May 1906.

31. Arthur O. Lovejoy, "Fourth Annual Meeting of the Western Philosophy Association," pp. 269–70; Arthur O. Lovejoy, "Fifth Annual Meeting of the Western Philosophy Association," p. 377; Arthur O. Lovejoy, "Sixth Annual Meeting of the Western Philosophy Association," p. 318. The papers he delivered at the annual meetings were, "Kant's Antithesis of Dogmatism and Criticism" (1904), "The Influence of the Self-Conscious on Volition" (1906), and his presidential address, "The Obsolescence of the Eternal" (1909).

32. AOL to WWL, 12 October 1905; AOL and others to W. S. Chaplin, 21 May 1906, Washington University Archives.

33. Frederick J. E. Woodbridge to AOL, 28 May 1907; W. S. Chaplin to AOL, 3 June 1907, Washington University Archives; AOL to W. S. Chaplin, 4 June 1907 and 5 June 1907, Washington University Archives.

34. AOL to Emmeline D. Lovejoy, 25 September 1907; AOL to WWL, 4 October 1907; AOL to Wallace and Emmeline Lovejoy, 23 November 1907.

35. *Missouri University Catalogue* (1908–9), pp. 157–59, University of Missouri Archives.

36. AOL to Emmeline D. Lovejoy, 24 January 1910, 30 January and 1 February 1910; Arthur O. Lovejoy, "The Service Pension of the Carnegie Foundation," pp. 299–300; Arthur O. Lovejoy, "The Retrospective Anticipations of the Carnegie Foundation," pp. 414–15.

37. AOL to WWL, 18 December 1909, 1 January 1910.

38. AOL to WWL, [February 1910]; John B. Watson to AOL, 27 February 1910; AOL to WWL, [March 1910]; Ira Remsen to AOL, 18 March 1910 and 29 March 1910; AOL to WWL, 3 April 1910.

39. E. F. Buchner to AOL, 12 April 1910; John B. Watson to AOL, 18 April [1910]; Ira Remsen to AOL, 18 April 1910; Edward H. Griffin to AOL, 18 April 1910; E. F. Buchner to AOL, 18 April 1910; AOL to Emmeline D. Lovejoy, 28 April 1910.

40. George Holmes Howison, "The Harmony of Determinism and Freedom," pp. 354–55.

41. AOL to George Holmes Howison, 20 May 1901, 27 July 1901, Howison Papers; Howison, "Harmony of Determinism and Freedom," p. 356.

42. Arthur O. Lovejoy, "Religion and the Time-Process," pp. 439–40, 447–48.

43. Ibid., pp. 453–61.

44. Ibid., p. 468.

45. Arthur O. Lovejoy, "The Desires of the Self-Conscious," pp. 29–30.

46. Ibid., pp. 31–32, 31n.

47. Ibid., pp. 32–33.

48. Ibid., pp. 33–35.

49. Ibid., pp. 38–39.

50. Lovejoy, "Pragmatism and Theology," pp. 40–44, 68–70.

51. Ibid., pp. 71, 74–77.

52. Arthur O. Lovejoy, "The Obsolescence of the Eternal," pp. 482, 489–90, 497.

CHAPTER III
IDEALISM, PRAGMATISM, AND TEMPORALISM

1. [Arthur O. Lovejoy], "Romantic Philosophy," pp. 140–41; AOL to William James, 15 February [1910], James Papers.
2. Arthur O. Lovejoy, ["Essay on the Real"], pp. 2–15.
3. Ibid., pp. 17–21.
4. Ibid., pp. 21–24, 27–28.
5. Ibid., pp. 28–35.
6. Arthur O. Lovejoy, "Some Concluding Criticisms on the 'Total Experience' Account of Reality, with special reference to the 'Moment of Arrest,' " pp. 1–2.
7. Ibid., pp. 4–9.
8. Ibid., pp. 10–23.
9. Ibid., pp. 24–26, 35–36.
10. Ibid., pp. 36–52.
11. Ibid., pp. 53–56.
12. AOL to George Holmes Howison, 9 October 1898, Howison Papers.
13. Ibid.
14. Ibid.
15. AOL to George Holmes Howison, 20 May 1901, Howison Papers.
16. AOL to George Holmes Howison, 27 July 1901, Howison Papers.
17. Ibid.
18. Most of Lovejoy's articles on pragmatism were collected in Arthur O. Lovejoy, *The Thirteen Pragmatisms and Other Essays*.
19. Arthur O. Lovejoy, "Pragmatism *Versus* the Pragmatist," in *The Thirteen Pragmatisms*, p. 190.
20. AOL to William James, 1 January 1908, James Papers.
21. William James to AOL, 22 December 1907; AOL to William James, 1 January 1908, James Papers.
22. AOL to William James, 27 August 1909, James Papers.
23. William James, *A Pluralistic Universe*, pp. 212–13, 217–19, 272; William James to AOL, 4 September 1909.
24. AOL to William James, 27 August 1909, James Papers.
25. Arthur O. Lovejoy, "The Problem of Time in Recent French Philosophy," p. 12.
26. William James, *Some Problems of Philosophy*, p. 172; Lovejoy, "Time in French Philosophy," p. 544.
27. Lovejoy, "Time in French Philosophy," p. 545; AOL to William James, 27 August 1909, James Papers.
28. AOL to William James, 23 August 1907, James Papers.
29. Arthur O. Lovejoy, "The Thirteen Pragmatisms," in *The Thirteen Pragmatisms*, pp. 1–29; the article first appeared in *The Journal of Philosophy* 5 (1908):5–12, 29–39.
30. Lovejoy, "Thirteen Pragmatisms," pp. 2, 29.
31. Ibid., pp. 3–10.
32. William James, *Pragmatism*, p. 201; Lovejoy, "Thirteen Pragmatisms," pp. 10–12, 26.

33. Lovejoy, "Thirteen Pragmatisms," pp. 14–21.
34. Ibid., pp. 16–17.
35. James, *Pragmatism*, pp. 210–11; Lovejoy, "Thirteen Pragmatisms," pp. 23–24.
36. Arthur O. Lovejoy, "Pragmatism and Theology," pp. 68–71.
37. Lovejoy, "Pragmatism *Versus* the Pragmatist," pp. 136–45, 152–53.
38. Ibid., pp. 167–68.
39. John Dewey, "Realism without Monism or Dualism," pp. 316–17, 356.
40. Lovejoy, "Pragmatism *Versus* the Pragmatist," pp. 174–79.
41. Ibid., pp. 179–80.
42. Ibid., pp. 184–85.
43. Ibid., pp. 185–86.
44. Arthur O. Lovejoy, "The Obsolescence of the Eternal," pp. 483–84, 489.
45. Lovejoy, "Time in French Philosophy," pp. 11–12.
46. AOL to Henri Bergson, 24 May 1911.
47. Lovejoy, "Time in French Philosophy," pp. 323–24.
48. Ibid., pp. 329–30; AOL to Henri Bergson, 24 May 1911.
49. Lovejoy, "Time in French Philosophy," pp. 335–36; AOL to Henri Bergson, 24 May 1911.
50. Lovejoy, "Time in French Philosophy," pp. 333–35.
51. Ibid., pp. 337–38.
52. Henri Bergson to AOL, 10 May 1911, 6 June 1911, 4 July 1911.
53. Arthur O. Lovejoy, "Bergson on 'Real Duration,' " pp. 190–95.
54. Arthur O. Lovejoy, "A Temporalistic Realism," pp. 87–89.
55. Lovejoy, "Time in French Philosophy," pp. 543–44; AOL to Henri Bergson, 24 May 1911.
56. Lovejoy, "Temporalistic Realism," p. 97.

CHAPTER IV
CRITICAL REALISM AND THE DUALISMS

1. Arthur O. Lovejoy, "A Temporalistic Realism," p. 97.
2. J. E. Creighton, "The Purposes of a Philosophical Association," pp. 221, 230.
3. Daniel J. Wilson, "Professionalization and Organized Discussion in the American Philosophical Association, 1900–1922," pp. 55–57, 60; Karl Schmidt, "The Tenth Annual Meeting of the American Philosophical Association," p. 97.
4. F.J.E. Woodbridge and others, "Report of the Committee on Definitions of the American Philosophical Association," p. 701.
5. H. A. Overstreet, "Eleventh Annual Meeting of the American Philosophical Association," p. 101; Josiah Royce, "On Definitions and Debates," pp. 97–100.
6. The Committee on Discussion, "The American Philosophical Association," pp. 615–16.
7. James Bissett Pratt, "The Twelfth Annual Meeting of the American Philosophical Association," pp. 91–94.
8. Wilson, "Professionalization and Organized Discussion," pp. 64–65.
9. Arthur O. Lovejoy, "On Some Conditions of Progress in Philosophical Inquiry," pp. 126–30.

10. Ibid., pp. 130–33.

11. Ibid., pp. 133, 137–41.

12. Ibid., p. 144.

13. Ibid., pp. 142, 148–49.

14. Ibid., pp. 150–53.

15. Ibid., pp. 153–55.

16. Ibid., pp. 155–58; Norman Kemp Smith, "How Far Is Agreement Possible in Philosophy?" p. 704.

17. Lovejoy, "Progress in Philosophical Inquiry," p. 159.

18. Ibid., pp. 159–60.

19. Ibid., p. 163.

20. Ernest Albee, Charles M. Bakewell, Theodore DeLaguna, William Ernest Hocking, Edmund H. Hollands, "Progress in Philosophical Inquiry and Mr. Lovejoy's Presidential Address," pp. 315–38; Wilson, "Professionalization and Organized Discussion," pp. 67–69.

21. Herbert W. Schneider, *Sources of Contemporary Philosophical Realism in America*, pp. 17–23; A. G. Ramsperger, "Critical Realism"; Durant Drake and others, *Essays in Critical Realism*; Edwin B. Holt and others, *The New Realism*; John Dewey and others, *Creative Intelligence*.

22. Durant Drake to AOL, 3 January 1917; Durant Drake to AOL, Macintosh, Pratt, Rogers, Sellars, Strong, and Santayana, 15 February 1917; Durant Drake to AOL, Macintosh, Pratt, Rogers, and Sellars, 24 February 1917; AOL to Durant Drake, 3 March 1917; Roy Wood Sellars, *Reflections on American Philosophy from Within*, pp. 44–45.

23. Durant Drake, "Memorandum of First Conference," summer 1917.

24. C. A. Strong to AOL, 21 September 1917; AOL to Fellow Collaborators, 15 January 1918; Durant Drake to AOL, 6 September 1919.

25. Lovejoy, "Progress in Philosophical Inquiry," p. 141; Durant Drake to AOL, 22 November [1917?]; C. A. Strong to AOL, 21 September 1917.

26. On this last point, see Durant Drake to AOL, 1 February 1920.

27. Philip P. Wiener, "The Central Role of Time in Lovejoy's Philosophy," pp. 290–91; Lewis S. Feuer, "The Philosophical Method of Arthur O. Lovejoy," pp. 493–95.

28. Lovejoy, "Progress in Philosophical Inquiry," pp. 141, 151.

29. Feuer, "Philosophical Method," pp. 495–96; Arthur O. Lovejoy, "Pragmatism *Versus* the Pragmatist," pp. 157, 168–69, 171, 185–90.

30. Arthur O. Lovejoy, "The Anomaly of Knowledge," pp. 241–42.

31. Ibid., pp. 245–46.

32. Ibid., pp. 249–50.

33. Ibid., pp. 251–52.

34. Ibid., pp. 260, 276–80.

35. Ibid., pp. 280–82.

36. Ibid., pp. 282–83.

37. Ibid., pp. 251–52, 283–86; see also Arthur O. Lovejoy, "On the Existence of Ideas," pp. 42–99.

38. On Lovejoy's conclusion that the revolt against dualism had failed, see Arthur O. Lovejoy, *The Revolt Against Dualism*, pp. 324–25.

39. Ibid., pp. 12–13.

40. Ibid., pp. 13–14.

41. Ibid., pp. 15–18.

42. Ibid., pp. 18–20.

43. Ibid., pp. 21–22.

44. Ibid., pp. 23–27.
45. Ibid., pp. 27–28.
46. Ibid., pp. 28–29.
47. Ibid., pp. 30–32.
48. Ibid., pp. 32–33.
49. Ibid., pp. 33–34.
50. Ibid., pp. 34–38.
51. Ibid., pp. 38–40.
52. Ibid., pp. 40–41.
53. Ibid., pp. 323–25.
54. Ibid., pp. 328–29.
55. Ibid., pp. 378–79.
56. Ibid., pp. 380–86.
57. Ibid., pp. 386–90.
58. Ibid., pp. 393–94.
59. Ibid., pp. 394–98.

CHAPTER V
"THE BELLING OF CATS," 1910–1920

1. AOL to David Starr Jordan, 29 April 1901; Arthur O. Lovejoy, "Some Harvard Notes," pp. 114–16; Arthur O. Lovejoy, "The Social Rôle of the French University," pp. 134–46.

2. AOL to Emmeline D. Lovejoy, 24 January 1910; Arthur O. Lovejoy, "The Service Pension of the Carnegie Foundation," pp. 299–300.

3. Richard Hofstadter and Walter P. Metzger, *The Development of Academic Freedom in the United States*, pp. 470–75.

4. Ibid., pp. 475–76; Arthur O. Lovejoy and others, "The Case of Professor Mecklin," pp. 80–81. The other members of the committee were J. E. Creighton, W. E. Hocking, E. B. McGilvary, W. T. Marvin, G. H. Mead, and Howard C. Warren.

5. AOL to B. W. Kunkel, 2 December 1957; Hofstadter and Metzger, *Academic Freedom*, pp. 475–76.

6. AOL to B. W. Kunkel, 2 December 1957; Lewis S. Feuer, interview, Charlottesville, Va., 7 June 1979; Hofstadter and Metzger, *Academic Freedom*, p. 476; "A National Association of University Professors," p. 458.

7. "A National Association of University Professors," p. 459.

8. Ibid.; John Dewey and AOL to "Dear Sir," 7 December 1914, AAUP Archives; Josiah Royce to AOL, [December 1914], AAUP Archives; H. A. Overstreet, "Minutes of the Meeting for the Organization of the American Association of University Professors," 1 and 2 January 1915, AAUP Archives; Arthur O. Lovejoy, "The Association of University Professors," pp. 744–45; Arthur O. Lovejoy, "Organization of the American Association of University Professors," pp. 151–54; Lewis S. Feuer, interview, 7 June 1979.

9. AOL to John Dewey, 13 April 1914 and 9 May 1914; John Dewey to AOL, 22 June [1914] and 23 October 1914, AAUP Archives.

10. Arthur O. Lovejoy, "The Profession of the Professorate," pp. 189, 191; John Dewey, "The American Association of University Professors: Introductory Address," p. 149.

11. [E.R.A. Seligman] to Professor [William] MacDonald, 20 January 1916,

AAUP Archives; Edwin R. A. Seligman and others, "General Report of the Committee on Academic Freedom and Academic Tenure," pp. 17–43.

12. Seligman, "General Report," pp. 24–27; Laurence R. Vesey, *The Emergence of the American University*, pp. 76–81.

13. Seligman, "General Report," pp. 27–29.

14. Ibid., pp. 30–33.

15. Ibid., pp. 33–37.

16. Ibid., pp. 38–39.

17. Ibid., pp. 40–42.

18. Arthur O. Lovejoy, "Academic Freedom," *Nation*, p. 561.

19. AOL to Emmeline D. Lovejoy, 31 March 1912 and 21 April 1912; AOL to Owen R. Lovejoy, 29 March 1917.

20. AOL to WWL, 2 August 1914. The letter was written in Zurich, Switzerland. Arthur O. Lovejoy, "As to an Embargo on Arms," pp. 156–57.

21. Carol S. Gruber, *Mars and Minerva*, p. 52; George T. Blakey, *Historians on the Homefront*, pp. 9–11.

22. Lovejoy, "As to an Embargo on Arms," pp. 156–57.

23. Arthur O. Lovejoy, "German Scholars and 'Truth About Germany,' " p. 376. Arthur O. Lovejoy, "The Professorial Landsturm," p. 656–57; Gruber, *Mars and Minerva*, pp. 66–68.

24. Edwin R. A. Seligman and others, "Report of the Committee of Inquiry on Conditions at the University of Utah"; D. O. McGovney and others, "Report of the Committee of Inquiry Concerning Charges of Violation of Academic Freedom at the University of Colorado," pp. 3–71; Arthur O. Lovejoy and others, "Report of the Committee of Inquiry on the Case of Professor Scott Nearing of the University of Pennsylvania," pp. 7–57; Charles A. Kofoid and others, "Report of the Committee of Inquiry Concerning Charges of Violation of Academic Freedom, Involving the Dismissal of the President and three Members of the Faculty, at the University of Montana," pp. 3–52.

25. Norman Kemp Smith to AOL, 8 January 1917.

26. Gruber, *Mars and Minerva*, p. 117; Blakey, *Historians on the Homefront*, pp. 13–14, 16–33.

27. Blakey, *Historians on the Homefront*, pp. 26–33; Robert D. Ward, "The Origin and Activities of the National Security League, 1914–1919," pp. 51–65.

28. Albert Bushnell Hart and Arthur O. Lovejoy, *Handbook of the War for Public Speakers*, pp. 3–4.

29. Ibid., pp. 4, 40–81. The editors noted that President Wilson's speeches were not included, for "these, it has been assumed, are already in the possession—and it is to be hoped, are in the memories—of all Americans deserving the name" (p. 4). Lovejoy later edited a selection of Wilson's speeches, Woodrow Wilson, *America Joins the World*, edited with an introduction by Arthur O. Lovejoy, (1919).

30. Hart and Lovejoy, *Handbook*, p. 85.

31. Lovejoy, "German Scholars," p. 376; Hart and Lovejoy, *Handbook*, p. 85; Blakey, *Historians on the Homefront*, p. 62.

32. Gruber, *Mars and Minerva*, p. 120n; Minutes of the Committee on Activities, Educational Bureau, YMCA, 3 October 1918, Historical Library, YMCA, New York.

33. "Supplementary Statement Accompanying Application of A. O. Lovejoy," Lovejoy Papers; Maryland, Council of Defense, *Report of the Mary-*

land Council of Defense to the Governor and General Assembly of Maryland, pp. 64–65, 93.

34. Arthur O. Lovejoy, "Wheat for the Allies," p. 12; Arthur O. Lovejoy, "German Peace Drives Rightly Named 'Traps,'" pp. 4, 15; Arthur O. Lovejoy, "Benevolent Neutrality," pp. 229–30; Arthur O. Lovejoy, "Is a 'Peace of Conciliation' Possible?" pp. 257–59.

35. The material on this mission is collected in a scrapbook in the Lovejoy Papers. The first quotation is from a statement by Charles Belmont Davis, secretary of the mission. Lovejoy's statement is from a clipping of the *Paris Herald*, 6 May 1918.

36. Minutes of the Committee on Activities, Educational Bureau, YMCA, 3 October 1918 and 19 February 1919, Historical Library, YMCA, New York; U.S. Department of Interior, Bureau of Education, *Educational Work of the Young Men's Christian Association*, 1916–1918, written by William Orr, pp. 15–19; AOL to Department Educational Directors, [fall 1918], Lovejoy Papers; Ernest H. Wilkins to AOL, 5 March 1919, AAUP Archives; A. O. Lovejoy and E. H. Wilkins, "Some Facts About the British," 7 March 1919, AAUP Archives.

37. Arthur O. Lovejoy, "To Conscientious Objectors," pp. 187–88. The letter of Norman Thomas and the other conscientious objectors appeared in *New Republic*, 11 (1917):109–11.

38. AOL to Allyn A. Young, 9 October 1917.

39. Allyn A. Young to AOL, 27 October 1917 and 5 November 1917; Arthur O. Lovejoy with Edward Capps and A. A. Young, "Report of the Committee on Academic Freedom in Wartime," p. 47. One member of the full Committee on Academic Freedom, Frank H. Hodder of the University of Kansas, dissented from the report on the grounds that the restrictions endangered the very concept of academic freedom. F. H. Hodder to Allyn A. Young, 29 January 1918.

40. Lovejoy, Capps, and Young, "Academic Freedom in Wartime," pp. 30–32.

41. Ibid., pp. 32–34.

42. Ibid., pp. 34–37.

43. Ibid., pp. 37–39.

44. Ibid., p. 40.

45. Ibid., pp. 40–42.

46. Ibid., pp. 43–44.

47. Ibid., p. 46.

48. "The Professors in Battle Array," p. 255; Arthur O. Lovejoy, "Academic Freedom in Wartime," p. 402.

49. Blakey, *Historians on the Homefront*, p. 140.

50. Arthur O. Lovejoy, "Annual Message of the President," pp. 3–7.

51. Ibid., pp. 9–10.

52. Ibid., pp. 10–11.

53. Ibid., pp. 11–13.

54. Ibid., pp. 14–15.

55. Ibid., pp. 15–19; AOL to W. C. Curtis, 29 March 1920, AAUP Archives.

56. Arthur O. Lovejoy, "Teachers and Trade-Unions," pp. 106–20.

57. Arthur O. Lovejoy and others, "Report of the Committee of Inquiry on Conditions in Washburn College," pp. 66–137; Arthur O. Lovejoy and others, "Report of the Committee of Inquiry Concerning Clark University," pp. 40–107.

CHAPTER VI
THE MORAL OF *The Great Chain of Being*

1. This chapter, with minor revisions, is reprinted with the permission of *The Journal of the History of Ideas*, c. 1980, vol. 41, no. 2.
2. ACL to WWL, 2 June [1895].
3. Arthur O. Lovejoy, "Religion and the Time-Process," pp. 440, 443–44.
4. Ibid., pp. 444–46.
5. Ibid., pp. 448, 455–62.
6. Arthur O. Lovejoy, "The Dialectic of Bruno and Spinoza," pp. 144–45.
7. Ibid., pp. 150–52.
8. Ibid., pp. 154–57.
9. Ibid., pp. 145, 173.
10. Arthur O. Lovejoy, *The Great Chain of Being*, p. viii.
11. AOL to WWL, 3 April 1896 and [summer 1896]; Arthur O. Lovejoy, "The Entangling Alliance of Religion and History," pp. 265–69; Lovejoy, *Chain of Being*, p. 329.
12. Lovejoy, "Religion and the Time-Process," pp. 457–58; Arthur O. Lovejoy, "A Temporalistic Realism," pp. 88–89; Arthur O. Lovejoy, "Some Eighteenth Century Evolutionists," pp. 238–51, 323–40. Several of Lovejoy's articles on evolution were brought together in Bentley Glass, Owsei Temkin, and William Strauss, Jr., eds., *Forerunners of Darwin*.
13. Lovejoy, "Religion and the Time-Process," pp. 457–59; Lovejoy, *Chain of Being*, pp. 268–69.
14. Lovejoy, "Religion and the Time-Process," pp. 461–62.
15. Arthur O. Lovejoy, "Schiller and the Genesis of German Romanticism," pp. 1–10, 134–46; Arthur O. Lovejoy, "On the Discrimination of Romanticisms," pp. 229–53; Lovejoy, *Chain of Being*, pp. 325–26.
16. Arthur O. Lovejoy, "The Anomaly of Knowledge," p. 286; Arthur O. Lovejoy, "Reflections on the History of Ideas," pp. 3, 8.
17. Lovejoy, "Reflections on the History of Ideas," pp. 16–21; Lovejoy, *Chain of Being*, p. 47.
18. Arthur O. Lovejoy, "Some Concluding Criticisms on the 'Total Experience' Account of Reality, with special reference to the 'Moment of Arrest,'" pp. 6–8; Lovejoy, *Chain of Being*, pp. viii, 46–47.
19. Lovejoy, *Chain of Being*, p. 23. William James, in speaking of the mind's quest of tranquility in rationality, employed the same image of finding to end "in wandering mazes lost." William James, "The Sentiment of Rationality," p. 341.
20. Lovejoy, *Chain of Being*, pp. 24–25, 35–41.
21. Ibid., pp. 45–52.
22. Ibid., pp. 55–58.
23. Ibid., pp. 58–59.
24. Ibid., pp. 59–66.
25. Ibid., pp. 96–98.
26. Ibid., pp. 144, 154; Arthur O. Lovejoy, "The Obsolescence of the Eternal," pp. 489, 497.
27. Lovejoy, *Chain of Being*, pp. 183, 200, 204, 208, 211, 215, 232.
28. [Arthur O. Lovejoy], "Prolegomena," ca. 1958, Lovejoy Papers; Lovejoy, *Chain of Being*, pp. 242–45.
29. Lovejoy, *Chain of Being*, pp. 245–46, 288.
30. Ibid., pp. 288–89.

31. Ibid., pp. 293–94.
32. Ibid., pp. 312–13.
33. Ibid., pp. 325–26.
34. Ibid., pp. 327–29, 331.
35. Lovejoy, "Concluding Criticisms," p. 6; Lovejoy, *Chain of Being*, p. 332.

CHAPTER VII
EVOLUTION AND THE NATURE OF MAN

1. AOL to WWL, 2 June [1895].
2. Arthur O. Lovejoy, "Some Eighteenth Century Evolutionists," pp. 238–40.
3. Arthur O. Lovejoy, "The Argument for Organic Evolution Before 'The Origin of Species,'" p. 499.
4. Ibid., pp. 501–4.
5. Ibid., p. 499.
6. Thomas S. Kuhn, *The Structure of Scientific Revolutions*, pp. 67–68.
7. Lovejoy, "Argument for Organic Evolution," p. 549.
8. Arthur O. Lovejoy, "The Unity of Science," p. 32.
9. Ibid., p. 2.
10. Ibid., pp. 6, 8–9.
11. Ibid., pp. 17–19.
12. Ibid., pp. 26–29.
13. Ibid., pp. 30–31.
14. Ibid., pp. 31–32; AOL to H. S. Jennings, 15 March 1912. Lovejoy employed the phrase "the first morning of creation wrote what the last dawn of reckoning shall read" without quotation marks. However, it is a direct quotation from Edward FitzGerald's "The Rubáiyát of Omar Khayyám" (stanza 73). To complicate matters, William James, in a similar context in "The Dilemma of Determinism," quoted the entire stanza, though without attributing it to FitzGerald (p. 150).
15. Arthur O. Lovejoy, "The Discontinuities of Evolution," pp. 174–76.
16. Ibid., pp. 176–78.
17. Ibid., pp. 178–82.
18. Ibid., pp. 183–85.
19. Ibid., pp. 186–88.
20. Ibid., pp. 189–92.
21. Ibid., pp. 194–95.
22. Ibid., pp. 195–97.
23. Ibid., pp. 198–207.
24. Ibid., pp. 207–8.
25. Ibid., p. 209.
26. Ibid., p. 218.
27. Arthur O. Lovejoy, "The Meanings of 'Emergence' and Its Modes," pp. 20–33.
28. Ibid., pp. 22–23.
29. Ibid., pp. 23–24.
30. Ibid., pp. 20–21, 25.
31. Ibid., pp. 26–28.
32. Ibid., p. 30.
33. Ibid., pp. 30–33.

34. *Reflections on Human Nature*, which contains Lovejoy's historical treatment of these matters, was originally given as a series of lectures at Swarthmore College in 1941. They were not published in their final form until 1951.

35. Arthur O. Lovejoy, *Reflections on Human Nature*, pp. 11–12, 14–15, 22–23.

36. Ibid., pp. 46–53, 64.

37. Ibid., pp. 129, 131, 134.

38. Ibid., pp. 153–54, 157, 181, 190.

39. Ibid., pp. 181–84.

40. Ibid., p. 190.

41. Ibid., pp. 247–48.

42. Ibid., pp. 248–52.

43. Ibid., pp. 252–53.

44. Ibid., pp. 257–58.

45. Ibid., pp. 258–62.

46. Ibid., pp. 262–63.

47. Ibid., pp. 263–64.

48. Arthur O. Lovejoy, "Terminal and Adjectival Values," pp. 594–96.

49. Ibid., pp. 596–97, 599; Lovejoy, *Reflections on Human Nature*, p. 72.

50. Lovejoy, "Terminal and Adjectival Values," pp. 598, 602.

51. Ibid., pp. 602–3.

52. Ibid., pp. 603–4.

53. Ibid., pp. 604–5.

54. A. Clutton-Brock, "Pooled Self-Esteem," pp. 721–31.

55. Lovejoy, *Reflections on Human Nature*, pp. 117–18.

56. Ibid., pp. 125–27.

57. George Boas, interview, Baltimore, Md., 7 November 1975.

58. AOL to William James, 27 August 1909, James Papers.

CHAPTER VIII
TO THE RAMPARTS AGAIN, 1930–1962

1. A. L. Hammond, "Brief History of the Department of Philosophy, 1876–1938," pp. 11–12; George Boas, interview, Baltimore, Md., 27 February 1979.

2. George Boas, interviews, 16 January 1975, 23 January 1976; Marjorie Nicolson, "A. O. Lovejoy as Teacher," pp. 428–32; Frank N. Trager, interview, New York, N.Y., 17 July 1979.

3. George Boas, interview, 27 February 1979; Frank N. Trager, interview, 17 July 1979; Lewis S. Feuer, interview, Charlottesville, Va., 7 June 1979.

4. Arthur O. Lovejoy, H. C. Lancaster, and D. M. Robinson, "Constitution of the History of Ideas Club"; George Boas, Minutes of the second meeting of the History of Ideas Club, 1 March 1923; AOL to Dorothy Stimson, 1 December 1952.

5. Dorothy Stimson, "The History of Ideas Club," pp. 186–87; George Boas, interview, 16 January 1975.

6. Arthur O. Lovejoy and George Boas, *Primitivism and Related Ideas in Antiquity*, vol. 1 of *A Documentary History of Primitivism*, pp. ix–xi.

7. George Boas, "A. O. Lovejoy: Reason-in-Action," p. 539; Frank N. Trager, interview, 17 July 1979; AOL to Raymond Dexter Havens, 9 August [1936], Havens Papers.

8. Bruce Kuklick, *The Rise of American Philosophy*, pp. 409–11.

9. AOL to George Boas, 16 October 1932; Lewis S. Feuer, "Arthur O. Lovejoy," pp. 358–59; Lewis S. Feuer, interview, 7 June 1979.

10. AOL to James Houghton Woods, 19 February 1932, 6 March 1932, Philosophy Department Files, Harvard Archives; Feuer, "Arthur O. Lovejoy," pp. 361–62; Lewis S. Feuer, interview, 7 June 1979.

11. AOL to William Ernest Hocking, 24 March [1937], Philosophy Department Files, Harvard Archives; Arthur O. Lovejoy, "Philosophical Anthropology," syllabus; Victor Lowe, interview, Baltimore, Md., 26 February 1979.

12. George Boas to Isaiah Bowman, 15 December 1937, Johns Hopkins Archives; Isaiah Bowman to AOL, 16 May 1938, Johns Hopkins Archives; George Boas, interview, 27 January 1976; Frank N. Trager, interview, 17 July 1979; Lovejoy quoted in "Dr. A. O. Lovejoy to Leave Hopkins," *Baltimore Sun*, 7 January 1938, pp. 9, 22.

13. George Sarton to AOL, 29 May 1937; AOL to George Sarton, 2 June 1937, Sarton Papers.

14. Philip P. Wiener, "Lovejoy's Rôle in American Philosophy," pp. 169–70; Philip P. Wiener, interview, Philadelphia, Pa., 20 May 1979.

15. AOL to Roy Harvey Pearce, 13 June 1946, 6 August 1946, 6 March [1956]; Roy Harvey Pearce to Daniel J. Wilson, 13 March 1979.

16. Arthur O. Lovejoy, *Essays in the History of Ideas*, p. xi; Arthur O. Lovejoy, "The Historiography of Ideas," pp. 531, 537–39; Arthur O. Lovejoy, "Reflections on the History of Ideas," pp. 4, 7. Lovejoy once told Lewis Feuer that he had "'picked up' the idea of the historical tracing of unit-ideas" from Wilhelm Windelband's *A History of Philosophy*. Feuer, "Arthur O. Lovejoy," p. 365; Lewis S. Feuer, interview, 7 June 1979.

17. AOL to Raymond Dexter Havens, 2 November 1932, Havens Papers; Frank N. Trager, interview, 17 July 1979.

18. Arthur O. Lovejoy, *Hitler as Pacifist*, pp. 3, 7, 9–15, 18.

19. Boas, "A. O. Lovejoy: Reason-in-Action," p. 535; George Boas, interview, 13 September 1974; Maryland Committee for Concerted Peace Efforts, minutes, 19 June 1939; Maryland Committee for Non-Participation in Japanese Aggression, Executive Committee, minutes, 19 December 1939.

20. Arthur O. Lovejoy, letters to the editor of the *Baltimore Evening Sun*, 6 February 1940, and the *Baltimore Sun*, 31 May 1940, p. 12, 15 January 1941, p. 12; Arthur O. Lovejoy, "Address to Maryland Congressional Delegation," pp. 2090–91.

21. Richard W. Steele, "Preparing the Public for War," p. 1642.

22. [Arthur O. Lovejoy], EM 10, G.I. Roundtable: *What Shall Be Done About Germany After the War?* pp. 5–19; [Arthur O. Lovejoy], EM 12, G.I. Roundtable: *Can We Prevent Future Wars?* pp. 4–17, 20–23.

23. Ralph Barton Perry, *Final Report on the Work of the Committee, 1942–1945*, pp. 5–6, 9–11, 16, 30–31.

24. [Arthur O. Lovejoy], *Should There Be an International Organization for General Security Against Military Aggression, and Should the United States Participate in Such an Organization?* Problem IV, pp. 1, 3; Arthur O. Lovejoy, *The Dumbarton Oaks Proposals: The Enforcement of Peace*, Problem XVIII, pp. 2, 34–36.

25. Arthur O. Lovejoy, "The Draft Charter of the United Nations," speech to the Baltimore Bar Association, 1 May 1945.

26. Arthur O. Lovejoy, "Academic Freedom in War Time," p. 402.

27. Lewis S. Feuer, interview, 7 June 1979; Frank N. Trager, interview, 17 July 1979.

28. AOL to Frank N. Trager, 23 October [1941]. Lovejoy added that the same principles would apply to "members of the Nazi or the Italian Fascist parties."

29. "*The American Scholar* Forum: Communism and Academic Freedom," pp. 323–54. This forum included a factual summary of the case, statements by the president of the university, Raymond B. Allen, and the dismissed professors, and commentary by Lovejoy, Max Lerner, T. V. Smith, and Helen M. Lyrd.

30. Arthur O. Lovejoy, "Communists *versus* Academic Freedom," pp. 332–33.

31. Ibid., p. 333.

32. Ibid., pp. 334–36.

33. Victor Lowe, "A Resurgence of 'Vicious Intellectualism,'" pp. 436, 438, 442, 4–6.

34. Victor Lowe, interview, 26 February 1979; AOL to Philip P. Wiener, 7 March [1952]; Arthur O. Lovejoy, "On a Supposed Resurgence of Vicious Intellectualism," pp. 85–87.

35. Sidney Hook to Daniel J. Wilson, 27 April 1979; Christopher Lasch, *The Agony of the American Left*, pp. 82–83; George S. Counts, Paul R. Hays, Sidney Hook, and Arthur O. Lovejoy to the editor of the *New York Times*, 13 July 1953, 4:10.

36. Lowe, "'Vicious Intellectualism,'" pp. 441–42; Victor Lowe, "In Defense of Individualistic Empiricism," pp. 103–5, 111.

37. "Professor Lovejoy and the University of Maryland," *Baltimore Sun*, 18 March 1951, p. 14; "Lovejoy Sees Opposition to Appointment," *Baltimore Sun*, 17 March 1951, p. 24; "Lovejoy Denied Approval by Senate Group," *Baltimore Sun*, 1 April 1951, p. 26.

38 "Byrd Bows and Senate Approves Dr. Lovejoy," *Baltimore Sun*, 3 April 1951 p. 30; "Dr. Lovejoy Hits Athletic Scholarships," *Baltimore Sun*, 28 November 1951, p. 36; George Boas, interview, 13 September 1974; "Lovejoy, With Reluctance,' Resigns as U. of M. Regent," *Baltimore Sun*, 2 October 1955, p. 38; AOL to Theodore McKeldin, 26 September 1955, University of Maryland, Board of Regents.

39. AOL to Roy Harvey Pearce, 16 March 1958; AOL to Philip P. Wiener, 30 May 1958.

40. AOL to Raymond Dexter Havens, 22 July 1950, 2 August 1950, Havens Papers.

41. Arthur O. Lovejoy, "Prolegomena," ms fragment, ca. 1958.

42. Arthur O. Lovejoy, "Academic Freedom," *Encyclopedia of the Social Sciences*, 1:384–88.

BIBLIOGRAPHY

MANUSCRIPT COLLECTIONS

Baltimore, Maryland
  The Johns Hopkins University, Ferdinand Hamburger, Jr., Archives
  The Johns Hopkins University, Special Collections
    Arthur O. Lovejoy Papers
    Raymond Dexter Havens Papers
Berkeley, California
  Registrar, University of California, Berkeley
  University Archives, Bancroft Library, University of California, Berkeley
    George Holmes Howison Papers
Cambridge, Massachusetts
  Harvard University Archives
    Files of the Department of Philosophy, Harvard University
  Houghton Library, Harvard University
    George Sarton Papers
    William James Papers
Columbia, Missouri
  University of Missouri Archives
New York, New York
  Historical Library, Young Men's Christian Association
St. Louis, Missouri
  Washington University Archives, W. S. Chaplin Files
Stanford, California
  Stanford University Archives, David Starr Jordan Papers
Washington, D.C.
  The American Association of University Professors Archives

PUBLISHED WRITINGS OF ARTHUR O. LOVEJOY

Lovejoy, Arthur O. "Academic Freedom." Encyclopedia of the Social
    Sciences, 1:384–88.
———. "Academic Freedom." Nation 103 (1916): 561.
———. "Academic Freedom in War Time." Nation 106 (1918): 401–2.
———. "Address to Maryland Congressional Delegation." Congressional
    Record, 76th Cong., 1st sess., 1939, appendix, 84, pt. 12: 2090–91.

Bibliography

————. Introduction to *America Joins the World: Selections from the Speeches and State Papers of President Wilson, 1914–1918*. New York: Association Press, 1919.

————. "Annual Message of the President." *Bulletin of the American Association of University Professors* 5 (1919): 10–40.

————. "The Anomaly of Knowledge." In *The Thirteen Pragmatisms and Other Essays*, pp. 236–86. Baltimore: Johns Hopkins University Press, 1963.

————. "The Argument for Organic Evolution Before 'The Origin of Species.' " *Popular Science Monthly* 75 (1909): 499–514, 537–49.

————. "The Association of University Professors." *Science*, n.s. 40 (1914): 744–45.

————. "As to an Embargo on Arms." *New Republic* 4 (1915): 156–57.

————. "Benevolent Neutrality." *New Republic* 10 (1917): 229–30.

————. "Bergson on 'Real Duration.' " In *The Reason, the Understanding and Time*, pp. 185–202. Baltimore: Johns Hopkins University Press, 1961.

[————.] *Can We Prevent Future Wars?* EM 12, G.I. Roundtable. Washington, D.C.: U.S. Government Printing Office, 1944.

————. "Christian Ethics and Economic Competition." *Hibbert Journal* 9 (1911): 324–44.

————. "Communism *versus* Academic Freedom." *American Scholar* 18 (1949): 332–37.

————. "The Desires of the Self-Conscious." *Journal of Philosophy, Psychology and Scientific Methods* 4 (1907): 29–39.

————. "The Dialectic of Bruno and Spinoza." *University of California Publications in Philosophy* 1 (1904): 141–74.

————. "The Discontinuities of Evolution." *University of California Publications in Philosophy* 5 (1924): 173–220.

————. *The Dumbarton Oaks Proposals: The Enforcement of Peace.* Problem XVIII. Boston: The Universities Committee on Post-War International Problems, 1944.

————. "Ecclesiastes Instructed." *University of California Magazine* 8 (1902): 285.

————. "The Entangling Alliance of Religion and History." *Hibbert Journal* 5 (1907): 258–76.

————. ["Essay on the Real."] MS essay, circa 1896. Arthur O. Lovejoy Papers, Johns Hopkins University.

————. *Essays in the History of Ideas.* Baltimore: Johns Hopkins University Press, 1948.

————. "Fifth Annual Meeting of the Western Philosophy Association." *Journal of Philosophy, Psychology, and Scientific Methods* 2 (1905): 377.

————. "Fourth Annual Meeting of the Western Philosophy Association." *Journal of Philosophy, Psychology, and Scientific Methods* 1 (1904): 269–70.

————. "German Peace Drives Rightly Named 'Traps.' " *New York Times Magazine*, 28 July 1918, pp. 4, 15.

————. "German Scholars and 'Truth About Germany.' " *Nation* 99 (1914): 376.

————. *The Great Chain of Being: A Study of the History of an Idea.* Cambridge: Harvard University Press, 1936, 1964.

————. "The Historiography of Ideas." *Proceedings of the American*

Bibliography

Philosophical Society 78 (1938): 529–43.

———. *Hitler as Pacifist.* Baltimore: American Jewish Conference, Baltimore Branch, 1934.

———. "Increase in the President's Power." *Addresses Before the Public Questions Club of St. Louis*, pp. 99–106. St. Louis: The Public Questions Club, 1907.

———. "Is a 'Peace of Conciliation' Possible?" *New Republic* 16 (1918): 257–59.

———. "James Burnett, Lord Monboddo." *University of California Magazine* 1 (1895): 68–79.

———. "The Meanings of 'Emergence' and Its Modes." *Proceedings of the Sixth International Congress of Philosophy*, pp. 20–33. New York: Longmans, Green and Company, 1927.

———. "Monboddo and Rousseau." In *Essays in the History of Ideas*, pp. 38–61. Baltimore: Johns Hopkins University Press, 1948.

[———.] "The North Broadway Social Settlement." St. Louis: The Settlement, 1902.

———. "The Obsolescence of the Eternal." *Philosophical Review* 18 (1909): 479–502.

———. "On a Supposed Resurgence of Vicious Intellectualism." *Journal of Philosophy* 49 (1952): 85–89.

———. "On Some Conditions of Progress in Philosophical Inquiry." *Philosophical Review* 26 (1917): 123–63.

———. "On the Discrimination of Romanticisms." In *Essays in the History of Ideas*, pp. 228–53. Baltimore: Johns Hopkins University Press, 1948.

———. "On the Existence of Ideas." In *Three Studies in Current Philosophical Questions*, pp. 42–99. Baltimore: Johns Hopkins University Press, 1914.

———. "Organization of the American Association of University Professors." *Science*, n.s. 41 (1915): 151–54.

———. "The Origins of Ethical Inwardness in Jewish Thought." *American Journal of Theology* 11 (1907): 228–49.

———. "Pragmatism and Theology." In *The Thirteen Pragmatisms and Other Essays*, pp. 40–78. Baltimore: Johns Hopkins University Press, 1963.

———. "Pragmatism *Versus* the Pragmatist." In *The Thirteen Pragmatisms and Other Essays*, pp. 133–90. Baltimore: Johns Hopkins University Press, 1963.

———. "The Problem of Time in Recent French Philosophy." *Philosophical Review* 21 (1912): 11–31, 322–43, 527–45.

———. "The Profession of the Professorate." *Johns Hopkins Alumni Magazine* 2 (1914): 181–95.

———. "The Professorial Landsturm." *Nation* 99 (1914): 656–57.

———. "Rain at Dusk." *University of California Magazine* 1 (1895): 23.

———. *The Reason, the Understanding and Time.* Baltimore: Johns Hopkins University Press, 1961.

———. *Reflections on Human Nature.* Baltimore: Johns Hopkins University Press, 1961.

———. "Reflections on the History of Ideas." *Journal of the History of Ideas* 1 (1940): 3–23.

———. "Religion and the Time-Process." *American Journal of Theology* 6 (1902): 439–72.

Bibliography

——. "The Retrospective Anticipations of the Carnegie Foundation."
Science, n.s. 31 (1910): 414–15.
——. *The Revolt Against Dualism: An Inquiry Concerning the Existence
of Ideas*. 2nd ed. LaSalle, Ill.: Open Court Publishing Company, 1960.
[——.] "Romantic Philosophy." *Nation* 90 (1910): 140–41.
——. "Schiller and the Genesis of German Romanticism." In *Essays in
the History of Ideas*, pp. 207–27. Baltimore: Johns Hopkins University
Press, 1948.
——. "The Service Pension of the Carnegie Foundation." *Science*, n.s.
31 (1910): 299–300.
[——.] *Should There Be an International Organization for General
Security Against Military Aggression, and Should the United States
Participate in Such an Organization?* Problem IV. Boston: Universities
Committee on Post-War International Problems, 1943.
——. "Sixth Annual Meeting of the Western Philosophy Association."
Journal of Philosophy, Psychology, and Scientific Methods 3 (1906):
318.
——. "Social Legislation in Missouri." *Charities and the Commons*, 22
June 1907, pp. 326–28.
——. "The Social Rôle of the French University." *University of California
Magazine* 6 (1900): 134–46.
——. "Some Concluding Criticisms on the 'Total Experience' Account of
Reality, with special reference to the 'Moment of Arrest.' " MS essay,
8 June 1896. Arthur O. Lovejoy Papers, Johns Hopkins University.
——. "Some Eighteenth Century Evolutionists." *Popular Science Monthly*
65 (1904): 238–51, 323–40.
——. "Some Harvard Notes." *University of California Magazine* 2 (1896):
111–18.
——. "Teachers and Trade-Unions." *Educational Review* 60 (1920):
106–20.
——. "A Temporalistic Realism." In *Contemporary American Philosophy:
Personal Statements*, edited by George P. Adams and William P.
Montague, 2: 85–105. New York: Macmillan, 1930.
——. "Terminal and Adjectival Values." *Journal of Philosophy* 47 (1950):
593–608.
——. "The Thirteen Pragmatisms." In *The Thirteen Pragmatisms and
Other Essays*, pp. 1–29. Baltimore: Johns Hopkins University Press,
1963.
——. *The Thirteen Pragmatisms and Other Essays*. Baltimore: Johns
Hopkins University Press, 1963.
——. "To Conscientious Objectors." *New Republic* 11 (1917): 187–89.
——. "The Unity of Science." *University of Missouri Bulletin, Science
Series* 1 (1912): 1–34.
——. *What Shall Be Done About Germany After the War?* EM 10, G.I.
Roundtable. Washington, D.C.: U.S. Government Printing Office, 1944.
——. "Wheat for the Allies." *New York Times*, 3 April 1917, 12.
——. "William James as Philosopher." In *The Thirteen Pragmatisms and
Other Essays*, pp. 79–112. Baltimore: Johns Hopkins University Press,
1963.
Lovejoy, Arthur O., and Boas, George. *Primitivism and Related Ideas in
Antiquity*. A Documentary History of Primitivism and Related Ideas,
edited by Arthur O. Lovejoy, Gilbert Chinard, George Boas, and

Bibliography

Ronald S. Crane, vol. 1. Baltimore: Johns Hopkins University Press, 1933.

Lovejoy, Arthur O., with Capps, Edward, and Young, A. A. "Report of the Committee on Academic Freedom in Wartime." *Bulletin of the American Association of University Professors* 4 (1918): 29–47.

Lovejoy, Arthur O., and others. "The Case of Professor Mecklin: Report of the Committee of Inquiry of the American Philosophical Association and the American Psychological Association." *Journal of Philosophy, Psychology, and Scientific Methods* 11 (1914): 67–81.

Lovejoy, Arthur O., and others. "Report of the Committee of Inquiry Concerning Clark University." *Bulletin of the American Association of University Professors* 10 (1924): 40–107.

Lovejoy, Arthur O., and others. "Report of the Committee of Inquiry on Conditions in Washburn College." *Bulletin of the American Association of University Professors* 7 (1921): 66–137.

Lovejoy, Arthur O., and others. "Report of the Committee of Inquiry on the Case of Professor Scott Nearing of the University of Pennsylvania." *Bulletin of the American Association of University Professors* 2 (1916): 5–57.

OTHER PUBLISHED SOURCES

Albee, Ernest; Bakewell, Charles M.; DeLaguna, Theodore; Hocking, William Ernest; and Hollands, Edmund H. "Progress in Philosophical Inquiry and Mr. Lovejoy's Presidential Address." *Philosophical Review* 26 (1917): 315–38.

"The American Scholar Forum: Communism and Academic Freedom." *American Scholar* 18 (1949): 323–54.

"Annual Report of the North Broadway Social Settlement." St. Louis: The Settlement, 1903.

Bertocci, Peter A. "George Holmes Howison." *The Encyclopedia of Philosophy*, 4: 66.

Blakey, George T. *Historians on the Homefront: American Propagandists for the Great War.* Lexington: University Press of Kentucky, 1970.

Boas, George. "A. O. Lovejoy: Reason-in-Action." *American Scholar* 29 (1960): 535–42.

Brown, Rollo Walter. *Harvard Yard in the Golden Age.* New York: Current Books, Inc., 1948.

Buckham, John W., and Stratton, George M. *George Holmes Howison: Philosopher and Teacher. A Selection from his Writings with a Biographical Sketch.* Berkeley: University of California Press, 1934.

"Byrd Bows and Senate Approves Dr. Lovejoy." *Baltimore Sun*, 3 April 1951, p. 30.

Clutton-Brock, A. "Pooled Self-Esteem." *Atlantic Monthly* 128 (1921): 721–31.

The Committee on Discussion. "The American Philosophical Association." *Journal of Philosophy, Psychology, and Scientific Methods* 9 (1912): 615–16.

Conmy, Peter Thomas. "History of the Entrance Requirements of the Liberal Arts Colleges of the University of California, 1860–1927." *University of California Publications in Education* 2 (1928): 251–337.

Bibliography

Creighton, J. E. "The Purposes of a Philosophical Association." *Philosophical Review* 11 (1902): 219–37.

Daily Palo Alto (Palo Alto, Calif.), 1899–1901.

Davis, Allen F. *Spearheads for Reform: The Social Settlements and the Progressive Movement, 1890–1914.* New York: Oxford University Press, 1967.

Dewey, John. "The American Association of University Professors: Introductory Address." *Science,* n.s. 41 (1915): 147–51.

————. "Realism without Monism or Dualism." *Journal of Philosophy* 19 (1922): 309–17, 351–61.

Dewey, John, and others. *Creative Intelligence: Essays in the Pragmatic Attitude.* New York: Henry Holt and Company, 1917.

"Dr. A. O. Lovejoy to Leave Hopkins." *Baltimore Sun,* 7 January 1938, pp. 9, 22.

"Dr. Lovejoy Hits Athletic Scholarships." *Baltimore Sun,* 28 November 1951, p. 36.

Drake, Durant, and others. *Essays in Critical Realism: A Cooperative Study of the Problem of Knowledge.* London: Macmillan and Company, Ltd., 1920.

Elliott, Orin Leslie. *Stanford University: The First Twenty-Five Years.* Palo Alto, Calif.: Stanford University Press, 1937.

Ferrier, William Warren. *Origin and Development of the University of California.* Berkeley: The Sather Gate Book Shop, 1930.

Feuer, Lewis S. "Arthur O. Lovejoy." *American Scholar* 46 (1977): 358–66.

————. "John Dewey and the Back to the People Movement in American Thought." *Journal of the History of Ideas* 20 (1959): 545–68.

————. "The Philosophical Method of Arthur O. Lovejoy: Critical Realism and Psychoanalytical Realism." *Philosophy and Phenomenological Research* 23 (1963): 493–510.

FitzGerald, Edward. "The Rubáiyát of Omar Khayyám." In *The Norton Anthology of English Literature,* Revised, 2: 1179–90. Edited by M. H. Abrams. New York: W. W. Norton and Company, 1968.

Flower, Elizabeth, and Murphey, Murray G. *A History of Philosophy in America,* vol. II. New York: G. P. Putnam's Sons, 1977.

Furner, Mary O. *Advocacy and Objectivity: A Crisis in the Professionalization of American Social Science, 1865–1905.* Lexington: University Press of Kentucky, 1975.

Glass, Bentley; Temkin, Owsei; and Strauss, William L., Jr., eds. *Forerunners of Darwin: 1745–1859.* Baltimore: Johns Hopkins University Press, 1959.

Greven, Philip J., Jr. *Four Generations: Population, Land, and Family in Colonial Andover, Massachusetts.* Ithaca, N.Y.: Cornell University Press, 1970.

Gruber, Carol S. *Mars and Minerva: World War I and the Uses of Higher Learning in America.* Baton Rouge: Louisiana State University Press, 1975.

Hammond, A. L. "Brief History of the Department of Philosophy, 1876–1938." Baltimore: For the Department of Philosophy, Johns Hopkins University, 1938.

Hart, Albert Bushnell, and Lovejoy, Arthur O. *Handbook of the War for Public Speakers.* New York: National Security League, 1917.

Harvard University Catalogue. Cambridge: Harvard University, 1895–97.

Bibliography

Hofstadter, Richard, and Metzger, Walter P. *The Development of Academic Freedom in the United States.* New York: Columbia University Press, 1955.

Holt, Edwin B., and others. *The New Realism: Cooperative Studies in Philosophy.* New York: The Macmillan Company, 1912.

Howison, George Holmes. "The Harmony of Determinism and Freedom." In *The Limits of Evolution and Other Essays*, pp. 313–80. New York: The Macmillan Company, 1901.

James, William. "The Dilemma of Determinism." In *The Will to Believe and Other Essays in Popular Philosophy*, pp. 145–83. New York: Longmans, Green and Company, 1910.

——. "The Ph.D. Octopus." In *Memories and Studies*, pp. 329–47. New York: Longmans, Green and Company, 1924.

——. *A Pluralistic Universe.* London: Longmans, Green and Company, 1909.

——. *Pragmatism: A New Name for Some Old Ways of Thinking.* New York: Longmans, Green and Company, 1907.

——. "The Sentiment of Rationality." *Mind* 4 (1879): 319–46.

——. *Some Problems of Philosophy: A Beginning of an Introduction to Philosophy.* New York: Longmans, Green and Company, 1911.

Janik, Allan, and Toulmin, Stephen. *Wittgenstein's Vienna.* New York: Simon and Schuster, A Touchstone Book, 1973.

Johnson, Laurence. *A Medical Formulary.* New York: William Wood and Company, 1881.

Kofoid, Charles A., and others. "Report of the Committee of Inquiry Concerning Charges of Violation of Academic Freedom, Involving the Dismissal of the President and Three Members of the Faculty, at the University of Montana." *Bulletin of the American Association of University Professors* 3 (1917): 3–52.

Kuhn, Thomas S. *The Structure of Scientific Revolutions.* 2nd ed., enlarged. Chicago: University of Chicago Press, 1962.

Kuklick, Bruce. *The Rise of American Philosophy: Cambridge, Massachusetts, 1860–1930.* New Haven: Yale University Press, 1977.

Leland Stanford, Jr., University, *Ninth Annual Register, 1899–1900.*

Lasch, Christopher. *The Agony of the American Left.* New York: Vintage Books, 1966.

Lovejoy, Clarence Earle. *The Lovejoy Genealogy with Biographies and History, 1460–1930.* By the author, 1930.

"Lovejoy Denied Approval by Senate Group." *Baltimore Sun*, 1 April 1951, p. 26.

"Lovejoy Sees Opposition to Appointment." *Baltimore Sun*, 17 March 1951, p. 24.

"Lovejoy 'With Reluctance,' Resigns as U. of M. Regent." *Baltimore Sun*, 2 October 1955, p. 38.

Lowe, Victor. "In Defense of Individualistic Empiricism: A Reply to Messrs. Lovejoy and Hook." *Journal of Philosophy* 49 (1952): 100–111.

——. "A Resurgence of 'Vicious Intellectualism.' " *Journal of Philosophy* 48 (1951): 435–47.

McGovney, D. O., and others. "Report of the Committee of Inquiry Concerning Charges of Violation of Academic Freedom at the University of Colorado." *Bulletin of the American Association of University Professors* 2 (1916): 3–71.

Bibliography

Maryland, Council of Defense. *Report of the Maryland Council of Defense to the Governor and General Assembly of Maryland.* 1920.

Missouri University Catalogue. Columbia: Missouri University, 1908–9.

Mohr, James C. "Academic Turmoil and Public Opinion: The Ross Case at Stanford." *Pacific Historical Review* 39 (1970): 39–62.

"A National Association of University Professors." *Science*, n.s. 39 (1914): 458–59.

Nicolson, Marjorie. "A. O. Lovejoy as Teacher." *Journal of the History of Ideas* 9 (1948): 428–37.

Overstreet, H. A. "Eleventh Annual Meeting of the American Philosophical Association." *Journal of Philosophy, Psychology, and Scientific Methods* 9 (1912): 101–10.

Palmer, George Herbert, and Perry, Ralph Barton. "Philosophy, 1870–1929." In *The Development of Harvard University Since the Inauguration of President Eliot: 1869–1929.* Edited by Samuel Eliot Morison. Cambridge: Harvard University Press, 1930.

Perry, Ralph Barton. *Final Report on the Work of the Committee, 1942–1945.* Boston: Universities Committee on Post-War International Problems, 1945.

Pratt, James Bisset. "The Twelfth Annual Meeting of the American Philosophical Association." *Journal of Philosophy, Psychology, and Scientific Methods* 10 (1913): 91–95.

"Professor Lovejoy and the University of Maryland." *Baltimore Sun*, 18 March 1951, p. 14.

"The Professors in Battle Array." *Nation* 106 (1918): 255.

The Prospect Union, 1891–1899. Cambridge, Mass.: The Union, 1899.

Ramsperger, A. G. "Critical Realism." *The Encyclopedia of Philosophy*, 2: 261–63.

Royce, Josiah. *The Letters of Josiah Royce.* Edited with an introduction, John Clendenning. Chicago: University of Chicago Press, 1970.

——. "On Definitions and Debates." *Journal of Philosophy, Psychology, and Scientific Methods* 9 (1912): 85–100.

Schmidt, Karl. "The Tenth Annual Meeting of the American Philosophical Association." *Journal of Philosophy, Psychology, and Scientific Methods* 8 (1911): 91–103.

Schneider, Herbert W. *Sources of Contemporary Philosophical Realism in America.* Indianapolis: The Bobbs-Merrill Company, Inc., The Library of Liberal Arts, 1964.

Seligman, Edwin R. A., and others. "General Report of the Committee on Academic Freedom and Academic Tenure." *Bulletin of the American Association of University Professors* 1 (1915): 17–43.

Seligman, Edwin R. A., and others. "Report of the Committee of Inquiry on Conditions at the University of Utah." The American Association of University Professors, 1915.

Sellars, Roy Wood. *Reflections on American Philosophy from Within.* Notre Dame, Ind.: University of Notre Dame Press, 1969.

Sibley, Robert, ed. *The Golden Book of California.* Berkeley: The California Alumni Association, 1937.

Sinclair, Upton. *The Goose-Step: A Study of American Education.* Rev. ed. Pasadena, Calif.: By the author, 1923.

Smith, Norman Kemp. "How Far Is Agreement Possible in Philosophy?"

Bibliography

Journal of Philosophy, Psychology, and Scientific Methods 9 (1912): 701–11.

Steele, Richard W. "Preparing the Public for War: Efforts to Establish a National Propaganda Agency, 1940–41." *American Historical Review* 75 (1970): 1640–53.

Stimson, Dorothy. "The History of Ideas Club." In *Studies in Intellectual History*, pp. 174–96. Baltimore: Johns Hopkins University Press, 1953.

Thirty-Fifth Annual Report of the Boston Children's Aid Society, 1899. Boston: Rockwell and Churchill Press, 1899.

U.S. Department of the Interior. *Educational Work of the Young Men's Christian Association, 1916–1918.* Prepared for the Bureau of Education by William Orr. Washington, D.C.: U.S. Government Printing Office, 1919.

Vesey, Laurence R. "The American Academic Revolution, 1880–1910." Lecture given at Johns Hopkins University, 17 November 1975.

———. *The Emergence of the American University.* Chicago: University of Chicago Press, Phoenix Books, 1970.

Ward, Robert D. "The Origin and Activities of the National Security League, 1914–1919." *Mississippi Valley Historical Review* 47 (1960): 51–65.

Wiener, Philip P. "The Central Role of Time in Lovejoy's Philosophy." *Philosophy and Phenomenological Research* 23 (1963): 480–92.

———. "Lovejoy's Rôle in American Philosophy." In *Studies in Intellectual History*, pp. 161–73. Baltimore: Johns Hopkins University Press, 1953.

Wilson, Daniel J. "Professionalization and Organized Discussion in the American Philosophical Association, 1900–1922." *Journal of the History of Philosophy* 17 (1979): 53–69.

Woodbridge, F.J.E., and others. "Report of the Committee on Definitions of the American Philosophical Association." *Journal of Philosophy, Psychology, and Scientific Methods* 8 (1911): 701–8.

Woods, Robert A., and Kennedy, Albert J. *Handbook of Settlements.* New York: Charities Publication Committee, 1911.

INDEX

Absolute, 60–62, 73, 78, 143–44, 149–
51, 155, 170. *See also* Absolute Experience; Otherworldliness
Absolute Experience, 56–57; Lovejoy's
critique of, 58–62
Academic freedom: at Stanford, 36–
38; and AAUP, 114–16, 118–21,
129–37; during World War I, 123,
129–35; and communism, 201–6
Addams, Jane, 17
Albee, Ernest, 94
Alexander, Samuel, 98, 100
American Association of University
Professors (AAUP), 190, 202, 212;
and academic freedom, 115–16,
118–21, 123, 129–35; formation of,
116–18; and professionalization,
118–21, 135–38; Lovejoy as president of, 135–38, 211; and unioni-
zation, 135, 137–38
American Committee for Cultural
Freedom, 204–5
American Council of Learned Socie-
ties, 190, 192, 207
American Federation of Labor, 137–
38
American Historical Association: His-
torical Service Board, 197–98
American Philosophical Association
(APA), 116; professionalization in
85–94; organized discussion in, 86–
87, 91–92, 94; Lovejoy as president
of, 88–94, 211
American Psychological Association,
116
Ames, Joseph, 117
Andover, Mass., 3
Andover Theological Seminary, 24–25
Antiintellectualism, 101; of James, 67–
70, 185; of Bergson, 79–84
Approbativeness: Lovejoy's theory of,
50–51, 174–75, 179–85; in the
eighteenth century, 175–79; and

Hume and Smith, 176–79
Aristotle, 143, 147, 151

Babbitt, Irving, 27
Bakewell, Charles M., 94
Baltimore, Md., 45, 117, 121, 187,
192, 196
Baltimore Sun, 206
Becker, Carl, 174
Becoming, idea of, 53, 147, 149–51,
155–56, 167, 184
Behaviorism, 98, 166, 171
Bergson, Henri, 47, 49, 77, 113; Love-
joy's critique of, 79–84
Berlin, Germany, 4–5
Bloomfield, Maurice, 117
Boas, George, 186–87, 189, 192, 196
Boston, Mass., 3–5, 6–7, 18, 23–24
Boston Children's Aid Society, 23–24
Bowman, Isaiah, 192
Bradley, F. H., 62, 78, 112; *Appear-
ance and Reality*, 58–61
Broad, C. D., 171
Bruno, Giordano, 142–44, 151, 158
Bryan, William Jennings, 36
Buchner, E. F., 46
Buffon, G. L. L., comte de, 157
Bull, Mrs. Ole, 23
Butterworth, Joseph, 202
Byrd, H. C., 206–7

Cambridge, Mass., 19, 22–23, 26, 32
Cambridge Conferences, 23
Capps, Edward, 129–34
Carnegie Foundation, 44, 115
Carus Lectures. *See* Lovejoy, Arthur
O., *Revolt Against Dualism*
Cattell, J. McKeen, 117, 129
Chain of being, idea of, 145, 147, 167,
184; development of, 149–51; in
eighteenth century, 152–54; tem-
poralizing of, 153–54; and roman-
ticism, 154–55; moral of, 155–56

243

Index

Chambers, Robert: and *Vestiges of the Natural History of Creation*, 159-60
Chaplin, W. S., 38-39
Children's Protective Alliance, 42
Choice, theology of, 52-53
Christ, 17, 19, 24-25, 30-32, 34
Christianity, 17, 19-20, 22; Lovejoy's critique of, 30-33, 47-49, 146; Lovejoy's historical essays on, 33-35, 47-49, 141; and socialism, 42-43
City College of New York, 45, 194
Clutton-Brock, A., 183-84
Cognition: intertemporal, 74-75, 101-3, 105, 110-11; rational, 101-2. *See also* Epistemology; Knowledge, problem of
Columbia University, 117, 129; Lovejoy as teacher at, 44
Communism: and academic freedom, 201-6. *See also* Marxism
Communist party, 201-6
Conscientious objection, 129, 131
Constitution, United States, 174
Continuity, idea of, 146-47, 150-53, 157
Cooperation: in philosophy, 86-97; in history of ideas, 189-90, 192, 195
Counts, George S., 204-5
Creighton, James Edwin, 86

Danton, Georges Jacques, 91
Darwin, Charles, 146, 158; and *Origin of Species*, 157, 159
Davis, Allen F., 17
Deism, 48, 141-42, 146
Descartes, René, 109
Devenir réel, doctrine of, 66, 79
Dewey, John, 42, 67, 84, 211-12; Lovejoy's critique of, 73-77, 98; and AAUP, 117-18
Diversity, idea of, 59, 89, 145, 151, 154-56, 166-67
Drake, Durant, 94-96
Dualism: epistemological, 74-76, 82-84, 95-96, 98-113, 147-48, 156; psychophysical, 74-76, 103-4, 107-9, 156, 168; and critical realism, 95-96

Einstein, Albert, 161
Ely, Richard T., 118
Emergence, theory of, 169-72, 184. *See also* Evolution
Encyclopedia of the Social Sciences, 212
England: in World War I, 122-23, 125-26, 128
Enlightenment, 49, 145-47, 149, 152-53, 156, 173-74; Lovejoy's admiration for, 152-53, 209
Epistemology, 65; pragmatic, 52, 71-76; monistic, 74-76; dualistic, 74-

76, 82-84, 98-113, 147-48; of critical realists, 94-96
Error, problem of, 56-58, 90-91, 97, 111
Eternity, idea of, 53, 77-78, 149, 152, 155
Ethics: Lovejoy and rational, 49-52, 173, 179-85; and evolution, 158, 172-73; of Hume and Smith, 176-79
Everett, Charles C., 22, 28
Evolution: history of theories of, 15, 43-44, 47, 145-47, 158-60; and religious thought, 48, 53, 142, 146; Lovejoy's theories of, 157-72, 184; discontinuities in, 158, 160, 163-69, 184; emergent, 160, 163-72, 184

Feuer, Lewis S., 97-98, 230 (n. 16)
Fichte, Johann Gottlieb, 55
FitzGerald, Edward, 228 (n. 14)
France: Lovejoy visits, 27-28, 126-28; in World War I, 122, 125
Freud, Sigmund, 173
Furner, Mary, 37

Gelsemium, fluid extract of, 6, 216 (nn. 11, 12)
Germantown, Pa., 7-8, 12
Germany: and Lovejoy's childhood, 4-5, 7; in World War I, 122-26; scholarship in, 122-23, 128; in World War II, 195-98
Gilman, Daniel Coit, 13, 195
Gilman, Elizabeth, 195
God, 30-31, 155; Howison's view of, 14, 46-47; as creator, 46, 52, 54, 56, 184; Lovejoy's view of, 31-32, 62-65, 184, 206. *See also* Christ
Good, idea of, 49, 141, 150-51, 155
Gradation, idea of, 146-47, 150-51, 157
Graduate Club (Harvard), 22
Graduate Philosophical Society (Harvard), 22
Gruber, Carol, 122, 124

Hamburg, Germany, 4-5
Harper, William Rainey, 12
Hart, Albert Bushnell, 124-26
Harvard University, 13, 28-29, 32-33, 35-36, 43, 55, 87, 117, 169; Lovejoy as student at, 18-26, 62; philosophy at, 20-22; Lovejoy visiting professor at, 190-92
Hays, Paul R., 204-5
Hegel, G. F., 55
Herder, J. G., 157-58
Hinckley, Frank E., 16-17
History, philosophy of, 47-48
History of ideas, 15, 33-35, 47-49, 139-49, 157-60, 188-90, 192-95, 230 (n. 16)

244

Index

Index

Index

Royce, Josiah, 25, 28, 65, 70, 78, 87, 91, 98, 149, 190, 212; as teacher of Lovejoy, 20–21, 56–62, 112; idealism of, 56, 60–62; and AAUP, 117

Russell, Bertrand, 103

St. Louis, Mo., 38–40, 44
Santayana, George, 20–21, 95–96
Sarton, George, 192
Schaper, William, 129
Schauffler, Margaret (sister of Sara Lovejoy), 4, 6, 216 (n. 8)
Schelling, Friedrich, 155
Science: unity of, 160–63, 169; discontinuities in, 161–63
Self-consciousness: Lovejoy's theory of, 49–52, 58, 63, 158, 162–63, 181; and evolution, 158, 162–63
Self-esteem: and approbativeness, 174–75, 179, 183–85; in ethics of Hume and Smith, 179; pooled, 183–84
Self-subsistence, idea of, 56–57, 59, 61–62
Seligman, E. R. A., 118–19
Sellars, Roy Wood, 95
Settlement work: and Lovejoy, 16–17, 23–24, 39–42; religious motivation of, 17; secular rationale for, 40–43
Smith, Adam, 51, 158, 175; ethical theories of, 176–79; and *Theory of Moral Sentiments*, 176, 178–79
Smith, Norman Kemp, 92, 123
Sorbonne, 27
Souls, 47, 63–64
Spinoza, 142–44, 149, 151–52, 158
Stanford, Jane, 36–37
Stanford University, 26, 30, 114–15, 205; Lovejoy as teacher at, 28–29, 35–38; Ross affair at, 36–38
Strong, C. A., 94–96
Switzerland, 122

Temporalism, 65–66, 85; and Christianity, 30–33; and Howison, 47; introduced into world history, 47–49, 141–42; and Lovejoy's ethics, 51–52, 179–80; opposed to eternalism, 53, 77–78, 152; and pragmatism, 68–70, 72–73; defined by Lovejoy, 78–79; and rationalism, 78–79; and Bergson, 79–84; and problem of knowledge, 100–103; and history of ideas, 141–42, 146–47; and evolution, 146–47, 164; and chain of being, 153–56
Theology, rational: in Lovejoy's critique of Christianity, 33–35; Lovejoy's theory of, 46–54; and pragmatism, 66
Thing-in-itself, conception of, 57–58

This-worldliness, 150–51. *See also* Otherworldliness
Thomas, Norman, 129
Totality, idea of, 58–61
Toy, Crawford H., 22
Trager, Frank N., 187, 189
Truth, theories of, 57–58; pragmatic, 70–73

Uniformitarianism, 154
Unionism: among professors, 135, 137–38
Unitarianism, 32–33, 39
United Nations, 200
United States, War Department, 124, 126, 197
Unit-idea, 195; development of, 33–34, 48, 150, 230 (n. 16)
Universe, conceptions of: in Plato, 149–50; in eighteenth century, 152–53; Lovejoy's, 166–67, 184
Universities Committee on Post-War International Problems, 198–200
University of California, Berkeley, 8, 12, 98, 163; Lovejoy as student at, 12–16
University of California Magazine, 15–16, 41
University of Maryland Board of Regents, 206–7
University of Missouri: Lovejoy as teacher at, 44, 161
University of Washington, 202, 204

Values, adjectival and terminal: in Hume, 177; in Lovejoy, 180–83
Vernes, Maurice, 27
Voltaire, 153, 175
Voluntarism, 66

Wallace, Alfred Russel, 160
Warfield, E. D., 116
Washington University, 38–39, 44, 115
Watson, John B., 46
Western Philosophy Association, 44, 211
Whitehead, Alfred North, 103, 109
Wiener, Philip P., 97, 194
Wilkins, Ernest H., 128
Wilson, Woodrow, 128, 225 (n. 29)
Windelband, Wilhelm, 230 (n. 16)
Woodbridge, F. J. E., 87
World War I, 122–35; academic response to, 123–24, 130, 134–35
World War II: isolationism before, 195–97; Lovejoy in, 197–200
Worth, theory of, 47–49, 141–42

YMCA, 124, 128
Young, Allyn A., 129–34

Zeno's paradox, 84

248